LaTeX for Complete Novices

Nicola L. C. Talbot

W0007216

VOLUME 1 OF
THE DICKIMAW LaTeX SERIES

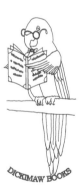

Dickimaw Books

SAXLINGHAM NETHERGATE

British Library Cataloguing in Publication Data
Talbot, Nicola L. C., b. 1970
LaTeX for Complete Novices
Volume 1 of The Dickimaw LaTeX Series

ISBN 978-1-909440-00-5
BIC: UGD — Desktop publishing
1. LaTeX (Computer file); 2. Computerized typesetting.

Published by Dickimaw Books.

This book is a rewrite of the author's on-line LaTeX tutorial formerly located at http://theoval.cmp.uea.ac.uk/~nlct/latex/novices/ (2004–2012). Accompanying web resources are now available from http://www.dickimaw-books.com/latex/novices/ (including source code). Version 1.4. Copyright © 2004 Nicola L. C. Talbot

Permission is granted to copy, distribute and/or modify this document under the terms of the GNU Free Documentation License, Version 1.2 or any later version published by the Free Software Foundation; with no Invariant Sections, no Front-Cover Texts, and one Back-Cover Text: "If you choose to buy a copy of this book, Dickimaw Books asks for your support through buying the Dickimaw Books edition to help cover costs." A copy of the license is included in the section entitled "GNU Free Documentation License".

CONTENTS

LIST OF FIGURES

LIST OF TABLES

LIST OF EXERCISES

CHAPTER 1

INTRODUCTION

The aim of this book is to introduce LaTeX to a non-technical person. LaTeX is excellent for producing professional looking documents, however it is a *language* not a word processor, so it can take a bit of getting used to, particularly if you have never had any experience using programming languages.

[FAQ: Why is TeX not a WYSIWYG system?]

LaTeX does take a while to learn, so why should you use it? Here are a few reasons but it is not an exhaustive list:

LaTeX is far better at typesetting mathematical equations than word processors. I wrote my Ph.D. thesis back in the days of LaTeX2.09 (the old version of LaTeX) and given the high quantity of mathematics that I had to typeset, it would have taken me considerably longer to write it in a word processor, and the resulting document wouldn't have looked nearly as good. Even Microsoft have acknowledged TeX's high-quality mathematical typography [12].

EXAMPLE:

Here's an equation taken from some kernel survival analysis:

$$\frac{\partial^2 \mathcal{L}}{\partial z_i^{\rho 2}} = -\frac{\partial \rho_i}{\partial z_i^{\rho}} \left(\frac{\partial v_i}{\partial \rho_i} \frac{e^{v_i}}{1 - e^{v_i}} + v_i \frac{e^{v_i} \frac{\partial v_i}{\partial \rho_i}(1 - e^{v_i}) + e^{2v_i} \frac{\partial v_i}{\partial \rho_i}}{(1 - e^{v_i})^2} \right)$$

↑ Output

↓ Output

(You can find out how to create this equation on page 174 in Section 9.4.9.)

That's all very well and good if you want to typeset some equations, but if your work doesn't involve maths, does that mean that LaTeX is not for you? Although I am a mathematician, I have written plenty of documents with no maths in at all, including prose, poetry, newsletters, posters and brochures, but I still opt for LaTeX because using LaTeX ensures consistent formatting, and the style of the document can be completely changed by simply using a different class file, or loading additional packages. This means that I can concentrate on writing the document, rather than worrying about how it will look. It also means that if, after having written a 200 page document, I then find that I need to change all the figure captions so that they are labelled "Fig" instead of "Figure", all I need to do is edit a single line, rather than going through 200 pages to individually edit every single figure caption.[1.1]

[1.1]Sure, you could use a search and replace function, but a sweeping replace-all can have unexpected side effects. For example, your document may include the sentence, "Figures from the last quarter showed improvement", which would get changed to, "Figs from the last quarter showed improvement".

1

Serious fiction writers are taught never to remind the reader that they're reading a book. Poor formatting is just as much a reminder of this as authorial intrusion.

LATEX makes it very easy to cross-reference chapters, sections, equations, figures, tables etc, and it also makes it very easy to generate a table of contents, list of figures, list of tables, index, glossary[1.2] and bibliography. You don't need to worry about numbering anything, as this is done automatically, which means that you can insert new sections or swap sections around without having to worry about updating all the section numbering etc. Furthermore, if you use BIBTEX[1.3] in combination with LATEX, and you have, say, 100 or more citations, it doesn't matter if you are then told that the citations have to be re-ordered (say, in order of citation rather than alphabetically). All that is required is a minor edit to change the appropriate style file rather than ploughing through the entire document changing all the citations by hand.

When you are editing a document using a word processor, the word processor has to work out how to reformat the document every time you type something. If you have a large document with a great many inserted objects (such as figures and equations), the response to keyboard input can become very slow. You may find that after typing a few words you will have to wait until the computer catches up before you can see what you have typed. With LATEX you type in your code using an ordinary text editor. The document doesn't get formatted until you pass it to LATEX, which means that you are not slowed down by constant reformatting.

Lastly, there's the fact that LATEX follows certain typographical rules, so you can leave most of the typesetting to LATEX. You rarely need to worry about minor things such as inter-sentence spacing. The default is English spacing, but if you have a publisher who disapproves of this, you can switch if off with a single command. (See Section 2.13.)

LATEX will also automatically deal with f-ligatures.[1.4] That is, if any of the following combination of letters are found: fl, ffl, ff, fi, ffi, they will automatically be converted into the corresponding ligatures: fl, ffl, ff, fi, ffi. Note the difference between fluffier (2 ligatures) and fluffier (no ligatures). These points may seem minor but they all contribute towards the impact of the entire document. When writing technical documents, the presentation as well as the content is important. All too often examiners or referees are put off reading a document because it is badly formatted. This provokes an immediate negative reaction and provides little desire to look favourably upon your work.

To give you an idea of what you can do with LATEX, this book was written in LATEX.[1.5] The PDF versions (including this paperback version) were generated using PDFLATEX and **makeindex** and the HTML version was generated using the LATEX2HTML[1.6] converter.

[FAQ: Conversion from (La)TeX to HTML]

[1.2] Glossaries are covered in *Using LATEX to Write a PhD Thesis* [13].

[1.3] Automating bibliographies is covered in *Using LATEX to Write a PhD Thesis* [13].

[1.4] Ligatures can be suppressed using the microtype package if necessary

[1.5] The source code is available at http://www.dickimaw-books.com/latex/novices/, but it really is *not* the place to start if you are a beginner, as it contains LATEX and Perl code beyond the scope of this tutorial.

[1.6] http://www.latex2html.org/

For more reasons as to why you might want to use LATEX instead of a word processor, have a look at http://www.ctan.org/what_is_tex.html#whytex.

1.1. Class and Package Documentation

There are hundreds of classes and packages available on the Comprehensive TEX Archive Network[1.7] (CTAN). These are made available by many volunteers. Some provide detailed documentation to accompany their contribution, while others only provide a few notes in a README file or comments in the source files. This book only provides an introductory look at a small selection of these contributions. If you want further details on how to use a particular class or package you should check the documentation that accompanies it. You can use the texdoc application to search for the documentation. This is a command line application, which means you need a terminal or command prompt (see Section 2.5).

To use texdoc, you need to type (at the command prompt) texdoc followed by a space followed by the name of the class or package you want information about. For example, to read the memoir documentation, type the following at the command prompt (press the return/enter key ⏎ at the end of the line):

```
texdoc memoir
```

Some packages come with more than one set of documentation. For example, the glossaries package comes with the main user manual, a short guide for beginners and the documented code for advanced users. Just doing

```
texdoc glossaries
```

will display the advanced documented code. To list all available documentation for a package, use the -l option:

```
texdoc -l glossaries
```

Then type the number corresponding to the file you want to view. If you can remember the file name (for example glossaries-user) you can type that next time you want to view it:

```
texdoc glossaries-user
```

There is also a Perl/Tk-based graphical user interface (GUI) called texdoctk, which is distributed with TeX Live, that you can use instead of texdoc if you can't work out how to use a terminal or prefer a GUI approach.

Failing that, you can also check on CTAN [1] using the URL ctan.org/pkg/ ⟨name⟩, where ⟨name⟩ is the name of the package or class. For example, if you want to look up the documentation for the memoir package, you can find it at http://ctan.org/pkg/memoir or go to http://mirror.ctan.org/ and search for the package or class.

[1.7] http://mirror.ctan.org/

Another alternative recently made available is to use the URL `texdoc.net/pkg/`⟨*name*⟩. For example, `http://texdoc.net/pkg/memoir` will fetch the documentation for the memoir class.

However, it's better to use `texdoc` or `texdoctk` to read the documentation installed with the class or package on your computer to ensure it matches the installed class or package version.

Note that it is important to remember that the TEX world is mostly supported by volunteers. CTAN [1] itself is maintained by a very small group (currently two people). It's not like a commercial company with 24/7 support and hundreds of paid employees constantly updating the software. At its core, TEX is a community effort. While some volunteers actively maintain and update their classes or packages, some people move on to other things and stop maintaining their work. Occasionally, if the class or package is popular, someone else might take over maintenance. There is no dedicated helpdesk to go to, but there are many ways of getting help, see Appendix C (Need More Help?)

1.2. Overview

This document is structured as follows:

Chapter 2 (Some Definitions) defines terms that will be used throughout this document. I strongly suggest that you look through this chapter before you start so that you understand the terminology used in this document. At the very least, you should read the first part that details how corresponding input and output is displayed in this document — you need to understand the difference between "input" (source code) and "output" (how the source code will appear in the typeset document).

Chapter 3 (From Source Code to Typeset Output) details the software that you will need to use LATEX and describes how to use the software.

Chapter 4 (Creating a Simple Document) shows you how to create a very basic document.

Chapter 5 (Structuring Your Document) shows you how to create chapters and other sectional units so that you end up with a fully structured document.

Chapter 6 (The graphicx Package) shows you how to include external image files and how to scale and rotate text.

Chapter 7 (Floats) describes how to create figures and tables.

Chapter 8 (Defining Commands) describes how to define your own commands, and redefine existing commands.

Chapter 9 (Mathematics) describes how to typeset mathematics.

Chapter 10 (Defining Environments) describes how to define new environments.

Chapter II (Counters) discusses how numbers are stored in counters, how to change their values, and how to define your own counter.

Appendix A (Downloading and Installing Packages) shows you how to download and install additional packages that weren't installed with your TeX distribution.

Appendix B (Common Errors) documents possible errors you may encounter, and gives advice on how to fix them.

Appendix C (Need More Help?) gives pointers on where to go for help.

Throughout this document there are pointers to related topics in the UK List of TeX Frequently Asked Questions[1.8] (UK FAQ). These are displayed in the margin in square brackets, as illustrated on the right. You may find these resources useful in answering related questions that are not covered in this book. To find the resources, go to http://www.tex.ac.uk/faq and either look for the question title in the list, or enter a keyword in the search field. *[FAQ: What is LaTeX?]*

This book and associated files, including solutions to the exercises, are available on-line at: http://www.dickimaw-books.com/latex/novices/.

1.3. Recommended Reading

This document is designed as an introductory text, not a comprehensive guide. For further reading try some of the following: *[FAQ: Books on LaTeX]*

LaTeX: A Document Preparation System [9] is the user guide and reference manual for LaTeX, and is a good basic text for anyone starting out, however it doesn't cover AMSTeX, so anyone who needs to typeset more than basic mathematics may prefer either *A Guide to LaTeX* [7] or *The LaTeX Companion* [3]. Both these books cover AMSTeX, BibTeX and makeindex. *[FAQ: What are the AMS packages?]*

In the same series as *The LaTeX Companion*, there is also *The LaTeX Graphics Companion* [5] which details how to illustrate documents with LaTeX and PostScript, including a chapter on colour (coloured text, background, tables and slides). This is recommended to anyone who is contemplating heavy use of graphics, but you do need a basic knowledge of LaTeX before delving into it.

The final book in the "Companion" series which you may find useful is *The LaTeX Web Companion* [4]. This is recommended for those interested in creating documents for the web, either as HTML or PDF. It details how to convert LaTeX documents into HTML using various applications such as LaTeX2HTML and TeX4ht, and how to create PDF documents using PDFLaTeX, including how to create active links within your document using the hyperref package. *[FAQ: What is PDFTeX?]*

There are two new LaTeX books that I haven't read but have been recommended to me: *LaTeX Beginner's Guide* [8] and *LaTeX and Friends* [20].

Note that the UK TeX User Group[1.9] (UK TUG) has a 25% book discount scheme for members. See http://uk.tug.org/membership for more details of that and other

---

[1.8]http://www.tex.ac.uk/faq
[1.9]http://uk.tug.org/

associated benefits. If you're not in the UK, have a look at `http://www.tug.org/usergroups.html` to see if there is a local user group in your area.

[FAQ: How to get help]

There is also a wealth of LaTeX-related information on the Internet. CTAN [1] is a good place to start. You can check the on-line catalogue [22] for information about available software and, as mentioned earlier, there is also the list of frequently asked questions which I recommend you try if you have any queries. See also Appendix C (Need More Help?)

CHAPTER 2

SOME DEFINITIONS

As mentioned in Chapter 1 (Introduction), LaTeX is a language, so you can't simply start typing and expect to see your document appear before your very eyes. You need to know a few things before you can get started, so it's best to define a few terms first. Don't worry if there seems a lot to take in, there will be some practical examples later, which should hopefully make things a little clearer.

[FAQ: Why is TeX not a WYSIWYG system?]

Throughout this book, source code is illustrated in a typewriter font with the word Input placed in the margin, and the corresponding output (how it will appear in the PDF document) is typeset with the word Output in the margin.

EXAMPLE:

A single line of code is displayed like this:

```
This is an \textbf{example}.
```

Input

The corresponding output is illustrated like this:

This is an **example**.

Output

Segments of code that are longer than one line are bounded above and below, illustrated as follows:

```
Line one\par
Line two\par
Line three.
```

⊤ Input

↓ Input

with corresponding output:

Line one
Line two
Line three.

⊤ Output

↓ Output

Take care not to confuse a backslash \ with a forward slash / as they have different meanings.

Command definitions are shown in a typewriter font in the form:

```
\documentclass[⟨options⟩]{⟨class file⟩}
```

Definition

7

In this case the command being defined is called \documentclass and text typed ⟨*like this*⟩ (such as ⟨*options*⟩ and ⟨*class file*⟩) indicates the type of thing you need to substitute. (Don't type the angle brackets!) For example, if you want the scrartcl class file you would substitute ⟨*class file*⟩ with scrartcl and if you want the letterpaper option you would substitute ⟨*options*⟩ with letterpaper, like this:

Input   \documentclass[letterpaper]{scrartcl}

But more on that later.

Sometimes it can be easy to miss a space character when you're reading this kind of book. When it's important to indicate a space, the visible space symbol ␣ is used. For example:

Input   A␣sentence␣consisting␣of␣six␣words.

When you type up the code, replace any occurrence of ␣ with a space.

One other thing to mention is the comment character % (the percent symbol). Anything from the percent symbol up to, and including, the end of line character is ignored by LaTeX. Thus

Input ⊤
```
A simple % next comes a command to make some bold text
\textbf{example}
```
Input ⊥

will produce the output

Output   A simple **example**

The percent symbol is often used to suppress unwanted space resulting from line breaks[2.1] in the source code. For example, the following code

Input ⊤
```
Foo%
Bar
```
Input ⊥

will produce the output:

Output   FooBar

as opposed to

Input ⊤
```
Foo
Bar
```
Input ⊥

which will produce the output:

Output   Foo Bar

On the other hand, spaces at the start of a line of input are ignored, so

---

[2.1] LaTeX treats the end-of-line character as a space.

```
Foo%
    Bar
```

↑ Input

↓ Input

still produces:

FooBar

Output

2.1. Source Code

The *source code* consists of all the text and LaTeX commands that make up an entire document. The source code is typed in using a text editor, and saved with the file extension `.tex`. The source code may be contained in just one file, or it might be split across several files.

[FAQ: TeX-friendly editors and shells]

2.2. Output File

The LaTeX application reads in your source code and creates the typeset document, the *output file*. This book assumes that you will be using the version of LaTeX that produces PDF files (PDFLaTeX). If you are using TeXWorks (see Chapter 3 (From Source Code to Typeset Output)), you need to select the "PDFLaTeX" item from the drop-down list. If you are using TeXnicCenter, select the "LaTeX⇒PDF" build profile. If you are using WinEdt, when you want to build your document click on the button marked "PDFLaTeX" rather than the one marked "LaTeX". If you are using a terminal or command prompt, use the command `pdflatex` rather than `latex`. (TeXnicCenter, WinEdt and using the terminal or command prompt approach are described in the supplemental material.)[2.2]

2.3. DVI File

TeX (and subsequently LaTeX) originally created *DVI (DeVice Independent) files* instead of PDF files.[2.3] However, although there are free DVI viewers, not many people have them installed, so it's really only TeX users who can read them. Also, you can't embed image files in a DVI file or have fancy effects, such as rotation. Instead, people can use TeX/LaTeX to create a DVI file and then use an application to convert the DVI file to PostScript.

These days PDF is the preferred platform-independent format, and with the advent of PDFTeX, modern TeX/LaTeX users can directly create PDF documents rather than going through the DVI route. Some people still prefer to create DVI files as an intermediate step, particularly if they want to embed PostScript instructions (as is done by the pstricks package). For simplicity, this book assumes that you have a modern TeX distribution and are using PDFLaTeX rather than LaTeX⇒DVI.

[2.2]`http://www.dickimaw-books.com/latex/novices/html/supplemental.html`
[2.3]There was no PDF back then.

2.4. Auxiliary Files

When LaTeX creates your output file, it not only creates a PDF file but also creates other associated files. The most common of these are the log file, which has the extension .log, and the *auxiliary file*, which has the extension .aux.

The log file contains a transcript of the most recent LaTeX run. It lists all the files that have been loaded, including the class file and any packages that your document has used. There should also be the class or package version number and date, although this is dependent on the class or package author. If you ever want to ask for help, you need to say what version you are using.

For example, this book uses the scrbook class, so the log file includes the lines:

```
(/usr/local/texlive/2010/texmf-dist/tex/latex/koma-script/scrbook.cls
Document Class: scrbook 2010/06/17 v3.06 KOMA-Script document class
(book)
```

(This is actually now out-of-date as the latest version at the time of writing this is version 3.11a dated 2012/07/05.)

Error messages, warnings and general information messages are also written to the log file as well as the document statistics. You can delete this log file if you like. It will be created again the next time you run LaTeX.

The auxiliary file contains all the information needed for cross-referencing (covered in Section 5.5). This is needed to ensure all your cross-references are up-to-date. You can delete this file, but you will need at least two LaTeX runs to ensure your cross-references are correct the next time you create your output file.

TeXWorks also creates a file with the extension .synctex.gz. This file allows you to jump to and from the source code and the appropriate part of the output file. If you delete this file, you will have to run LaTeX again before you can use this function.

Other files that may be created include the table of contents file (.toc), the list of figures file (.lof) and the list of tables file (.lot). Some class files or packages create additional files. If your operating system hides file extensions, you might want to switch off this behaviour, if possible, to make it easier to distinguish between all the various files.

TeXWorks has a menu item File→Remove AUX Files that will remove the auxiliary files.

2.5. Terminal or Command Prompt

Sometimes you may find that you need to use a command-line application. This is an application that doesn't have a graphical user interface. This isn't specific to TeX, but the TeX distribution comes with a number of them. In fact, front-ends (such as TeXWorks) run some of these applications for you when click on the typeset or build button.

Most operating systems provide a *terminal* or command prompt where you can type the command-line application name and any associated information. For example, Figure 2.1 shows a terminal running under Fedora on Linux.

Windows To open the MSDOS Prompt, go to the Start menu, then "All Programs", then "Accessories" and click on "MSDOS Prompt".

Mac OSX To open the Mac Terminal, go to your "Applications" folder, open "Utilities" and double click on "Terminal".

Unix etc The Terminal is usually located either in the "Applications" menu or in the "System Tools" subdirectory of the "Applications" menu.

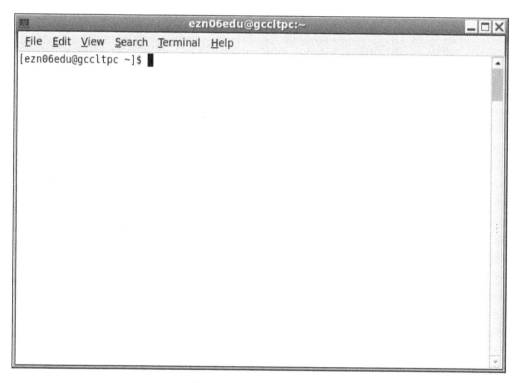

Figure 2.1. A Terminal

EXAMPLE:

One such command-line application you are likely to need is texdoc. This is mentioned in more detail in Section 1.1, but to use texdoc you need to open the terminal or command prompt as described above and type texdoc followed by a package or class name, for example:

```
texdoc scrbook
```

(see Figure 2.2 on the following page) then press the Enter or Return ⏎ key.

Other TEX-related command-line applications include pdflatex, bibtex, makeindex, xindy and kpsewhich.

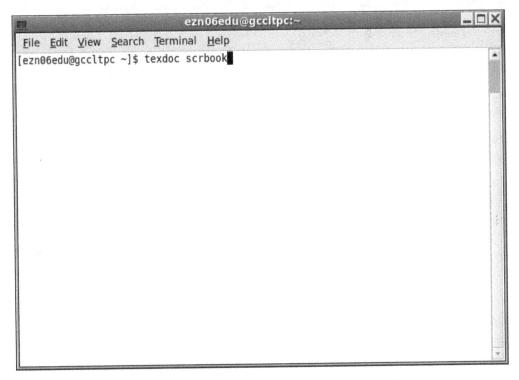

Figure 2.2. Running texdoc From a Terminal

2.6. Commands

A *command* is used to tell LaTeX to do a particular thing at that point in the document. These are the basic forms a command can take:

1. **A Control Word.**

   This is a backslash \ followed by letters (A,…,Z,a,…,z). There can be no non-alphabetical characters in the command, apart from the initial backslash, and the name is always **case-sensitive** so, for example, \gamma and \Gamma have different meanings. One command that often trips up new users is \LaTeX, which prints the LaTeX logo: LaTeX. This command has three captial letters and two lower case letters. If you get the case of any of the letters incorrect, you will get an "undefined control sequence" error.

   [FAQ: Commands gobble following space]

   There must be no space between the backslash and the start of the command name. Some command names are made up of two or more names joined together, such as \tableofcontents. *Make sure you don't insert any spaces in the control word.* This will either lead to an error or an unexpected result. For example,

   \appendixname

   displays "Appendix" but

   \appendix name

   switches to the appendices and then prints the word "name".

   Most LaTeX commands have fairly self-explanatory names. (For example, \chapter starts a new chapter and \rightarrow prints an arrow pointing to the right.) However, in most cases, you need to use U.S. spelling (for example, \color rather than \colour).

   This is the most common form of command. Any spaces immediately following a command of this type are ignored, so for example

   \TeX nician

   Input

   will produce

   TeXnician

   Output

   whereas

   \TeX{} nician

   Input

   will produce

   TeX nician

   Output

But the following will cause an "undefined control sequence" error:

✗   `\TeXnician`

There is one command that you must use in every document you create, and that is the `\documentclass` command. This command must be placed at the very start of your document, and indicates what type of document you are creating. This command is described in more detail in Chapter 4 (Creating a Simple Document).

2. A Starred Command

Some commands have variants that are indicated by an asterisk at the end of the name. For example, `\chapter` makes a numbered chapter whereas `\chapter*` is makes an unnumbered chapter. A *starred command* is the version of the command with the asterisk. (On a UK keyboard the asterisk character is usually located on the same key as the digit 8.)

This may seem like a different form to a control word, described above. After all, I've just said that a control word can only contain alphabetical characters. However a starred command is actually a control word (such as `\chapter`) followed by an asterisk. The control word checks to see if the next character is an asterisk. If it is, it performs one action, otherwise it performs another action.

This type should therefore just come under the previous category, but as you will often hear of "starred commands" it seemed better to have a separate category.

3. A Control Symbol.

This is a backslash followed by a single non-alphabetical character. For example `\%` will print a percent symbol. Spaces are not ignored after this type of command, for example

`17.5\% VAT`

will produce

17.5% VAT

It's also possible to have starred forms of control symbols. For example `\\` forces a line break. If it's not followed by an asterisk a page break is allowed at that line break, but if it is followed by an asterisk `\\*` no page break is allowed at that line break. (If a page break is needed, it will be made at the end of the previous line instead.)

4. Character Sequence.

Some special sequences of characters combine to form an instruction. For example ffi is the command to produce the ffi ligature, and the sequence of symbols ! ' is the command to produce the upside down exclamation mark ¡

5. **An Internal Command.**

This is like the first type, a control word, but the @ character appears in the command name (for example \c@section) *however* internal commands should only be used in class files or packages. The @ symbol takes on a special meaning when a file is included using \documentclass (a class file) or \usepackage (a package).

For example, in a class file or package \c@section is an internal representation of the section counter, whereas in a .tex file \c@section is interpreted as the command \c (the cedilla accent command) that takes the character @ as its argument, followed by section, which produces the rather odd looking @section.

Don't be tempted to use internal commands until you have first grasped the basics. You have been warned!

[FAQ: \@ and @ in macro names]

2.7. Grouping (or Scope)

A segment of code may be *grouped* by placing it within { and } (curly braces). Most commands that occur within a group will be local to that group. For example, \bfseries changes the font weight to bold, so the following segment of code:

```
Here is some text. {This text \bfseries is in a group.} Here is some more
text.
```

↑ Input
↓ Input

will appear in the typeset document looking like:

Here is some text. This text **is in a group.** Here is some more text.

Output

As can be seen, the font change only stays in effect until it reaches the end of the group (signified by the closing curly brace }.) For a command to be in the same *scope* as another command, both commands must be within the same group. For example, in the following, \bfseries and \itshape are in the same scope:

```
{\bfseries Some bold \itshape and italic text}
```

Input

But below, they are in different scopes:

```
{\bfseries Some bold text} {\itshape and some italic text}
```

Input

Environments form an implicit scope.

2.8. Arguments (also called "Parameters")

Some commands take one or more *arguments*. This provides a way to give LaTeX additional information so that it is able to carry out the command. There are two types of arguments: mandatory and optional.

2.8.1. Mandatory Arguments

Mandatory (or compulsory) arguments are arguments that *have* to be specified.

EXAMPLES:
1. If you want a footnote, you need to use the \footnote command, which has a mandatory argument that specifies the contents of the footnote. Like this:

Input

    Here is a footnote.\footnote{This is the footnote text.}

Output

    Here is a footnote.[2.4]

2. If you want to start a new chapter, you need to use the \chapter command, but you also need to tell LaTeX the title of this new chapter. So the \chapter command takes one mandatory argument that specifies the title.

    For example, the following code:

Input

    \chapter{Some Definitions}

    was used to generate the heading for the current chapter (at the top of page 7).

3. The command \textbf typesets its argument in a bold font (as opposed to the declaration \bfseries which switches to a bold font.)

    For example, the following code:

Input

    \textbf{Some bold text.}

    produces the output

Output

    Some bold text.

NOTES:
1. LaTeX takes the first non-space object following the command name as the argument, which is why in the above examples the arguments have to be grouped.

    Suppose the last example above didn't have a group, so instead the code was:

Input

    \textbf Some bold text.

    then only the "S" would be the argument because it's the first object following the command, in which case the output would look like:

Output

    Some bold text.

[2.4]This is the footnote text.

2. If you want the argument to be blank, use empty braces: {}. For example, suppose you want to have a chapter without a title[2.5] you would need to do:

`\chapter{}`

2.8.2. Optional Arguments

Some commands may have one or more *optional arguments*. Unlike mandatory arguments, optional arguments must always be enclosed in square brackets [ ].

EXAMPLE:
The command \\ ends a line. So the following segment of code:

`Line one\\Line two.` Input

will produce the following output:

Line one
Line two.

Output

However the \\ command also has an optional argument that allows you to specify how big the gap between the two lines should be. So the following segment of code:

`Line one\\[1cm]Line two.` Input

will produce the following output:

Line one

Line two.

Output

Incidentally, note the difference between the previous example, and the following example:

`Line one\\{[1cm]} Line two.` Input

Line one
[1cm] Line two.

Output

In this example the [1cm] has been placed inside a group, so it is no longer considered to be an optional argument, and since the command \\ does not take a mandatory argument, the [1cm] is simply interpreted as ordinary text.

[FAQ: Start of line goes awry]

[2.5]The numbers for chapters, sections etc are automatically inserted by LaTeX, so this example would produce a numbered chapter without a title.

EXAMPLE:

The command \framebox (which will be covered later in Section 4.7.1) takes a mandatory argument and two optional arguments. \framebox puts a frame around the contents of its mandatory argument:

Input   \framebox{Some Text}

Output   Some Text

The first optional argument can be used to make the box a specified width:

Input   \framebox[4cm]{Some Text}

Output   Some Text

The second optional argument specifies the justification of the text (left, right or centred) within the box:

Input   \framebox[4cm][r]{Some Text}

Output   Some Text

In general, if a command has both optional and mandatory arguments, the optional arguments are usually specified first (although there are a few exceptions).

2.9. Moving Arguments and Fragile Commands

Certain types of commands, called *fragile commands*, can seriously mess things up when they are used in what is termed a *moving argument*. These types of argument are generally those whose contents are copied to another part of the document. For example, section headings appear at the start of a section, but they can also appear in the table of contents. The \footnote command is a fragile command, so

\section{A heading\footnote{with a footnote}}

[FAQ: An extra '}'??]

will cause an error.

If there is no other command to use in its place, you should use \protect immediately before the fragile command:

Input   \section{A heading\protect\footnote{with a footnote}}

[FAQ: Footnotes in LaTeX section headings]

This, however, is a contrived example, because it isn't a good idea to have a footnote in a section heading, as it will also end up in the table of contents, and possibly in page headings.

2.10. Robust Commands

A *robust command* is a command that is not a fragile command.

2.11. Short and Long Commands

A *short command* is a command whose argument may not contain a paragraph break (either as a blank line or using \par.) Conversely, a *long command* is a command whose argument may contain a paragraph break.

Using short commands helps to test for forgotten braces, so it is recommended that when you define a new command (see Chapter 8 (Defining Commands)) you should always make the command a short command, unless there is a chance that the argument may need to contain a paragraph break.

2.12. Declarations

The term *declaration* is used to refer to a command that affects the document from that point onwards. The declaration itself does not produce any text and, in most cases, its effect can be localised by placing the declaration within a group. For example, \bfseries is a declaration that switches the current font weight to bold, so the following code

```
Here is some normal text.
\bfseries Here is some bold text.
```

↑ Input

↓ Input

will appear in the typeset document looking like:

Here is some normal text. **Here is some bold text.**

Output

Some declarations don't immediately have a visible effect. For example, the declarations

```
\raggedright \raggedleft \centering
```

Definition

only set the paragraph justification to ragged-right, ragged-left or centred, respectively, if the declaration is still in effect at the end of the paragraph. That is, if it is still in effect at the next \par or blank line.

EXAMPLE:

```
This is an example paragraph illustrating the paragraph justification
declarations. The default justification is fully justified. \raggedright
The paragraph justification can be switched to ragged-right or
\raggedleft ragged-left. \par
```

↑ Input

↓ Input

Output ↑
> This is an example paragraph illustrating the paragraph justification declarations. The default justification is fully justified. The paragraph justification can be switched to ragged-right or ragged-left.

Output ↓

Above, the justification at the paragraph break is ragged-left, so that's the justification used for the entire paragraph. Compare with:

Input ↑
```
{This is an example paragraph illustrating the paragraph justification
declarations. The default justification is fully justified. \raggedright
The paragraph justification can be switched to ragged-right or
\raggedleft ragged-left.} \par
```
Input ↓

Output ↑
> This is an example paragraph illustrating the paragraph justification declarations. The default justification is fully justified. The paragraph justification can be switched to ragged-right or ragged-left.

Output ↓

Above, the justification at the paragraph break is fully-justified, since both the declarations \raggedright and \raggedleft are cancelled when their local scope (signified by the curly braces) ends. This type of mistake most often occurs when people try to centre text doing something like:

✗
```
{\centering Some text that is supposed to
be centred.
}

Next paragraph.
```

The paragraph break (blank line) must go before the closing brace.

✔
```
{\centering Some text that is supposed to
be centred.

}
Next paragraph.
```

⚠ While we're on the subject of centred text, don't be tempted to use \centerline. It's obsolete [16].

2.13. Inter-Sentence Spacing

Inter-sentence spacing refers to the default type of space to be inserted between adjacent sentences within a paragraph. There is disagreement over what size this space should be. French spacing uses the same space as used between words. English spacing uses an en-space (half an em[2.6]-space). With proportional fonts (such as this one), the en-space is slightly larger than a single space. The difference is shown here:

↑ Input
```
X X

X\enspace X
```
↓ Input

↑ Output

X X
X X

↓ Output

(Note that with fully-justified paragraphs, in both cases the spaces may be stretched to ensure the sides of the paragraph are flushed.)

TeX (and LaTeX) defaults to English spacing, but you can switch to French spacing using the declaration:

```
\frenchspacing
```
Definition

and switch back again using

```
\nonfrenchspacing
```
Definition

There was no en-space on a typewriter, so typists started using two spaces in an attempt to emulate that slightly larger than one space look. This habit has spread to word-processor users as well, and now many people incorrectly assume English spacing means adding two spaces after a full stop, which is too wide and looks ugly, but this error shouldn't be used as a criticism against English spacing.

There has been a gradual trend towards French spacing over the last century, and some publishers insist on it. I think this may in part be due to a backlash against the ugliness of two spaces in typewritten and word-processed documents. In fact the Oxford Style Manual [11] simply states, "In text, only use a single space after all sentence punctuation."

Personally, I prefer English spacing, particularly in reference books. I have many reference books on my shelf, but I haven't read any of them from cover-to-cover. I flick to a particular section and skim through the paragraphs until I reach the desired bit of information. Sometimes I've already looked something up, so I have a vague idea as to where to find the information. The extra space between sentences makes it easier to locate a particular sentence.

This isn't so much of an issue with books designed to be read from beginning to end, such as a novel. However, I have read one such book that used a font where the

[2.6] see Section 2.17

commas had tiny tails and most of the sentences contained multiple proper nouns, which made it very difficult to read as it wasn't clear where the sentences ended. Is that a full stop followed by a new sentence that happens to start with a proper noun, or is it a comma whose tiny tail is blurred by my short-sighted eyes followed by a clause that happens to start with a proper noun? A well-written, well-presented document should not interrupt the reader, forcing them to continually go back to re-parse a sentence.

However, if you are writing a document, whether prose or technical, with the intention of having it published you must check with the publisher's guidelines to see if they insist on a particular style.

NOTES:
An end of sentence punctuation mark can be one of: a full stop (.), exclamation mark (!) or question mark (?).

1. If an end of sentence punctuation mark follows a lower case character, TEX assumes the punctuation mark indicates the end of the sentence. For example, as in:

   Input

   ```
   Did you see that? I certainly did.
   ```

2. Where this isn't the case, use \␣ (backslash followed by a space).

   Input ↑

   Input ↓

   ```
   This can happen when a sentence contains a lower case abbreviation,
   e.g.\␣like this one.
   ```

3. If an end of sentence punctuation mark follows an upper case character, TEX assumes the sentence hasn't ended at that point. For example, as in:

   Input

   ```
   The G.P. said it was only hypochondria.
   ```

4. Where the sentence actually ends with an upper case letter, add \@ after the letter and before the punctuation mark.

   Input ↑

   Input ↓

   ```
   Yesterday, I saw my G.P\@. Tomorrow I'm going to see the
   specialist.
   ```

NOTE ON TYPEWRITER FONTS
Note that \nonfrenchspacing in a monospaced font will insert two spaces between sentences, emulating a typewritten document.

⊤ Input

```
\ttfamily
\nonfrenchspacing x. x.

\frenchspacing x. x.
```

⊥ Input

⊤ Output

```
    x.  x.
    x.  x.
```

⊥ Output

2.14. Hyphenation

Words sometimes require *hyphenation* to help justify paragraphs and prevent overly large areas of white space or protrusions into the right margin. Some word processors by default don't hyphenate words in fully-justified paragraphs, which has led some people to believe that hyphenation is bad. Just because word processors do something a certain way, doesn't mean that it's the correct way. TEX has an excellent hyphenation algorithm, but the default hyphenation pattern is designed for English. If you are writing in another language, use the babel package to switch the hyphenation pattern (see Section 5.8).

Despite using an excellent algorithm, TEX occasionally gets the hyphenation wrong, particularly where the hyphenation is context sensitive. There are two ways of setting the hyphenation for a given word.

1. For all occurrences of the word, use

   ```
   \hyphenation{⟨hyphenated word⟩}
   ```
   Definition

   inserting a hyphen - at all possible hyphenation points. For example:

   ```
   \hyphenation{gal-axy}
   ```
   Input

2. For a particular instance of a word, use \- at the hyphenation point within the word. For example:

⊤ Input

```
There once was a little alien called Uiop who lived in the faraway
gal\-axy of Zxcv.
```

⊥ Input

2.15. Environments

An *environment* is a block of code contained within the commands

Definition   \begin{⟨*env-name*⟩}

and

Definition   \end{⟨*env-name*⟩}

where ⟨*env-name*⟩ is the name of the environment. The block of code is then formatted in a method specific to that environment. For example, the bfseries[2.7] environment will typeset the contents of the environment in a bold font. The following code:

Input   \begin{bfseries}Here is some bold text.\end{bfseries}

will appear in the typeset document looking like:

Output   **Here is some bold text.**

Some environments also supply commands that may only be used within that environment.

EXAMPLE:
The itemize environment provides a command called \item so that you can specify individual items within an unordered list:

Input ⊤
```
Shopping List:
\begin{itemize}
  \item Cabbages
  \item Bananas
  \item Apples
\end{itemize}
```
Input ↓

The above will produce the following output:

Output ⊤

Shopping List:

- Cabbages

- Bananas

- Apples

Output ↓

[2.7] Note there is no backslash in the environment name.

2.16. The Preamble

The *preamble* is the part of the source code that comes after the \documentclass command and before \begin{document} (the start of the document environment). Only a few special commands may be placed in the preamble (such as \title), and there are a few special commands that may only go in the preamble (such as \usepackage). Nothing that generates text (for example, \maketitle) may go in the preamble.

```
\documentclass{...}
                    ⟵── This bit in here is the preamble.
\begin{document}
```

2.17. Lengths

A *length* register stores dimensions (such as 1in, 5cm, 8.25mm). Like control words, length registers start with a backslash and only contain alphabetical characters in their name. These registers are used to determine page layouts etc. For example, the paragraph indentation is given by the length register \parindent. Acceptable units of measurement are listed in Table 2.1. The two relative units "em" and "ex" are dependent on the current font. (The em-value used to be the width of an "M" and the ex-value was the height of the letter "x", but these days the values are more arbitrary [6].) Use em for widths and ex for heights if you want to use relative values.

Table 2.1. Units of Measurement

pt	TeX point: 72.27pt = 1in
in	inch: 1in = 25.4mm
mm	millimetre: 1mm=2.845pt
cm	centimetre: 1cm = 10mm
ex	the "x-height" of the current font
em	the width of a "quad" in the current font
sp	scaled point: 1sp = 65536pt
bp	big point (or PostScript point): 72bp = 1in
dd	didôt point: 1dd=0.376mm
pc	pica: 1pc=12pt
cc	cicero: 1cc=12dd
mu	math unit: 18mu = 1em

To change a length you can use the command:

\setlength{⟨*cmd*⟩}{⟨*length*⟩}   Definition

where ⟨*cmd*⟩ is the register (for example, \parindent) and ⟨*length*⟩ is the new length. Alternatively, you can add a value to a length using:

Definition   \addtolength{⟨*cmd*⟩}{⟨*length increment*⟩}

The value of a length register can be displayed in your document using

Definition   \the⟨*register*⟩

[FAQ: Zero paragraph indent]

A *rubber length* is a length that has a certain amount of elasticity. This enables you to specify your desired length but allows LaTeX to stretch or contract the space to get the body of text as flushed with the margins as possible.

For example, the paragraph gap \parskip is usually set to 0pt plus 1pt. This means that the preferred gap is 0pt but LaTeX can stretch it up to 1pt to help prevent the page from having a ragged bottom. For example:

Input ↑

```
\setlength{\parindent}{0pt}
\setlength{\parskip}{10pt plus 1pt minus 1pt}

This is the first paragraph.

This is the second paragraph.
The paragraph indentation is \the\parindent.
```

Input ↓

This now produces:

Output ↑

This is the first paragraph.

This is the second paragraph. The paragraph indentation is 0.0pt.

Output ↓

In this example, the preferred paragraph gap is 10pt but it will allow for a deviation of up to plus or minus 1pt.

Note that it's generally best not to change \parskip explicitly as it can cause unexpected complications. If you use one of the KOMA-Script classes, such as scrreprt, you can use the parskip class option that can take the following values: parskip=full (a full line height) parskip=half (half a line height).[2.8]

EXAMPLE:

Input   \documentclass[parskip=full]{scrbook}

If you want to change any of the page layout lengths (such as \textwidth), the easiest way to do it is to use the geometry package. This package should have been

---

[2.8]There are also variants that have +, - or * as a suffix. See the KOMA-Script documentation for further details.

installed when you installed your TEX distribution. For example: suppose you want the total text area to be 6.5in wide and 8.75in high with a left margin of 0.4in, then you would do:

`\usepackage[body={6.5in,8.75in},left=0.4in]{geometry}` Input

2.18. Class File

The *class file* (`.cls`) defines the page layout, heading styles and various commands and environments needed for a particular type of document. The class file is specified using the command

`\documentclass[⟨options⟩]{⟨class-name⟩}` Definition

where ⟨*class-name*⟩ is the name of the file without the `.cls` extension. All LATEX documents must start with this command. This book uses the scrbook class.

2.19. TEX

TEX is the typesetting language written by Donald Knuth. He wrote a format of TEX called Plain TEX, but many people find Plain TEX complicated, so Leslie Lamport wrote a format of TEX called LATEX to make it a bit easier to use. You can think of LATEX as a go-between converting your instructions into TEX. This book mostly uses the term LATEX, even if the matter is more general to TEX, to avoid complicating matters. Some error messages you may see will be LATEX messages, some will be TEX messages. LATEX error messages tend to be a bit easier to understand than TEX messages. There are other formats of TEX, such as ConTeXt, but this book does not cover them.

[FAQ: What is TeX?]

[FAQ: Should I use Plain TeX or LaTeX?]

[FAQ: How does LaTeX relate to Plain TeX?]

[FAQ: What is ConTeXt?]

2.20. Perl

TEX-distributions such as `TeX Live` and `MiKTeX` also include some helper applications that you may find useful. For example, `texdoc` (Section 1.1) helps you access installed documentation and `makeindex` helps generate an index for your document. Some of the helper applications are written in a scripting language called *Perl*, and you must have the `perl` application installed to be able to use them. Unix-like operating systems should already have it installed. Windows users can choose between several Perl distributions. The most popular seem to be `Strawberry Perl`[2.9] and `Active Perl`.[2.10] Perl scripts that come with TEX include: `epstopdf` (converts Encapsulated PostScript (EPS) files to PDF), `pdfcrop` (crops a PDF file), `xindy` (a more flexible indexing application than `makeindex`), `texcount` (counts the number of words in a

---

[2.9]`http://strawberryperl.com/`
[2.10]`http://www.activestate.com/activeperl`

LATEX document) and `latexmk` (runs LATEX and any associated applications, such as `bibtex`, the required number of times to ensure the document is fully up-to-date).

CHAPTER 3

FROM SOURCE CODE TO TYPESET OUTPUT

Every time you want to create or edit a LaTeX document, there are three basic steps you will always need to follow:

1. Write or edit the source code.

2. Pass the source code to the `latex` or `pdflatex` application ("LaTeX the document").

    - If there are any error messages, return to Step 1.
    - If there are no error messages, a PDF file is created.

3. View the PDF file to check the result. If you need to modify your document, go back to Step 1.

You will therefore need:

1. A text editor (to perform Step 1). For example Vim,[3.1] Emacs[3.2] or Gedit.[3.3]

2. The TeX software (to perform Step 2). If you don't already have TeX on your machine, you will need to install it. The most convenient way to do this is to install from the TeX Collection DVD ROM, which is distributed to all TeX User Group[3.4] (TUG) members, but you can also download and install free TeX distributions, such as TeX Live, MiKTeX or MacTeX, from the Internet (see on the following page). There is also proTeXt, an enhancement of MiKTeX that aims to be an easy-to-install TeX Distribution. For more information including up-to-date links, go to http://www.ctan.org/starter.html. *[FAQ: (La)TeX for different machines]*

3. A PDF viewer (to perform Step 3). For example Adobe Reader,[3.5] Sumatra,[3.6] Evince[3.7] or Okular.[3.8]

[3.1]http://www.vim.org/
[3.2]http://www.gnu.org/software/emacs/
[3.3]http://projects.gnome.org/gedit/
[3.4]http://tug.org/
[3.5]http://www.adobe.com/
[3.6]http://blog.kowalczyk.info/software/sumatrapdf/free-pdf-reader.html
[3.7]http://projects.gnome.org/evince/
[3.8]http://okular.kde.org/

This can be rather complicated for a beginner, especially for those with no experience writing computer code. Fortunately, there are some all-in-one applications (often called a *front-end*) that provide a text editor (for Step 1), buttons or menu items to run the latex or pdflatex command-line application (for Step 2) and, in some cases, a viewer to perform Step 3.

Section 3.1 describes one such front-end called TeXWorks.[3.9] I have chosen to describe TeXWorks because it is a free, cross-platform application. Binaries are available for Microsoft Windows, Mac OS X and GNU/Linux. The screen shots of TeXWorks in this book were taken from the Linux version running under Fedora. If you run TeXWorks on other operating systems, it may have a slightly different look, but it has the same functionality.

New versions of TeX Live and MiKTeX include TeXWorks for MS Windows, and new versions of MacTeX include TeXWorks for Mac OS X users. GNU/Linux users can use their Add/Remove Software utility to install TeXWorks. Alternatively, you can download TeXWorks by following the links provided at http://www.tug.org/texworks/.

If you're confused by all the options, let's keep things as simple as possible:

- MS Windows:

  You have a choice between MiKTeX (or proTeXt) and TeX Live. MiKTeX provides a smaller and quicker installation, but the downside is that you may not have the classes or packages you want to use. MiKTeX can install these whenever you try to LaTeX a document that uses them, but you need an Internet connection while it does this. TeX Live installs everything, so it takes longer and needs more space, but you should have the majority of packages and classes that you need.

TeX Live:

1. Fetch and unpack http://mirror.ctan.org/systems/texlive/tlnet/install-tl.zip

2. Run install-tl and follow the instructions. This can take an hour or more.

proTeXt:

1. Go to http://tug.org/protext/

2. Click on the "download the self-extract protext.exe" link to download and run the executable.

MiKTeX:

1. Go to http://www.miktex.org/

2. In the left-hand panel, there is a link to the download page for the latest version. At time of writing, it is MiKTeX 2.9. Click on that link.

[3.9]http://www.tug.org/texworks/

3. Scroll down to the section "Installing a basic `MiKTeX` system".

4. If you're happy with the selected mirror location, click on the "Download" button.

5. Run the executable.

- Mac OS X:

  1. Go to `http://tug.org/mactex/`

  2. Follow the instructions on that page.

- GNU/Linux:

  1. Fetch and unpack `http://mirror.ctan.org/systems/texlive/tlnet/install-tl-unx.tar.gz`

  2. Follow the instructions at `http://tug.org/texlive/quickinstall.html`

  3. Once `TeX Live` has finished installing, run your system's "Add/Remove Software" tool.

  4. Find "texworks", select the newest version and install.

If you run into problems, there are mailing lists at `http://tug.org/mailman/listinfo/tex-live` and `http://docs.miktex.org/manual/lists.html` for TeX Live and `MiKTeX`, and `MacTeX` help at `http://www.tug.org/mactex/help/`. There is also a list of places where you can ask for help in Appendix C (Need More Help?).

3.1. TeXWorks

Hopefully you've managed to successfully install TeX and TeXWorks as described above, so let's test it out.

First run TeXWorks. On Windows, you can access it via the Start menu. On GNU/Linux, it's probably located in Applications→Office, or you can type `texworks` in a terminal. You should now see the TeXWorks window. The button marked with a grey triangle in a green circle is the build or typeset function. It runs the application in the drop-down list next to it. This is set to pdfLaTeX, which is what we want for now.

It's a good idea to switch on the syntax highlighting, if it isn't already on. This is done via the Format→Syntax Coloring sub-menu. Make sure the LaTeX item is selected.

Next, type in the following sample source code, as shown in Figure 3.1 on page 33 (the commands used here will be described in more detail in Chapter 4 (Creating a Simple Document)):

Input ↑

```
\documentclass{scrartcl}

\begin{document}

This is an example document.

\end{document}
```

Input ↓

Pay close attention to the backslashes at the start of each command name. If you find the font is a bit too small for you, you can make it larger using the Format →Font menu item. *This doesn't affect the font size in your PDF file, just the font size of your code.* This displays the "Select Font" dialog box. Set the font size as appropriate.

Then save the document, using the File→Save As menu item. I called my document `example1.tex` (remember the `.tex` extension and stick to file names that only consist of alphabetical characters, digits and hyphens — don't uses spaces or underscores).

Now that you have saved the file, you can run pdfLaTeX. Make sure the drop-down list next to the build button has "pdfLaTeX" selected and click on the build button. If all goes well, a new window should open displaying the typeset document (Figure 3.2 on page 34).

Now let's see what happens if there is an error in the source code. In Figure 3.3 on page 35 I have misspelt the \documentclass command. This time, when I click on the build button, I get the error message:

```
! Undefined control sequence.
1.1 \documentclas
                  {scrartcl}
?
```

(Shown in Figure 3.4 on page 36.)

Here "Undefined control sequence" means an unrecognised command, and below that message, "1.1" means the error was encountered on line 1. An input line at the bottom of the window has appeared with a cursor. LATEX is in interactive mode and is awaiting a response. There are several responses, but I'm only going to mention two of them:

1. Type h and press the Return/Enter key ←┘. This displays a short help message and awaits a new response (see Figure 3.5 on page 37).

2. Type x and press Return/Enter. This aborts the LATEX run.

Notice that the green circle button with the grey triangle has turned into a red stop button. This button can be used to abort the process instead of typing x.

Now, there is a second tab at the bottom of the TeXWork's window (Figure 3.6 on page 39). This lists the error message and provides a link to the line where the

Figure 3.1. Source Code for an Example Document. (Syntax highlighting switched on.)

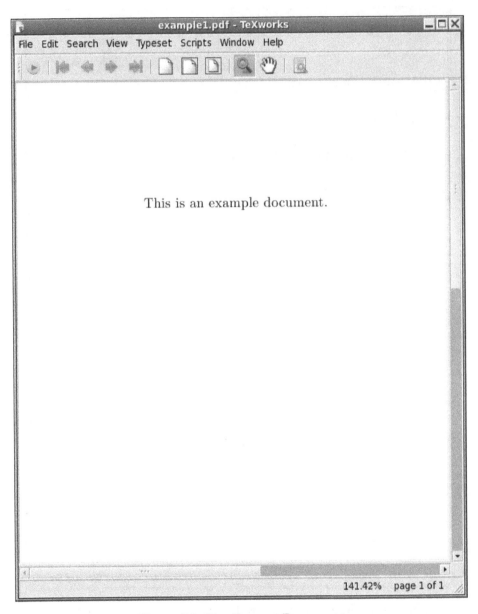

Figure 3.2. The Typeset Document

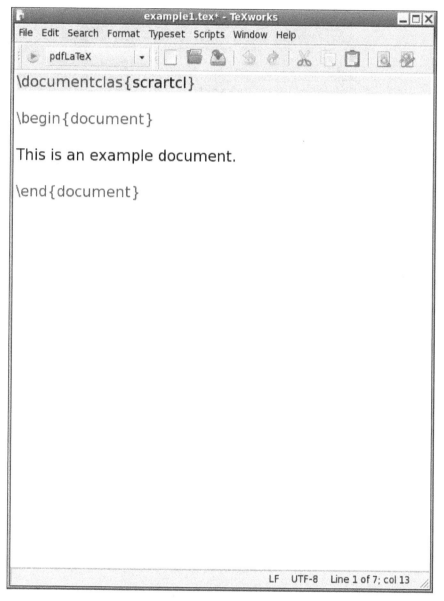

Figure 3.3. The Source Code Has a Misspelt Command

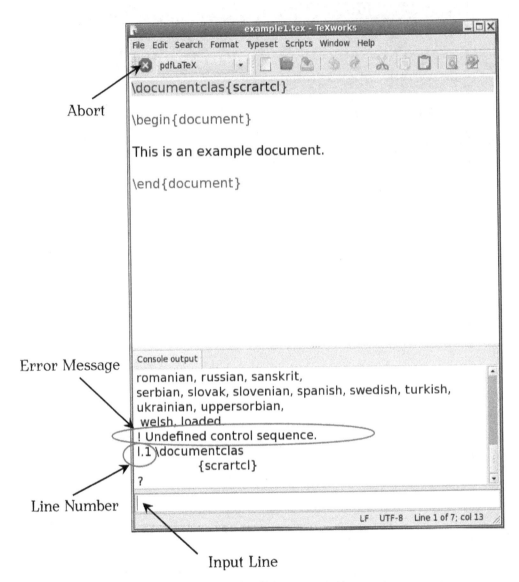

Figure 3.4. An Error Message is Displayed

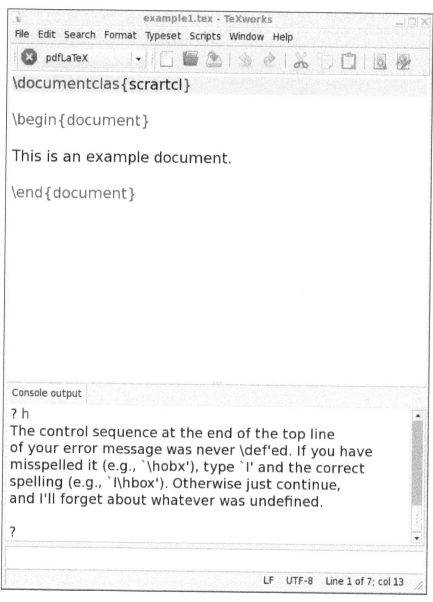

Figure 3.5. A Short Help Message

error occurred. Clicking on this link highlights line 1. Next I need to fix the error by correcting the spelling of the command. Once it's fixed, I can click on the build button.

Here's another error you might encounter: I'm now going to misspell the class name. It should be scrartcl, but in Figure 3.7 on page 40 it has been misspelt. This time, when I click on the build button, I get the error:

```
! LaTeX Error: File 'scrartc.cls' not found.
```

I have two choices: type in the correct name on the line below "Enter file name:" or I can abort the process using the red abort button. In either case I need to go back and fix the error in my code.

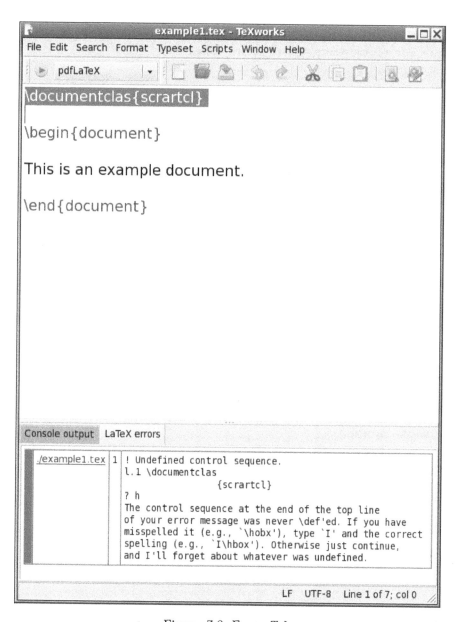

Figure 3.6. Error Tab

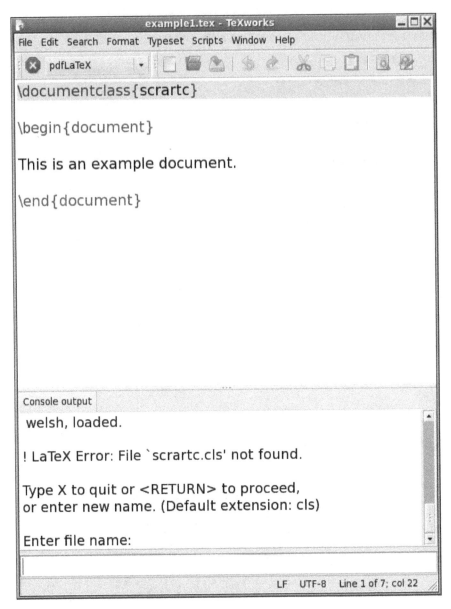

Figure 3.7. Misspelt Class File

CHAPTER 4

CREATING A SIMPLE DOCUMENT

Having installed and tested the software, let's now look at how to actually write the source code. The very first line of any document that you create must have the command:

\documentclass[⟨*option-list*⟩]{⟨*class-name*⟩}

Definition

This tells LaTeX what type of document you want to create (for example an article, a technical report or correspondence). The \documentclass command takes one mandatory argument, ⟨*class-name*⟩, that specifies the class file.

There are many class files available, and some publishers, institutions or journals provide their own custom classes (for example, the jmlr class for the Journal of Machine Learning Research). Popular classes include memoir (for books and reports) and those supplied in the KOMA-Script bundle (for books, reports, articles and correspondence). There's also beamer (for presentations) as well as classes for typesetting exams, flashcards, concert programmes etc. For simplicity, this book will concentrate on three of the KOMA-Script classes scrartcl (for articles), scrreprt (for technical reports, theses etc) and scrbook (for books).

We'll start with a very simple document, so let's use the scrartcl class file. In this case the very first line of the source code should be:

\documentclass{scrartcl}

Input

The \documentclass command also takes an optional argument, ⟨*option-list*⟩, which should be a comma separated list of options to be passed to the class file. This allows you to override the class file defaults. For example, the scrartcl class file by default uses A4 paper, but if you are in the USA you will probably want to use letter paper. This can be achieved using the option letterpaper. So you would need to edit the above line to:

\documentclass[letterpaper]{scrartcl}

Input

Let's change another option. The normal font size is 11pt by default, but we have the option to change it, so let's use 12pt:

\documentclass[letterpaper,12pt]{scrartcl}

Input

You can also change your document so that it is in a two-column format using the twocolumn option:

\documentclass[letterpaper,12pt,twocolumn]{scrartcl}

Input

After deciding what type of document you want, you now need to specify the contents of the document. This is done inside the document environment. The document is started with the command:

Input   `\begin{document}`

and ended with

Input   `\end{document}`

(LaTeX stops reading the file when it reaches the above line, so anything occurring after it is ignored.)

My source code now looks like:

Input ⊤
```
\documentclass[12pt]{scrartcl}

\begin{document}
```

Input ↓
```
\end{document}
```

Every document you create must have this form. You can't simply start typing the document text. You must first specify your class file, and then place the contents of the document inside the document environment.

So far so good, but at the moment we have an empty document, so we won't get any output. Let's now put some text into our document:

Input ⊤
```
\documentclass[12pt]{scrartcl}

\begin{document}

This is a simple document.
Here is the first paragraph.

Here is the second paragraph. As you
can        see it's
a rather
short paragraph, but not as short as the previous one.

\end{document}
```
Input ↓

TOP FIVE MISTAKES MADE BY NEW USERS

I first started teaching LaTeX in 1998, and these are the most common errors I've seen when people start learning LaTeX:

1. Missing out the backslash \ at the start of one or more of the commands.

2. Using a forward slash / instead of a backslash \.

3. Forgetting \end{document}.

4. Misspelling "document" (in \begin{document} and \end{document}).

5. Missing a closing brace }.

If you encounter any problems when you start out, go through that check list first. Then check Appendix B (Common Errors).

Whenever you start a new document, always type in the \documentclass, \begin{document} and \end{document} commands first (Figure 4.1 on the following page). Then move your cursor between the \begin and \end lines and type the document text (Figure 4.2 on the next page).

Exercise 1 (Simple Document)

Try typing the code in the above example into TeXWorks or the editor of your choice (see Chapter 3 (From Source Code to Typeset Output) if you can't remember what to do.) You can also download[4.1] a copy of this file, but I recommend that you try typing it in to give yourself some practice.

Things to note while you are typing: firstly, when you press the return character at the end of a line this end-of-line character is converted into a space in the output file. So the fact that I have some very ragged lines in my source code has no effect on the final result. (Note that some front-ends will reformat your lines as you type.) Whereas a completely blank line will be converted into a paragraph break (\par has the same effect).

Secondly, multiple spaces are converted into a single space, so the large gap between the words "can" and "see" is no different from having a single space.

Once you have typed up your source code, save your file (called, for example, exercise1.tex), and run PDFLaTeX as described in Section 3.1. If all goes well, TeXWorks should display the resulting PDF file in a new window, usually alongside the window containing the source code.

NOTES:

1. Each paragraph automatically starts with an indentation in the PDF.

2. There is no blank line between the paragraphs in the PDF document. (See what happens if you add the KOMA-Script class option parskip=full:

   \documentclass[12pt,parskip=full]{scrartcl}

   and rebuild the PDF.)

3. Move the mouse over one of paragraphs in the PDF viewer and pop-up the context menu (usually a right mouse click). Select Jump to Source. The window containing the source code should now gain the focus and the line of code matching the typeset line you clicked on in the PDF should now be highlighted.

[4.1]http://www.dickimaw-books.com/latex/novices/html/exercises/simpledoc.tex

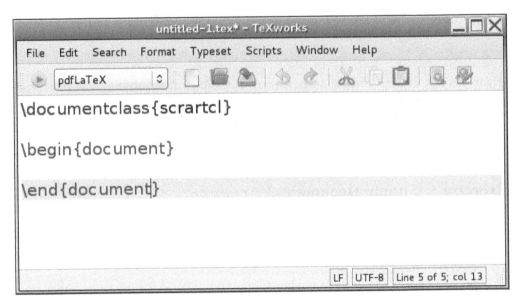

Figure 4.1. Starting a New Document: always type these three lines first.

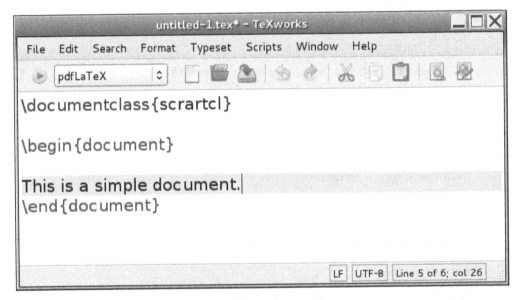

Figure 4.2. Starting a New Document: move the cursor inside the document environment and start typing the document text.

4.1. Using Simple Commands

[FAQ: Typesetting all those TeX-related logos]

Now let's try adding a few simple commands to our document. The command \LaTeX produces the LaTeX logo and the command \today prints the current date. LaTeX always ignores any spaces that follow a command name that consists of letters, as it uses the space to indicate the end of the command name. This means that if we want a space to occur immediately after the command, we need to explicitly say so using the command \␣ (recall from page 8 ␣ indicates a space character). So, for example:

`\LaTeX\␣logo`

Input

produces the output:

LaTeX logo

Output

Some people when starting out can get a bit confused by this and read it as the entity "\LaTeX\" whereas it is in fact two commands: "\LaTeX" (print the LaTeX logo) followed "\ " (print a space.)

Let's also try using a command that takes an argument. The command

`\footnote{⟨text⟩}`

Definition

takes one argument that specifies the text that should appear in the footnote. This command must be placed where you want the footnote marker to appear.

Exercise 2 (Using Simple Commands)

Edit the document you created in Exercise 1 (page 43), so that it looks like the following: (You can download[4.2] it if you like, but again it is better if you try typing it in yourself.)

```
\documentclass[12pt]{scrartcl}

\begin{document}

This is a simple \LaTeX\␣document. Here is the first paragraph.

Here is the second paragraph\footnote{with a footnote}. As you can see
it's a rather short paragraph, but not as short as the previous one. This
document was created on: \today.
\end{document}
```

↑ Code

↓ Code

[4.2]http://www.dickimaw-books.com/latex/novices/html/exercises/simple.tex

Now LaTeX your document and view the result. (Remember to check Appendix B (Common Errors) if you have a problem.) You should see the LaTeX logo, the footnote marker and the current date. If you scroll down to the bottom of the page, you should see the footnote.

4.2. Packages

[FAQ: What are LaTeX classes and packages?]

Packages are files with the extension .sty that either define new commands or redefine existing commands. They're like a type of add-on or plug-in. Most of the commonly used packages should have been installed when you installed your TeX distribution (see Chapter 3 (From Source Code to Typeset Output)). Appendix A (Downloading and Installing Packages) covers how to install new packages. Most packages come with documentation that can be accessed using the texdoc application described in Section 1.1.

Packages are loaded in the preamble (after \documentclass and before \begin{document}) using

Definition   \usepackage[⟨*option list*⟩]{⟨*package*⟩}

where ⟨*package*⟩ is the name of the package and ⟨*option list*⟩ is a list of comma-separated options. For example, to load the package graphicx with the draft option:

Input   \usepackage[draft]{graphicx}

Any applicable class options are also passed to packages, so in

Input ↑
Input ↓
```
\documentclass[draft]{scrartcl}
\usepackage{graphicx}
```

the draft option is set for both the scrartcl class and the graphicx package.

You can specify more than one package in the argument of \usepackage, where each package name is separated by a comma. For example:

Input   \usepackage{amsmath,amsfonts}

The graphicx package is covered in Chapter 6 (The graphicx Package) and the amsmath package is covered in Chapter 9 (Mathematics), so let's start out with a relatively simple example.

4.2.1. Changing the Format of \today

In the previous exercise, we used the \today command to produce the current date. By default, this command displays the date in US format. To illustrate how to use packages, this section will look at how to use the datetime package to change the way that \today displays the date.

The datetime package has various options that can be used to change the format of \today. For example, by default the datetime package redefines \today to display the date in the form: Tuesday 25th September, 2012. The option short will produce an abbreviated form, (for example Tue 25th Sept, 2012) and the option nodayofweek won't display the day of the week (for example 25th September, 2012). For those who don't like the raised ordinal, there is the level option. These can be passed as a comma separated list in the optional argument to the \usepackage command. It is also possible to use a declaration instead. For example, to redefine \today to display the date in the form 25/09/2012, you can either do

`\usepackage[ddmmyyyy]{datetime}`   *Input*

or

`\usepackage{datetime}`   *Input*
`\ddmmyyyydate`

The datetime package also defines the command

`\currenttime`   *Definition*

which displays the current time, where again the format can be changed by the package options. So the option 12hr will cause \currenttime to display the date in 12 hour format (for example, 7:33pm) and the option 24hr will cause \currenttime to display the date in 24 hour format (for example, 19:33).

Exercise 3 (Using the datetime Package)

Edit your document from Exercise 2 (page 45) so that it uses the datetime package. Experiment with the different package options, for example

`\usepackage[short,nodayofweek,level,12hr]{datetime}`   *Input*

and add the current time

`This document was created on: \today\␣at \currenttime.`   *Input*

You can download[4.3] an example. For a full list datetime of package options, see the datetime documentation. (Refer to Section 1.1 on how to find package documentation.)

4.3. Special Characters and Symbols

You can use most of the standard characters that you find on your keyboard, but the 10 symbols shown in Table 4.1 on the following page have a special meaning.

[4.3]http://www.dickimaw-books.com/latex/novices/html/exercises/datetime.tex

Table 4.1. Special Characters

{ } % & $ # _ ^ ~ \

We have already used the curly braces { and }. The percent symbol % is a comment character. Everything from the percent symbol up to the end of line is ignored by LaTeX. This means you can have comments in your source code to remind you what a particular part of your code is doing. We have also used the backslash symbol \ which indicates that we are using a LaTeX command, as in \LaTeX or \today. The meaning of the other special characters will be covered later.

So what do you do if you want one of these symbols to actually appear in your document? Table 4.2 lists commands that produce these and other symbols. Note that some of the commands have short cuts, such as --- instead of \textemdash and ?` instead of \textquestiondown.

[FAQ: Where can I find the symbol for ...?]

[FAQ: How to get copyright, trademark, etc]

The symbol ` is the backtick (or grave) symbol, as opposed to the apostrophe symbol '. The backtick symbol usually looks like ` on a keyboard, and on most UK keyboards it is situated to the left of the 1 key. The opening double quote is created using two adjacent backtick symbols and the closing double quote with two adjacent apostrophe symbols. This gives 66 and 99 style quotes, which you wouldn't get using the double quote symbol on your keyboard.

Note that the symbols | < and > have to be created using \textbar, \textless and \textgreater when in normal text mode. If you try to enter them using the corresponding keyboard characters you may get — ¡ and ¿. (They do however work if you are in maths mode.[4.4]) The slash character / may be used directly, as in "and/or", but no line break will be permitted at the slash, whereas \slash (as in "and\slash␣or") will allow a line break at that point.

Table 4.2. Symbols

\textbackslash	\	\slash	/	\textgreater	>
\textasciicircum	^	\$	$	\textbar	|
\textasciitilde	~	\{	{	\textless	<
\pounds	£	\}	}	\dag	†
\textregistered	®	\#	#	\ddag	‡
\texttrademark	™	\%	%	' or \textquoteright	'
\copyright	©	\&	&	` or \textquoteleft	`
\textbullet	•	\i	ı	'' or \textquotedblright	"
?` or \textquestiondown	¿	\j	ȷ	`` or \textquotedblleft	"
!` or \textexclamdown	¡	-	-	-- or \textendash	–
--- or \textemdash	—	\S	§	\textperiodcentered	·
\ldots	...	\P	¶	_ or \textunderscore	_

Ligatures and special symbols are shown in Table 4.3 on the facing page. (Note that, as mentioned in the introduction, the f-ligatures are automatically converted.)

[4.4]There are also some text fonts that will display them correctly, but don't rely on it.

When using a command in the middle of a word, take care that the command doesn't run into the rest of the word. For example, the British spelling of the word manœuvre has an œ-ligature in the middle of it. You will get an error if you try:

```
man\oeuvre
```

as LaTeX will interpret it as the command \oeuvre which doesn't exist.

There are several ways to code this in LaTeX:

1. Place a space after the command:

   ```
   man\oe␣uvre
   ```
   Input

2. Place an empty brace after the command:

   ```
   man\oe{}uvre
   ```
   Input

3. Group the command:

   ```
   man{\oe}uvre
   ```
   Input

   (This can adversely affect the kerning so is best avoided.)

Table 4.3. Ligatures and Special Symbols (Computer Modern Font)

\AE	Æ	\ae	æ	\OE	Œ	\oe	œ
fi	fi	ffi	ffi	fl	fl	ffl	ffl
\AA	Å	\aa	å	\L	Ł	\l	ł
\O	Ø	\o	ø	\SS	SS	\ss	ß

English speakers are by and large very lackadaisical when it comes to accents, but accents affect pronunciation, and so are just as important as the correct spelling. There is a big difference between putting your knife into someone's pâté (meat paste), and putting your knife into someone's pate (head)!

Accented letters are created by specifying which accent you want, and the letter on which to put the accent. The accent commands are listed in Table 4.4, and each command takes one mandatory argument. The command indicates what accent to use, and the argument indicates the letter on which to put the accent.

You may have noticed in Table 4.2 on the preceding page the commands \i and \j which produce a dotless i and j (ı and ȷ). With old versions of LaTeX (or TeX) an accent over a normal "i" or "j" left the original dot in, which is incorrect, so a dotless "ı" or "ȷ" were required. With modern distributions, an accented "i" or "j" is correctly rendered.

EXAMPLE:

Input ↑
Input ↓

```
It's na\"ive to think that eating mouldy p\^at\'e won't result in food
poisoning.
```

Result:

Output

It's naïve to think that eating mouldy pâté won't result in food poisoning.

Table 4.4. Accent Commands

Definition	Example Input	Example Output	Definition	Example Input	Example Output
\'{⟨object⟩}	\'{c}	ć	\={⟨object⟩}	\={c}	c̄
\`{⟨object⟩}	\`{c}	c̀	\.{⟨object⟩}	\.{c}	ċ
\^{⟨object⟩}	\^{c}	ĉ	\~{⟨object⟩}	\~{c}	c̃
\"{⟨object⟩}	\"{c}	c̈	\v{⟨object⟩}	\v{c}	č
\u{⟨object⟩}	\u{c}	c̆	\H{⟨object⟩}	\H{c}	c̋
\t{⟨object⟩}	\t{xy}	x͡y	\c{⟨object⟩}	\c{c}	ç
\d{⟨object⟩}	\d{c}	c̣	\b{⟨object⟩}	\b{c}	c̱
\r{⟨object⟩}	\r{c}	c̊			

This book only covers a very small subset of available symbol commands. If the command you want isn't here, try Scott Pakin's comprehensive symbol list [10]. Another useful resource is `detexify`.[4.5]

4.3.1. The inputenc Package

Instead of using the accent and ligature commands described above, you can use the inputenc package and enter the character directly, but you must ensure you match the encoding with that used by your text editor. For example, this book uses UTF8 encoding so I have loaded the inputenc package in the preamble with the `utf8` option:

Input

```
\usepackage[utf8]{inputenc}
```

Note that it's a good idea to also use the fontenc package as well. For example, if you want to use Type 1 fonts:

Input ↑
Input ↓

```
\usepackage[T1]{fontenc}
\usepackage[utf8]{inputenc}
```

Returning to an earlier example, I can directly enter the Unicode character (U+0153) for the lower case œ ligature:

[4.5]`http://detexify.kirelabs.org/classify.html`

manœuvre Input

Note that if you are collaborating on a document and you want to use this approach, you must ensure that all your co-authors use the same input encoding. For example, suppose you decide to use ISO Latin 1 encoding (latin1 option):

\usepackage[latin1]{inputenc} Input

but your co-author is using a UTF-8 editor and types:

naïve Input

where ï is the Unicode character U+00EF. UTF-8 characters use one to four 8-bit bytes whereas ISO Latin 1 uses an 8-bit single-byte character set. So the U+00EF binary sequence is interpreted by ISO Latin 1 encoding as two characters: Ã (0xC3) and ‾ (0xAF). Therefore the resulting PDF file will end up containing the rather odd looking:

naÃ‾ve

(If you are using TeXWorks, you can set your preferred encoding using Edit→ Preferences and select the "Editor" tab where there is an "Encoding" setting. Make sure this setting matches the inputenc option you use in your document.)

Exercise 4 (Using Special Characters)

Start a new file in TeXworks, and see if you can write the source code to create the output below. Choose whether you want to use the inputenc package or if you want to use commands such as \c, but in either case you need to be careful of the special characters listed in Table 4.1 on page 48.

Item #1: Our travel expenditure came to $2000.00 & our equipment expenditure came to £100.00 plus VAT @ 17.5%. ↑ Output
Chloë collected Zoë from the crèche. They stopped to admire the façade of a new café and then went to a matinée. ↓ Output

You can download[4.6] the source code if you can't work out how to do it, and remember to check Appendix B (Common Errors) if you have a problem.

4.4. Lists

Now you've had a go at using some commands, let's use some environments (recall Section 2.15). A good example of environments are the list making environments. There are three basic list making environments: itemize (for unordered lists), enumerate (for ordered lists) and description (for lists where you want to specify your own label.)

[4.6]http://www.dickimaw-books.com/latex/novices/html/exercises/spchar.tex

In each of these environments, each item in the list must be started with the command:

Definition   \item[⟨*marker*⟩]

The optional argument ⟨*marker*⟩ can be used to override the default marker for that particular item. (For example, to replace the bullet point for an individual item in an unordered list to make that item stand out from all the other items.) We will be looking at how to change the default marker in Section 8.2.

RELATED UK FAQ [19] TOPICS:

- Perhaps a missing \item?

- Fancy enumeration lists

- How to adjust list spacing

- Interrupting enumerated lists

- "Too deeply nested"

4.4.1. Unordered Lists

Unordered lists are created using the itemize environment.

EXAMPLE:

Input ↑
```
\begin{itemize}
\item Animal
\item Vegetable
\item Mineral
\end{itemize}
```
Input ↓

Output ↑

- Animal

- Vegetable

- Mineral

Output ↓

ANOTHER EXAMPLE:
Changing the default markers is covered in Section 8.2, but it's also possible to override the default marker for a particular item, as in this example (recall the double-dagger symbol command \ddag from Table 4.2 on page 48):

```
\begin{itemize}
\item Animal
\item[\ddag] Vegetable
\item Mineral
\end{itemize}
```

- Animal

‡ Vegetable

- Mineral

Be careful about using square brackets [] inside an optional argument. Grouping is required, as in:

```
\begin{itemize}
\item Animal
\item[{[X]}] Vegetable
\item Mineral
\end{itemize}
```

- Animal

[X] Vegetable

- Mineral

Similarly if the item starts with an open square bracket [, as in:

```
\begin{itemize}
\item Animal
\item {[sic]} Wegetable
\item Mineral
\end{itemize}
```

Output ↑

- Animal

- [sic] Wegetable

- Mineral

Output ↓

Nested Lists

It is also possible to nest itemize environments. The following example has three levels, each using its own default marker.

Input ↑
```
\begin{itemize}
\item Animal
\begin{itemize}
\item Mammals
\item Birds
\item Reptiles. For example:
\begin{itemize}
\item dinosaurs
\item crocodiles
\end{itemize}
\end{itemize}
\item Vegetable
\begin{itemize}
\item Cultivated
\item Wild
\end{itemize}
\item Mineral
\end{itemize}
```
Input ↓

Output ↑

- Animal

  - Mammals

  - Birds

  - Reptiles. For example:

    * dinosaurs
    * crocodiles

- Vegetable

- – Cultivated
- – Wild

- • Mineral

You might have noticed the code in the above example is a little difficult to read. Each new list item starts a new paragraph, so it doesn't matter if we have blank lines before each item. Also, recall from Chapter 2 (Some Definitions) that spaces at the start of each line of code are ignored, so it's possible to make the code more readable without affecting the final result:

```
\begin{itemize}

    \item Animal

    \begin{itemize}

        \item Mammals

        \item Birds

        \item Reptiles. For example:

        \begin{itemize}

            \item dinosaurs

            \item crocodiles

        \end{itemize}

    \end{itemize}

    \item Vegetable

    \begin{itemize}

        \item Cultivated

        \item Wild

    \end{itemize}
```

```
    \item Mineral

\end{itemize}
```

Input ↓

It's now a little easier to see which \begin{itemize} matches up with the corresponding \end{itemize}.

EXAMPLE (FOUR LEVELS)
This example has four levels, which is the maximum allowed by most classes.

Input ↑

```
\begin{itemize}
 \item Animal

 \begin{itemize}
  \item Mammal

   \begin{itemize}
   \item Placental

   \item Monotreme

   \begin{itemize}
     \item Platypus
   \end{itemize}

   \item Marsupial

   \begin{itemize}
    \item Kangaroo

    \item Koala
   \end{itemize}
  \end{itemize}

   \item Reptile
 \end{itemize}

 \item Vegetable

 \item Mineral
\end{itemize}
```

Input ↓

- Animal
  - Mammal
    * Placental
    * Monotreme
      · Platypus
    * Marsupial
      · Kangaroo
      · Koala
  - Reptile
- Vegetable
- Mineral

↑ Output

↓ Output

If you try adding a further level, LaTeX will give a "Too deeply nested" error.

4.4.2. Ordered Lists

Ordered lists are created using the enumerate environment. It has exactly the same format as the itemize environment described above.

We can use the same example as before, only this time use enumerate instead of itemize.

```
\begin{enumerate}
  \item Animal
  \item Vegetable
  \item Mineral
\end{enumerate}
```

↑ Input

↓ Input

The above input will produce the following output:

1. Animal

2. Vegetable

3. Mineral

↑ Output

↓ Output

As before, the marker for a particular item can be overridden:

Input ↑
```
\begin{enumerate}
  \item Animal
  \item[{[X]}] Vegetable
  \item Mineral
\end{enumerate}
```
Input ↓

Output ↑

   1. Animal

  [X] Vegetable

   2. Mineral

Output ↓

EXAMPLE (NESTED):

As with the itemize environment, most classes allow a maximum of four nested enumerate environments.

Input ↑
```
\begin{enumerate}
 \item Animal

 \begin{enumerate}
  \item Mammal

  \begin{enumerate}
  \item Placental

  \item Monotreme

  \begin{enumerate}
    \item Platypus
  \end{enumerate}

  \item Marsupial

  \begin{enumerate}
  \item Kangaroo

   \item Koala
  \end{enumerate}
 \end{enumerate}
```

```
  \item Reptile
\end{enumerate}

\item Vegetable

\item Mineral
\end{enumerate}
```

↓ Input

↑ Output

1. Animal
    a) Mammal
        i. Placental
        ii. Monotreme
            A. Platypus
        iii. Marsupial
            A. Kangaroo
            B. Koala
    b) Reptile
2. Vegetable
3. Mineral

↓ Output

4.4.3. Description Environment

The description environment has the same format as the itemize environment described in Section 4.4.1, only this time you need to specify a marker as an optional argument to the \item command, since there is no default marker for this environment. The marker may be a textual label, and most classes will typeset it in bold. The KOMA-Script classes, such as scrartcl, default to a bold sans-serif font, as illustrated in this next example:

↑ Input

```
\begin{description}
  \item[Animal] Living being

  \item[Vegetable] Plant

  \item[Mineral] Natural inorganic substance
\end{description}
```

↓ Input

Output ↑

Animal Living being

Vegetable Plant

Mineral Natural inorganic substance

Output ↓

The KOMA-Script classes provide a way of changing the font style in the description label markers. (The font changing commands \normalfont and \scshape will be covered in Section 4.5, and the KOMA-Script command \addtokomafont in Section 5.3.)

Input ↑

```
\addtokomafont{descriptionlabel}{\normalfont\scshape}
\begin{description}
  \item[Animal] Living being

  \item[Vegetable] Plant

  \item[Mineral] Natural inorganic substance
\end{description}
```

Input ↓

Output ↑

Animal Living being

Vegetable Plant

Mineral Natural inorganic substance

Output ↓

It is possible to nest all the listing environments, as long as you don't exceed four itemize and four enumerate environments. The description environment has no restriction on the number of times it can be nested. However, just because you can do something, doesn't mean you should. In general it's best to avoid an excessively complicated block of text in your document.

Example (Assorted Nesting):
This example uses each of the listing environments described above.

```
\begin{description}

  \item[Animal] Living being

  \begin{itemize}

    \item Mammals

    \item Birds

    \item Reptiles. For example:

    \begin{enumerate}

      \item dinosaurs

      \item crocodiles

    \end{enumerate}

  \end{itemize}

  \item[Vegetable] Plant

  \begin{itemize}

    \item Cultivated. For example:

    \begin{enumerate}

      \item Carrots

      \item Broccoli

      \item Potatoes

    \end{enumerate}

    \item Wild

  \end{itemize}

  \item[Mineral] Natural inorganic substance
```

Input ↓

```
\end{description}
```

Output ↑

Animal Living being

- Mammals
- Birds
- Reptiles. For example:
    1. dinosaurs
    2. crocodiles

Vegetable Plant

- Cultivated. For example:
    1. Carrots
    2. Broccoli
    3. Potatoes
- Wild

Mineral Natural inorganic substance

Output ↓

Exercise 5 (Lists)

Try writing the source code that will create the output shown below.

Output ↑

Village A small collection of dwelling places. Examples:

1. Marlingford
2. Saxlingham Nethergate

Town A large collection of dwelling places. Examples:

1. Great Yarmouth
2. Beccles

City A large town, usually containing a cathedral. Examples:

1. Norwich
2. Birmingham
3. London

Output ↓

You can download[4.7] the answer if you can't work out how to do it.

4.5. Fonts

LaTeX uses Donald Knuth's Computer Modern fonts by default. This supplies three font families: serif, sans-serif and a typewriter (or monospaced) font (as well as the maths fonts which are discussed in Section 9.4.1). With each font family, you can change the shape and weight, as well as the size.

[FAQ: Using PostScript fonts with TeX]

4.5.1. Changing the Font Style

There are two basic ways of changing fonts: you can either change the font for a small selection of text, for example, if you want to *emphasize* a word, or you may wish to change the font "from this point onwards". The commands shown in Table 4.5 on the following page are of the first type (text-block commands), whereas those shown in Table 4.6 on page 65 are of the second type — a declaration (or modal command).

NOTE:
Don't be tempted to use \bf, \md, \it, \sl, \sc, \sf, \tt or \rm. These commands are **obsolete** [16].

[FAQ: What's wrong with \bf, \it etc.?]

If you use an italic or slanted font declaration, such as \itshape, you will need to add an *italic correction* \/ at the end of the block of text, when the last letter of the sloping text leans too far over. This isn't necessary for text-block commands, such as \textit, just for the modal commands. The effect is more noticeable when part of a word is stressed, particularly with certain fonts.

EXAMPLE:
In the code below, the first instance of "repeated" doesn't have an italic correction but the second does:

{\itshape repeated}ly {\itshape repeated\/}ly

Input

Using Computer Modern:

*repeated*ly *repeated*ly

Output

Using Helvetica:

*repeated*ly *repeated*ly

Output

Using Antykwa Toruńska typeface:

*repeated*ly *repeated*ly

Output

Note that if you want to typeset an URL, rather than using \texttt it is better to use

---

[4.7] http://www.dickimaw-books.com/latex/novices/html/exercises/lists.tex

Table 4.5. Font Changing Text-Block Commands

Command	Example Input	Corresponding output (Computer Modern)
\textrm{⟨text⟩}	\textrm{roman} text	roman text
\textsf{⟨text⟩}	\textsf{sans serif} text	sans serif text
\texttt{⟨text⟩}	\texttt{typewriter} text	typewriter text
\textmd{⟨text⟩}	\textmd{medium} text	medium text
\textbf{⟨text⟩}	\textbf{bold} text	**bold** text
\textup{⟨text⟩}	\textup{upright} text	upright text
\textit{⟨text⟩}	\textit{italic} text	*italic* text
\textsl{⟨text⟩}	\textsl{slanted} text	*slanted* text
\textsc{⟨text⟩}	\textsc{Small Caps} text	SMALL CAPS text
\emph{⟨text⟩}	\emph{emphasized} text	*emphasized* text
\textnormal{⟨text⟩}	\textnormal{default} text	default text

Definition \url{⟨address⟩}

which is defined in the url package. For example:

Input \url{http://theoval.cmp.uea.ac.uk/~nlct/}

produces:

Output http://theoval.cmp.uea.ac.uk/~nlct/

(Note there is no need to do anything with the ~ (tilde) special character if you use it in the argument of \url.)

Environments can be used instead. Each environment has the same name as its corresponding declaration, but *without* the preceding backslash. For example:

Input \begin{sffamily}Some sans-serif text.\end{sffamily}

yields:

Output Some sans-serif text.

You can combine a font family with a given shape and weight using a variety of methods.

EXAMPLES:

1. Localised declarations:

Input {\sffamily\slshape Some slanted sans-serif text.}

2. Declarations that later get explicitly reset:

Input \sffamily\slshape Some slanted sans-serif text.\normalfont

Table 4.6. Font Changing Declarations

Declaration	Example Input	Corresponding output (Computer Modern)
\rmfamily	\rmfamily roman text	roman text
\sffamily	\sffamily sans serif text	sans serif text
\ttfamily	\ttfamily typewriter text	typewriter text
\mdseries	\mdseries medium text	medium text
\bfseries	\bfseries bold text	**bold text**
\upshape	\upshape upright text	upright text
\itshape	\itshape italic text	*italic text*
\slshape	\slshape slanted text	*slanted text*
\scshape	\scshape Small Caps text	SMALL CAPS TEXT
\em	\em emphasized text	*emphasized text*
\normalfont	\normalfont default text	default text

3. Mixing text-block and modal commands:

`\textsf{\slshape Some slanted sans-serif text.}`   Input

4. Nested commands:

`\textsf{\textsl{Some slanted sans-serif text.}}`   Input

5. Mixing environments and declarations:

```
\begin{sffamily}\slshape Some slanted sans-serif
text.\end{sffamily}
```
↑ Input

↓ Input

All of the above produce the same output:

Some slanted sans-serif text.   Output

Note that some combinations are not available, in which case LaTeX will give a
warning message, and will substitute the font for what it considers to be the closest
available match.

EXAMPLE:

`\textsc{\bfseries Text}`   Input

With the Antykwa Toruńska typeface, this appears as:

TEXT   Output

[FAQ: Warning: "Font shape … not available"]

whereas with Computer Modern, the result is:

Output **Text**

This is because Computer Modern doesn't have a bold small-caps font, so it just uses bold. LaTeX gives the following warning:

```
LaTeX Font Warning: Font shape 'T1/cmr/b/sc' undefined
(Font)                 using 'T1/cmr/b/n' instead on input line 2792.
```

Most sans-serif fonts don't provide a small-caps variant, so

Input `\textsf{\scshape Text}`

will either appear in regular sans-serif or small-caps serif, depending on the font in use. Using Libris sans-serif the result is:

Output Text

whereas using Computer Modern Sans, the result is:

Output TEXT

Emphasizing Words or Phrases

The command `\emph`, the declaration `\em` and the environment em behave slightly differently to the corresponding `\textit` command, `\itshape` declaration and itshape environment. The latter group simply use an italic font, whereas the former will toggle between sloping and upright. So if the surrounding font is upright then `\emph`, `\em` and em will use the sloping font, but if the surrounding font is italic or slanted, `\emph`, `\em` and em will use an upright font. This is particularly useful in abstracts where the abstract font varies between class files. It is recommended that if your intention is to emphasize something, you should use `\emph` etc. rather than `\textit` etc.

EXAMPLES:

1. Emphasized text in upright surrounding:

Input `Some \emph{emphasized} text.`

yields

Output Some *emphasized* text.

2. Emphasized text in italic surrounding:

Input `{\itshape Some \emph{emphasized} text.}`

yields

Output *Some* emphasized *text.*

3. Emphasized text in upright sans-serif surrounding:

   `{\sffamily Some \emph{emphasized} text.}` Input

   yields

   Some *emphasized* text. Output

4.5.2. Changing the Font Size

When you start writing a document, you need to decide what the base font size should be. The KOMA-Script classes default to 11pt, but this can be changed using the class options 8pt, 9pt, 10pt, 12pt, 14pt, 17pt or 20pt.

You can then change the font size *relative to* the base size, using one of the declarations shown in Table 4.7. That way, if you later decide to change the normal font size from, say, 11pt to 12pt, all you need do is change the class option (see page 41) and re-run LaTeX. Note that there are no equivalent text-block commands.

Table 4.7. Font Size Changing Declarations

Declaration	Example Input	Corresponding Output
\tiny	\tiny tiny text	tiny text
\scriptsize	\scriptsize script size	script size
\footnotesize	\footnotesize footnote size	footnote size
\small	\small small text	small text
\normalsize	\normalsize normal size	normal size
\large	\large large text	large text
\Large	\Large even larger	even larger
\LARGE	\LARGE larger still	larger still
\huge	\huge huge	huge
\Huge	\Huge extra huge	extra huge

Again, environments can be used instead, where each environment has the same name as its corresponding declaration, but *without* the preceding backslash. Font environments may be nested, for example:

```
\begin{itshape} Some italic text. \begin{Large}This text is
large.\end{Large} \end{itshape} Back to normal.
```
↑ Input
↓ Input

Output:

Some italic text. *This text is large.* Back to normal. Output

4.5.3. Changing Document Fonts

[FAQ: Choice of scalable outline fonts]

What if you don't want to use the default Computer Modern fonts? Some publishers and institutions insist on a combination of Times Roman (serif), Helvetica (sans-serif) and Courier (typewriter). To do this, you can load the following packages:

mathptmx (Times) Only affects \rmfamily and \textrm.

helvet (Helvetica) Only affects \sffamily and \textsf.

courier (Courier) Only affects \ttfamily and \texttt.

NOTES:

1. Don't be tempted to use the times package. It's obsolete [16]. Use mathptmx instead.

2. Although Times and Helvetica are commonly used together, they don't match, as illustrated below (temporarily switching from this book's fonts to Times and Helvetica):

Input

```
\rmfamily xx \sffamily xx
```

Results in:

Output

xx xx

The first two x's are in Times Roman and the second two are in Helvetica, which are somewhat larger. To compensate for this you need to scale the Helvetica font using the scaled option:

```
\usepackage[scaled=0.9]{helvet}
```

3. Loading helvet or courier doesn't change the default font family. Consider the following:

```
\documentclass{scrartcl}

\usepackage{helvet}

\begin{document}
This is a sample document.
\end{document}
```

Here, the text "This is a sample document" will be typeset in Computer Modern Roman. This is because \rmfamily is the default font and helvet only affects \sffamily, which hasn't been used. (See Section 8.2 to find out how to change the default font family.)

This book has used the following packages:

```
\usepackage[T1]{fontenc}
\usepackage[math]{anttor}
\usepackage{libris}
```

The fontenc package is used to switch to Type 1 font encoding, the anttor package is used to set the serif family to Antykwa Toruńska typeface, and the libris package is used to set the sans-serif family to the Libris ADF typeface. *[FAQ: Why bother with inputenc and fontenc?]*

Exercise 6 (Fonts)

Go back to the document you created in Exercise 1 (page 43) and change the first paragraph to a large bold font and the second paragraph to normal size italic. Emphasize the words "simple" and "short". (Again, you can download[4.8] the solution.)

If you like, you can try experimenting with loading different font packages, such as mathptmx, to change the default typeface. The LaTeX Font Catalogue [2] provides a useful list of fonts, although you may not have all of them installed.

4.6. Aligning Material in Rows and Columns

Text can be aligned in rows and columns using the tabular environment.

`\begin{tabular}[⟨pos⟩]{⟨column specifiers⟩}`   Definition

This environment has a mandatory argument ⟨*column specifiers*⟩ that specifies how to align each column. Within ⟨*column specifiers*⟩, there must be a specifier for each column. The three basic are: r (right aligned), l (left aligned) and c (centred). (Make sure you don't confuse l (the letter "ell") with 1 (the digit one).) The optional argument ⟨*pos*⟩ is covered in Section 4.7.

EXAMPLE:
Three columns (left, centred, centred):

`\begin{tabular}{lcc}`   Input

ANOTHER EXAMPLE:
Four columns (left, centred, centred, right):

`\begin{tabular}{lccr}`   Input

The r, l and c specifiers don't allow line breaks or paragraphs within a cell. It's not a good idea to have too much text in a cell, but if it's required you can use

`p{⟨width⟩}`   Definition

which indicates a paragraph cell of the given width.

[4.8]http://www.dickimaw-books.com/latex/novices/html/exercises/fonts.tex

EXAMPLE:
Three columns (paragraph of width 1in, centred, right):

Input   `\begin{tabular}{p{1in}cr}`

The paragraph cell will be formatted fully justified, which is often inappropriate for a narrow block of text. The array package provides

Definition   `>{⟨declaration⟩}`

which can be used directly in front of the l, c, r or p column specifiers. This inserts ⟨declaration⟩ in front of the entries for that column, so it can be used to insert, say, `\raggedright`.

EXAMPLE:
Three columns, the first left justified where each entry is in bold, the second a paragraph column of width 1in set to ragged right and the third centered:

Input   `\begin{tabular}{>{\bfseries}l>{\raggedright}p{1in}c}`

The array package also provides

Definition   `<{⟨declaration⟩}`

which can be used directly after the l, c, r or p column specifiers. This inserts ⟨declaration⟩ after the entries for that column.

INTER-COLUMN GAP:
The gap between columns is given by twice the value of the length register:

Definition   `\tabcolsep`

A gap of `\tabcolsep` is also inserted before the first column and after the last column. This length can be changed using one of the commands described in Section 2.17. For example:

Input   `\setlength{\tabcolsep}{4pt}`

This will put an 8pt gap between columns and a 4pt gap before the first column and after the last column.
The column specifiers can also include:

Definition   `@{⟨inter-column text⟩}`

This inserts ⟨inter-column text⟩ at that place on each row of the table, replacing the default inter-column gap.

EXAMPLE:
Suppose we want a centred first column, a right justified second column and a left justified third column with a dot between the second and third columns:

Input   `\begin{tabular}{cr@{.}l}`

Alternatively, you may want a larger gap between groups of columns, for example, two groups of three left justified columns:

\begin{tabular}{lll@{\hspace{4\tabcolsep}}lll}

Input

This uses the command:

\hspace{⟨*length*⟩}

Definition

which inserts a horizontal space of a given length. In this case, four times the value of \tabcolsep. This makes the gap between the third and fourth columns twice as wide as the gap between the other columns.

4.6.1. Column and Row Separation

Remember the special characters mentioned in Section 4.3? The ampersand character & is used to separate column entries. Rows are separated using:

\\[⟨*vertical space*⟩]

Definition

where ⟨*vertical space*⟩ is extra vertical spacing between rows, if required. There is also a longer equivalent:

\tabularnewline

Definition

If you have used something like >{\raggedright}p{⟨*length*⟩} as the specifier for your last column, you must use \tabularnewline instead of \\ to indicate the row break otherwise you will get the following error:

[FAQ: Alignment tab changed to \cr]

! Extra alignment tab has been changed to \cr.
<recently read> \endtemplate

EXAMPLE:
Let's have two columns, the first left justified and the second right justified:

```
\begin{tabular}{lr}
Video & 8.99\\
CD & 9.11\\
DVD & 15.00\\
Total & 33.10
\end{tabular}
```

↑ Input

↓ Input

Video	8.99
CD	9.11
DVD	15.00
Total	33.10

↑ Output

↓ Output

Recall from Chapter 2 (Some Definitions) that LaTeX ignores spaces at the start of a line and treats multiple spaces as a single space, so I could just have easily done:

Input ↑

```
\begin{tabular}{lr}
  Video & 8.99\\
  CD    & 9.11\\
  DVD   & 15.00\\
  Total & 33.10
\end{tabular}
```

Input ↓

and still have got the same result, but now the code is easier to read.

Entries form implicit grouping, so declarations made within a tabular environment only have an effect up to the next & or \\.

EXAMPLE:

Input ↑

```
\begin{tabular}{lr}
  Video & 8.99\\
  CD    & 9.11\\
  DVD   & 15.00\\
  \bfseries Total & 33.10
\end{tabular}
```

Input ↓

Output:

Output ↑

Video	8.99
CD	9.11
DVD	15.00
Total	33.10

Output ↓

Let's add an extra column and a header row:

Input ↑

```
\begin{tabular}{lrr}
  Item  & ex VAT & inc VAT\\
  Video &   8.99 &  10.56 \\
  CD    &   9.11 &  10.70 \\
  DVD   &  15.00 &  17.63 \\
  \bfseries Total &  33.10 &  39.89
\end{tabular}
```

Input ↓

Output:

Item	ex VAT	inc VAT
Video	8.99	10.56
CD	9.11	10.70
DVD	15.00	17.63
Total	33.10	39.89

↑ Output

↓ Output

EXAMPLE (ALIGNING ON A DECIMAL POINT):
If you want to align on the decimal point, it's best to use the siunitx package. That's beyond the scope of this book, but for simple data this can be achieved using the @ inter-column specifier. For example:

```
\begin{tabular}{lr@{.}l}
  Video & 8 & 99\\
  CD    & 9 & 11\\
  DVD   & 15 & 00\\
  \bfseries Total & 33 & 10
\end{tabular}
```

↑ Input

↓ Input

Output:

Video	8.99
CD	9.11
DVD	15.00
Total	33.10

↑ Output

↓ Output

4.6.2. Spanning Columns

You may have noticed I omitted the column headers in the above example. The problem with rewriting the table using r@{.}l to align the decimal point is that the header now needs to span the last two columns. This can be done using the command:

[FAQ: Merging cells in a column of a table]

\multicolumn{⟨cols spanned⟩}{⟨col specifier⟩}{⟨text⟩}

Definition

The first mandatory argument ⟨cols spanned⟩ is the number of columns you want to span, the second argument ⟨col specifier⟩ indicates how to align this column-spanning entry, the third argument ⟨text⟩ indicates what should go in this entry. Note that ⟨col specifier⟩ should only have a single column specifier, such as {c} or {r}. We can use \multicolumn to modify an earlier example as follows:

Input ⊤

```
\begin{tabular}{lrr}
        & \multicolumn{2}{c}{Price (\pounds)}\\
   Item & ex VAT & inc VAT\\
   Video &   8.99 &  10.56 \\
   CD    &   9.11 &  10.70 \\
   DVD   &  15.00 &  17.63 \\
   \bfseries Total &  33.10 &  39.89
\end{tabular}
```

Input ↓

Output:

Output ⊤

	Price (£)	
Item	ex VAT	inc VAT
Video	8.99	10.56
CD	9.99	11.74
DVD	15.00	17.63
Total	33.98	39.93

Output ↓

Here we are spanning two columns, so the first argument to \multicolumn is {2}, we want the entry centred, so the second argument is {c} and the text to go in this entry is simply {Price (\pounds)}.

[FAQ: How to alter the alignment of tabular cells]

The \multicolumn command can also be used to override the alignment of individual entries. Consider the following example:

Input ⊤

```
\begin{tabular}{lrr}
        & Year1 & Year2 \\
Travel    & 100,000 & 110,000\\
Equipment & 50,000 & 60,000
\end{tabular}
```

Input ↓

Output:

Output ⊤

	Year1	Year2
Travel	100,000	110,000
Equipment	50,000	60,000

Output ↓

In this example, the headers "Year1" and "Year2" would look better centred, but the rest of the entries in the second and third columns look best right aligned. We can use \multicolumn to span just one column, and use the second argument of \multicolumn to override the column specification:

```
\begin{tabular}{lrr}
        & \multicolumn{1}{c}{Year1}
        & \multicolumn{1}{c}{Year2}\\
Travel  & 100,000 & 110,000\\
Equipment & 50,000 & 60,000
\end{tabular}
```

Output:

	Year1	Year2
Travel	100,000	110,000
Equipment	50,000	60,000

4.6.3. Rules

In general, vertical rules are considered superfluous [11]. Although Turabian [18] allows for the possibility of vertical rules for tabulated material containing more than two columns but still advises against having too many and deprecates the use of them at either end.

Horizontal rules may be used at the top and bottom of the tabulated material, but other horizontal rules should be kept to a minimum. In general, the top and bottom rule should be thicker than the mid rules.

The booktabs package provides:

`\toprule[⟨wd⟩]`

for the top horizontal rule,

`\bottomrule[⟨wd⟩]`

for the bottom horizontal rule, and

`\midrule[⟨wd⟩]`

for horizontal rules in between rows, such as after the header row.

These commands should all go at the start of the appropriate row. This means that if you want a bottom rule, you need to add \\ followed by \bottomrule at the end of the tabulated material.

EXAMPLE:

```
\begin{tabular}{lrr}
\toprule
        & \multicolumn{1}{c}{Year1}
```

```
            & \multicolumn{1}{c}{Year2}\\
\midrule
Travel     & 100,000 & 110,000\\
Equipment & 50,000 & 60,000\\
\bottomrule
\end{tabular}
```

Input ↓

results in:

Output ↑

	Year1	Year2
Travel	100,000	110,000
Equipment	50,000	60,000

Output ↓

The thickness of the top and bottom rule is given by the length register \heavyrulewidth, and the thickness of the mid rule is given by the length register \lightrulewidth. These rule thicknesses can be overridden using the optional argument ⟨wd⟩ for \toprule, \midrule and \bottomrule.

Exercise 7 (Aligning Material)

Go back to the document you created in Exercise 2 (page 45) (and later modified in Exercise 3 (page 47)), and add the following:

Output ↑

	Expenditure (£)	
	Year1	Year2
Travel	100,000	110,000
Equipment	50,000	60,000

Output ↓

Note that the tabular environment doesn't create a caption, all it does is arrange its contents in rows and columns. You can find out how to turn your tabular environment into a table in Section 7.2.

You can download[4.9] the solution to this exercise. (Remember to check Appendix B (Common Errors) if you encounter an error message.)

For more information about using the tabular environment see *LaTeX: A Document Preparation System* [9], *A Guide to LaTeX* [7] or *The LaTeX Companion* [3]. The *LaTeX Companion* also describes how to span rows using the multirow package. For information on how to create coloured tables using the colortbl package, see *The LaTeX Graphics Companion* [5].

[4.9]http://www.dickimaw-books.com/latex/novices/html/exercises/tabular.tex

RELATED UK FAQ [19] TOPICS:

- How to change a whole row of a table

- Merging cells in a column of a table

- Fixed width tables

- Variable-width columns in tables

- Spacing lines in tables

4.7. Boxes and Mini-Pages

TEX views everything on a page as a form of box. Each box has an associated width, height and depth, and the boxes are placed together on the page with *glue*. This is reminiscent of the days of manual typesetting, where each letter or symbol was on a wooden block, and the wooden blocks were glued in place. The simplest form of box is a single letter. Some letters, such as "a" only have a height and width, whereas other letters, such as "y" have a height, width and depth (see Figure 4.3).

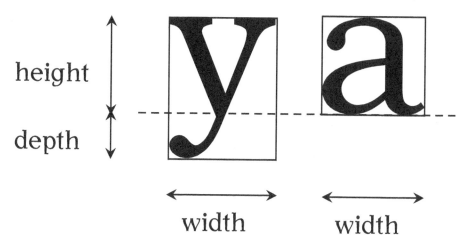

Figure 4.3. TEX Views Each Letter as a Box

For example, the phrase "cabbages and peas" is made up of 15 boxes:

cabbages and peas

whereas the word "cauliflower" consists of 10 boxes:[4.10]

cauliflower

[4.10]The fl-ligature is a single character, and so is one box not two.

More complicated boxes are made up of smaller boxes. We have already encountered one of these more complicated boxes: the tabular environment, discussed in the previous section. This type of box is called a *horizontal box*, which means that it can go in a line of text. For example:

Input ↑
Input ↓

```
Here is some text.
\begin{tabular}{cc}
A & B\\
C & D
\end{tabular}
The rest of the line.
```

produces:

Output ↑
Output ↓

> Here is some text. A B The rest of the line.
>   C D

Recall from the previous section that the tabular environment had an optional argument ⟨*pos*⟩. This governs the vertical alignment when the tabular environment occurs within a line of text. This can be one of c (centred — the default, as illustrated above), t (top) and b (bottom). For example,

Input ↑
Input ↓

```
Here is some text.
\begin{tabular}[b]{cc}
A & B\\
C & D
\end{tabular}
The rest of the line.
```

produces:

Output ↑
Output ↓

>   A B
> Here is some text. C D The rest of the line.

Since a box can't be broken across a line of text, you can use the box making command:

Definition \mbox{⟨*text*⟩}

to prevent ⟨*text*⟩ from spanning a line break.

EXAMPLE:
Compare:

```
\raggedright Some text at the beginning of a paragraph. Some text in the
middle of the paragraph. Some more text. \par
```
↑ Input
↓ Input

Some text at the beginning of a paragraph. Some text in the middle of the
paragraph. Some more text.

↑ Output
↓ Output

with:

```
\raggedright Some text at the beginning of a paragraph. \mbox{Some text
in the middle of the paragraph.} Some more text. \par
```
↑ Input
↓ Input

Some text at the beginning of a paragraph.
Some text in the middle of the paragraph. Some more text.

↑ Output
↓ Output

(If \raggedright had not been used, the text in the \mbox would've spilt out over the
edge of the page.)

Another type of box which can again be placed in a line of text, is the minipage
environment.

```
\begin{minipage}[⟨pos⟩][⟨height⟩]{⟨width⟩}
```
Definition

As the name suggests, this environment creates a "mini-page" of the given width.

EXAMPLE:

```
Some text.
\begin{minipage}{2in}
This is a mini-page. The text inside it is formatted as usual.

Paragraph breaks can also be used, but there is no indentation by
default\footnote{and this is how a footnote appears}.
\end{minipage}
The rest of the line.
```
↑ Input
↓ Input

which produces:

Output ↑

> Some text. | This is a mini-page. The text in-
> side it is formatted as usual.
> Paragraph breaks can also be
> used, but there is no indentation | The rest of the line.
> by default[a].
>
> ───────────
> [a]and this is how a footnote appears

Output ↓

You can optionally specify a height, and how the mini-page is aligned with the rest of the text. As with the tabular environment, the alignment option ⟨*pos*⟩ can be one of t (top), c (centred) or b (bottom). The default is c, which is why the above example has the mini-page centred vertically. This can be changed, for example:

Input ↑

```
Some text.
\begin{minipage}[t]{2in}
This is a mini-page. The text inside it is formatted as usual.

Paragraph breaks can also be used, but there is no indentation by
default\footnote{and this is how a footnote appears}.
\end{minipage}
The rest of the line.
```

Input ↓

which produces

Output ↑

> Some text. | This is a mini-page. The text in- | The rest of the line.
> side it is formatted as usual.
> Paragraph breaks can also be
> used, but there is no indentation
> by default[a].
>
> ───────────
> [a]and this is how a footnote appears

Output ↓

Note that the width can be specified relative to the current line width, using the length register \linewidth. For example,

```
\begin{minipage}{0.5\linewidth}
```

will start a mini-page that is half the width of the current line.

There is also a corresponding command

Definition

```
\parbox[⟨pos⟩][⟨height⟩]{⟨width⟩}{⟨text⟩}
```

which behaves in a similar way. So the above example can be rewritten using a \parbox:

```
Some text.
\parbox[t]{2in}{This is a parbox. The text inside it is formatted as
usual.

Paragraph breaks can also be used, but there is no indentation by
default.}
The rest of the line.
```

↑ Input

↓ Input

which produces

Some text. This is a parbox. The text inside The rest of the line.
it is formatted as usual.
Paragraph breaks can also be
used, but there is no indentation
by default.

↑ Output

↓ Output

You may have noticed that the \footnote command has not been used in the above example. The \parbox command is more restricted than the minipage environment, so you can't use the \footnote command in it. There are also certain environments, such as the list-making environments described in Section 4.4, that can be used in a minipage but not in a \parbox.

4.7.1. Framed Boxes

Recall the \framebox command described in Section 2.8.2:

\framebox[⟨*width*⟩][⟨*align*⟩]{⟨*text*⟩}

Definition

This treats ⟨*text*⟩ as a box of width ⟨*width*⟩ and puts a frame around it. The second optional argument may be one of: c (centred contents), l (left-aligned contents), r (right-aligned contents).

EXAMPLE:

Some \framebox[2in]{framed} text.

Input

Some | framed | text.

Output

There is a shorter related command with no optional arguments:

\fbox{⟨*text*⟩}

Definition

The fancybox package provides some additional framing commands:

\shadowbox{⟨*text*⟩}

Definition

Puts a shadow-style frame around its contents:

Input   Some \shadowbox{framed} text.

Output   Some ⌐framed⌐ text.

Definition   \doublebox{⟨*text*⟩}

Puts a double-lined frame around its contents:

Input   Some \doublebox{framed} text.

Output   Some ‖ framed ‖ text.

Definition   \ovalbox{⟨*text*⟩}

Puts a thin-lined oval frame around its contents:

Input   Some \ovalbox{framed} text.

Output   Some │ framed │ text.

Definition   \Ovalbox{⟨*text*⟩}

Puts a thick-lined oval frame around its contents:

Input   Some \Ovalbox{framed} text.

Output   Some │ framed │ text.

If you want a different frame effect, you will need to use a graphical package, such as pgf/tikz.

EXAMPLE:
This example uses commands beyond the scope of this book, but gives you an idea of what's possible.

Input

```
\documentclass{scrartcl}

\usepackage{tikz}
\usetikzlibrary{shapes}
\usetikzlibrary{decorations.pathmorphing}

\begin{document}

Some
\begin{tikzpicture}[baseline=(n.base),decoration=bumps]
\node[draw,ellipse,decorate] (n) {framed};
\end{tikzpicture}
```

```
text.

\end{document}
```

Input

Some 〜{ framed }〜 text.

Output

For further details, see the pgf documentation.

RELATED UK FAQ [19] TOPICS:

- Automatic sizing of minipage

- Float(s) lost

- Perhaps a missing \item?

CHAPTER 5

STRUCTURING YOUR DOCUMENT

Let's go back to the document we modified in Exercise 7 (page 76). In this chapter we shall edit that document step by step until we have a fully-fledged document with title, abstract, table of contents, sections etc.

5.1. Author and Title Information

The term *title page* is used to indicate the author, title and date information that can appear either on the front cover by itself or along the top of the first page of text. In order to do this, you must first specify the information. Once this information has been specified it can then be displayed.

The author, title and date are entered using the commands:

```
\author{⟨author names⟩}
\title{⟨title text⟩}
\date{⟨document date⟩}
```
Definition

The KOMA-Script classes also define:

```
\titlehead{⟨Title heading⟩}
\subject{⟨Subject⟩}
\subtitle{⟨Subtitle⟩}
\publishers{⟨Publisher⟩}
```
Definition

All these title-related commands only *store* information, they don't actually display anything. These commands can be put in the preamble. With most classes, you will typically need to use at least \author and \title.

[FAQ: The style of document titles]

Once you have used these commands, you can then display the information using the command:

```
\maketitle
```
Definition

This command should be placed where you want the title page to appear, which is normally at the start of the document environment.

Note that if you don't use the \date command, the current date will be inserted. If you want no date to appear, you need to specify an empty argument:

```
\date{}
```
Input

Multiple authors should be separated by the command \and. For example:

```
\author{A. Jones\\University of Somewhere \and
B. Smith\\University of Somewhere Else}
```

Within these titling fields, you can also use the command:

Definition

```
\thanks{text}
```

which produces a special type of footnote. For example:

Input

```
\title{A Great Project\thanks{funded by XYZ}}
```

Note that the footnote marker produced using \thanks is considered to have zero width, so if it occurs in the middle of a line, rather than the end, you will need to insert some extra space using \␣ (backslash space). The argument of \thanks is a moving argument.

Exercise 8 (Creating Title Pages)

Try editing the document you modified in Exercise 7 (page 76) to include title information. Modifications are illustrated in bold **like this**:

Code ⊤

```
\documentclass[12pt]{scrartcl}

\usepackage{datetime}

\title{A Simple Document}
\author{Me}

\begin{document}

\maketitle

This is a simple \LaTeX\␣document.
Here is the first paragraph.

Here is the second paragraph\footnote{with a footnote}.
As you can see it's a rather short paragraph, but not
as short as the previous one. This document was
created on: \today\␣at \currenttime.

\begin{tabular}{lrr}
 & \multicolumn{2}{c}{\bfseries Expenditure}\\
```

```
& \multicolumn{1}{c}{Year1} & \multicolumn{1}{c}{Year2}\\
\bfseries Travel & 100,000 & 110,000\\
\bfseries Equipment & 50,000 & 60,000
\end{tabular}

\end{document}
```

↓ Code

You can download[5.1] this document.

5.2. Abstract

The abstract environment is used to create an abstract for the document. The way in which the abstract is formatted depends on the class file. The scrreprt class file will put the abstract on a page by itself, some class files will indent the abstract and some will typeset the abstract in italic. Note also that some class files (such as scrbook) don't have an abstract environment. Abstracts traditionally go at the start of the document after the title, so the abstract environment should go after the \maketitle command.

[FAQ: 1-column abstract in 2-column document]

Exercise 9 (Creating an Abstract)

Try editing your document so that it has an abstract: Modifications are illustrated **like this**:

↑ Code

```
\documentclass[12pt]{scrartcl}

\usepackage{datetime}

\title{A Simple Document}
\author{Me}

\begin{document}

\maketitle

\begin{abstract}
A brief document to illustrate how to use \LaTeX.
\end{abstract}

This is a simple \LaTeX\ document.
```

[5.1]http://www.dickimaw-books.com/latex/novices/html/exercises/title.tex

```
Here is the first paragraph.

Here is the second paragraph\footnote{with a footnote}.
As you can see it's a rather short paragraph, but not
as short as the previous one. This document was
created on: \today\␣at \currenttime.

\begin{tabular}{lrr}
  & \multicolumn{2}{c}{\bfseries Expenditure}\\
  & \multicolumn{1}{c}{Year1} & \multicolumn{1}{c}{Year2}\\
\bfseries Travel & 100,000 & 110,000\\
\bfseries Equipment & 50,000 & 60,000
\end{tabular}


\end{document}
```

Code ↓

You can download[5.2] this document.

5.3. Chapters, Sections, Subsections ...

Chapters, sections, subsections etc can be inserted using the commands:

Definition
```
\part[⟨short title⟩]{⟨title⟩}
\chapter[⟨short title⟩]{⟨title⟩}
\section[⟨short title⟩]{⟨title⟩}
\subsection[⟨short title⟩]{⟨title⟩}
\subsubsection[⟨short title⟩]{⟨title⟩}
\paragraph[⟨short title⟩]{⟨title⟩}
\subparagraph[⟨short title⟩]{⟨title⟩}
```

[FAQ: How to create a \subsubsection]

All these commands have a moving argument (see Section 2.9), so fragile commands will need to be protected using \protect. The final two commands in the above list, \paragraph and \subparagraph, represent subsubsubsections and subsubsubsubsections, although most class files typeset their arguments as unnumbered running titles.

Note that the availability of these commands depends on the class file you are using. For example, the scrartcl class file that we have been using is designed for articles, so the \chapter command is not defined in that class, whereas it is defined in the scrreprt and scrbook class files.

[5.2]http://www.dickimaw-books.com/latex/novices/html/exercises/abstr.tex

Each of the commands above has a mandatory argument ⟨*title*⟩ and an optional argument ⟨*short title*⟩. The mandatory argument ⟨*title*⟩ is simply the title of the chapter/section/subsection etc. For example:

`\section{Introduction}` Input

If you are using the scrartcl class file, the output will look like:

1   Introduction
Output

Note that you don't specify the section number as LaTeX does this automatically. This means that you can insert a new section or chapter or swap sections around or even change a section to a subsection etc, without having to worry about updating all the section numbers.

[FAQ: The style of section headings]

If you are using a class file that contains chapters as well as sections, the section number will depend on the chapter. So, for example, the current section is the 3rd section of chapter 5, so the section number is 5.3. (Note that if you are using a class file where the section number depends on the chapter number, you must have a `\chapter` command before your first `\section` command, otherwise your section numbers will come out as 0.1, 0.2 etc.)

[FAQ: Why are my sections numbered 0.1 ...?]

Unnumbered chapters/sections etc are produced by placing an asterisk * after the command name. For example:

`\chapter*{Acknowledgements}` Input

You can switch to appendices using the command

`\appendix` Definition

then continue using \chapter, \section etc. For example (using the screprt class file):

[FAQ: Appendixes]

↑ Input

```
\appendix
\chapter{Derivations}
Some derivations.

\chapter{Tables}
Some tables.
```

↓ Input

NOTE:

The KOMA-Script classes have another type of sectioning command:

`\minisec{⟨heading⟩}` Definition

This provides an unnumbered heading not associated with any of the structuring levels. For example, the above was produce using:

Input ↑

```
\minisec{Note:}
The KOMA-Script classes have another type of sectioning command:
```

Input ↓

The next note below was produced using:

Input ↑

```
\minisec{Important Note:}
If you want to change the font style used by headings,
\emph{\bfseries do not} use font declarations in the sectioning
command arguments.
```

Input ↓

IMPORTANT NOTE:
If you want to change the font style used by headings, ***do not*** use font declarations in the sectioning command arguments. Don't do, for example:

✗   `\chapter{\itshape Introduction}`

The KOMA-Script classes provide the command:

Definition   `\addtokomafont{`⟨*element*⟩`}{`⟨*commands*⟩`}`

where ⟨*element*⟩ is the name of a structuring element (no backslash) and ⟨*commands*⟩ is the list of font changing declarations (see Table 4.6 on page 65) to apply to that element style. For example, this book uses the commands:

Input ↑

```
\addtokomafont{section}{\rmfamily\bfseries}
\addtokomafont{minisec}{\rmfamily\bfseries\scshape}
```

Input ↓

Exercise 10 (Creating Chapters, Sections etc)

Let's try editing our document so that it now has chapters, sections and an appendix. Since the scrartcl class file doesn't have chapters, let's change to the scrreprt class. Changes from our previous document are shown **like this**.

Code ↑

```
\documentclass[12pt]{scrreprt}

\usepackage{datetime}

\title{A Simple Document}
```

```
\author{Me}

\begin{document}
\maketitle

\begin{abstract}
A brief document to illustrate how to use \LaTeX.
\end{abstract}

\chapter{Introduction}

\section{The First Section}
This is a simple \LaTeX\ document.
Here is the first paragraph.

\section{The Next Section}
Here is the second paragraph\footnote{with a footnote}.
As you can see it's a rather short paragraph, but not
as short as the previous one. This document was
created on: \today\ at \currenttime.

\chapter{Another Chapter}

Here's another very interesting chapter.
We're going to put a picture here later.

\chapter*{Acknowledgements}

I would like to acknowledge all those
very helpful people who have assisted me in my work.

\appendix

\chapter{Tables}
We will turn this tabular environment into a table later.

\begin{tabular}{lrr}
 & \multicolumn{2}{c}{\bfseries Expenditure}\\
 & \multicolumn{1}{c}{Year1} & \multicolumn{1}{c}{Year2}\\
\bfseries Travel & 100,000 & 110,000\\
\bfseries Equipment & 50,000 & 60,000
\end{tabular}

\end{document}
```

↓ Code

(You can download[5.3] a copy of this file if you like, but I recommend that you try editing the file yourself to give you practice.)

———————

5.4. Creating a Table of Contents

Once you have all your sectioning commands, such as \chapter and \section, you can create a table of contents with the command

Definition   \tableofcontents

This command should go where you want your table of contents to appear (usually

[FAQ: The format of the Table of Contents, etc]

after \maketitle). The KOMA-Script classes provide two options that govern the format of the table of contents: toc=graduated and toc=flat. The first is the default and indents the different sectioning levels. The second doesn't use any indentation.

EXAMPLE:

Input   \documentclass[12pt,toc=flat]{scrreprt}

You may recall from the previous section that the sectioning commands all had an optional argument ⟨*short title*⟩. If your chapter or section title is particularly

[FAQ: My section title is too wide for the page header]

long, you can use ⟨*short title*⟩ to specify a shorter title that should go in the table of contents.[5.4] The longer title (given by the other argument ⟨*title*⟩) will still appear in the section heading in the main part of the document.

LaTeX processes all source code sequentially, so when it first encounters the \tableofcontents command, it doesn't yet know anything about the chapters, sections etc. So the first time the document is LaTeXed the necessary information is written to the table of contents (.toc) file (see Section 2.4). The subsequent pass reads the information in from the .toc file, and generates the table of contents. You will therefore need to LaTeX your document twice to make sure that the table of

[FAQ: Numbers too large in table of contents, etc]

contents is up-to-date.

ADDING EXTRA INFORMATION

The starred versions of the sectional commands (such as \chapter*) don't get added to the table of contents. It may be that you want to add it, in which case you need to use

Definition   \addcontentsline{⟨*toc*⟩}{⟨*section unit*⟩}{⟨*text*⟩}

after the heading. The first argument ⟨*toc*⟩ is the file extension without the dot. As mentioned above, the table of contents file has the extension .toc, so the first argument should be toc (later in Chapter 7 (Floats), we'll be adding a list of figures and a list of tables, and those have file extensions .lof and .lot, respectively). The second argument ⟨*section unit*⟩ is the name of the section unit. This is just the name

———————

[5.3]http://www.dickimaw-books.com/latex/novices/html/exercises/section.tex
[5.4]and in the page header, depending on the page style.

of the relevant sectioning command *without* the backslash. The final argument ⟨*text*⟩ is the entry text. For example (using scrreprt class):

```
\chapter*{Acknowledgments}
\addcontentsline{toc}{chapter}{Acknowledgements}
```

↑ Input

↓ Input

Exercise 11 (Creating a Table of Contents)

Try modifying your document so that it has a table of contents. Modifications from the previous exercise are illustrated **like this**:

↑ Code

```
\documentclass[12pt]{scrreprt}

\usepackage{datetime}

\title{A Simple Document}
\author{Me}

\begin{document}

\maketitle

\tableofcontents

\begin{abstract}
A brief document to illustrate how to use \LaTeX.
\end{abstract}

\chapter{Introduction}

\section{The First Section}

This is a simple \LaTeX\ document.  Here is the first paragraph.

\section{The Next Section}

Here is the second paragraph\footnote{with a footnote}.
As you can see it's a rather short paragraph, but not
as short as the previous one. This document was
created on: \today\ at \currenttime.

\chapter{Another Chapter}
```

```
Here's another very interesting chapter.
We're going to put a picture here later.

\chapter*{Acknowledgements}

I would like to acknowledge all those
very helpful people who have assisted
me in my work.

\appendix
\chapter{Tables}

We will turn this tabular environment into a table later.

\begin{tabular}{lrr}
 & \multicolumn{2}{c}{\bfseries Expenditure}\\
 & \multicolumn{1}{c}{Year1} & \multicolumn{1}{c}{Year2}\\
\bfseries Travel & 100,000 & 110,000\\
\bfseries Equipment & 50,000 & 60,000
\end{tabular}


\end{document}
```

Code ↓

If your table of contents doesn't come out right, try LaTeXing it again. (Again, you can download[5.5] this file.)

You might want to try experimenting with the toc=flat class options to see what difference it makes:

Input

```
\documentclass[12pt,toc=flat]{scrreprt}
```

5.5. Cross-Referencing

We have already seen that LaTeX takes care of all the numbering for the chapters etc, but what happens if you want to refer to a chapter or section? There's no point leaving LaTeX to automatically generate the section numbers if you have to keep track of them all, and change all your cross-references every time you add a new section. Fortunately LaTeX provides a way to generate the correct number. All you have to do is label the part of the document you want to reference, and then refer to this label when you want to cross-reference it. LaTeX will then determine the correct number

[FAQ: Referring to labels in other documents]

[5.5]http://www.dickimaw-books.com/latex/novices/html/exercises/toc.tex

that needs to be inserted at that point.

The first part, labelling the place you want to reference, is done using the command:

`\label{⟨string⟩}`   Definition

The argument ⟨*string*⟩ should be a unique textual label. This label can be anything you like as long as it is unique, but it's a good idea to make it something obvious so that, firstly, you can remember the label when you want to use it, and secondly, when you read through your code at some later date, it's immediately apparent to you to which part of the document you are referring. People tend to have their own conventions for labelling. I usually start the label with two or three letters that signify what type of thing I'm labelling. For example, if I'm labelling a chapter I'll start with ch, if I'm labelling a section I'll start with sec.

EXAMPLES:

1. Labelling a chapter:

   ```
   \chapter{Introduction}
   \label{ch:intro}
   ```

2. Labelling a section:

   ```
   \section{Technical Details}
   \label{sec:details}
   ```

Note that the `\label` command doesn't produce any text, it simply assigns a label. You can now refer to that object using the command:

`\ref{⟨string⟩}`   Definition

which will produce the relevant number.

EXAMPLE:

```
See Section \ref{sec:results} for an analysis of the results.
```

It is a typographical convention that you should never start a new line with a number. For example, if you have the text "Chapter 1" the "1" must be on the same line as the "Chapter". We can do this by using an *unbreakable space*, which will put a space but won't allow LaTeX to break the line at that point. This is done using the tilde (~) special character, so the example above should actually be:

Input `See Section~\ref{sec:results} for an analysis of the results.`

There is a similar command to reference the page number:

Definition `\pageref{⟨string⟩}`

EXAMPLE:

Input ↑

Input ↓
```
See Chapter~\ref{ch:def} on page~\pageref{ch:def} for a list of
definitions.
```

The label `ch:def` obviously needs to be defined somewhere:

Input ↑

Input ↓
```
\chapter{Definitions}
\label{ch:def}
```

In fact, I have done this in my source code for Chapter 2 (Some Definitions) of this document, so the above example would look like:

Output See Chapter 2 on page 7 for a list of definitions.

[FAQ:
Referring to
things by
their name]
　　It's not just chapters and sections that you can reference, most of the numbers that LaTeX automatically generates can be cross-referenced.

EXAMPLE:

The source code for footnote 5.4 on page 92 is:

Input ↑

Input ↓
```
\footnote{\label{ftn:header}and in the page header, depending on the page
style}
```

and it was referenced above using:

Input ↑

Input ↓
```
The source code for footnote~\ref{ftn:header} on
page~\pageref{ftn:header} is:
```

　　The varioref package provides a more convenient way of doing this using the command:

Definition `\vref{⟨label⟩}`

This is like `\ref` but also adds information about the location, such as "on page $⟨n⟩$" or "on the following page", if the corresponding `\label` occurs on a different page, so the above example can be changed to:

Input `The source code for footnote~\vref{ftn:header} is:`

which still produces

The source code for footnote 5.4 on page 92 is: Output

Compare with a reference to one of the labels in the next example:

See step~\vref{itm:edit}. Input

which produces:

See step 1 on the following page. Output

CAVEAT:

You can run into trouble if the \vref command occurs on a page break. When it tries to insert the location information, such as "on the next page", the information is no longer correct. This can cause an "Infinite loop" error. When this happens, either edit your paragraph so the reference no longer falls on the page break or use \ref instead of \vref for that instance.

ANOTHER EXAMPLE:

The enumerate environment described in Section 4.4.2 automatically numbers the items within an ordered list, so it's possible to label list items. Recall the numbered list of instructions at the start of Chapter 3 (From Source Code to Typeset Output). Here's the code:

Input

```
\begin{enumerate}

    \item\label{itm:edit} Write or edit the source code.

    \item Pass the source code to the \texttt{latex} or \texttt{pdflatex}
        application (''\LaTeX\ the document'').

        \begin{itemize}

            \item If there are any error messages,
                return to Step~\ref{itm:edit}.

            \item If there are no error messages, a PDF file
                is created, go to Step~\ref{itm:view}.
        \end{itemize}

    \item\label{itm:view} View the PDF file to check the result.

\end{enumerate}
```

Input

Output:

Output ↑

1. Write or edit the source code.

2. Pass the source code to the `latex` or `pdflatex` application ("LATEX the document").

   - If there are any error messages, return to Step 1.
   - If there are no error messages, a PDF file is created, go to Step 3.

3. View the PDF file to check the result.

Output ↓

The `\ref` and `\pageref` commands may come before or after the corresponding `\label` command. As with the table of contents, LATEX first writes out all the cross-referencing information to another file (the auxiliary (`.aux`) file, see Section 2.4) and then reads it in the next time, so you will need to LATEX your document twice to get everything up-to-date.

If the references aren't up-to-date, you will see the following message at the end of the LATEX run:

```
LaTeX Warning: Label(s) may have changed.
Rerun to get cross-references right.
```

The following warning

```
LaTeX Warning: There were undefined references.
```

means that LATEX found a reference to a label that does not appear in the auxiliary file. This could mean that it's a new label, and the warning will go away the next time you LATEX your document, or it could mean that either you've forgotten to define your label with the `\label` command, or you've simply misspelt the label. The undefined references will show up as two question marks ?? in the output file.

[FAQ: "Rerun" messages won't go away]

Very occasionally, if you have cross-references and a table of contents, you might have to LATEX your document three times to get everything up to date. Just check to see if the `Label(s) may have changed` warning appears.

If you find it inconvenient having to remember to click the typeset button twice, you can use `latexmk`. This will run LATEX the required number of times to ensure the document is up-to-date. To do this in TeXWorks, change the drop-down menu to "LaTeXmk", as illustrated in Figure 5.1 on the next page. Note that `latexmk` is a Perl script, so you need to make sure you have `perl` installed (see Section 2.20).

If `latexmk` isn't listed in the drop-down menu, you can add it via Edit→Preferences. This opens the dialog box shown in Figure 5.2 on page 101. You can add a new tool as follows:

1. To the right of the box labelled "Processing Tools" there is a button marked with a plus (+) sign. Click on it to open the tool configuration dialog, shown in Figure 5.3 on page 102.

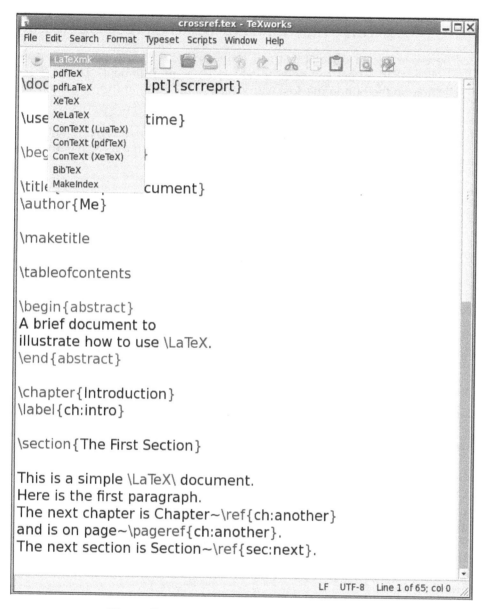

Figure 5.1. Selecting LaTeXmk in TeXWorks

2. Fill in the name "LaTeXmk" in the box labelled "Name" and either type in the location of `latexmk` in the box labelled "Program" or use the "Browse" button to locate it on your filing system. (See Figure 5.4 on page 102.) This will vary depending on your operating system and TeX-distribution, but it will probably be in a subdirectory (folder) called bin somewhere in the TeX-distribution tree.

3. There are lots of options that can be passed to `latexmk`, but if you want to produce PDF output you need to add -pdf as an argument. This is done by clicking on the button marked with a plus to the right of the "Arguments" box and type -pdf, as shown in Figure 5.5 on page 103.

4. Another argument needs to be added that specifies the basename of the LaTeX file. This is done by again clicking on the plus button and typing $basename, as shown in Figure 5.6 on page 103 .

5. Click on "OK" to close the Tool Configuration dialog.

6. If you want to set `latexmk` to be your default processing tool, you can select it from the drop-down list labelled "Default".

7. Click "OK" when you're done.

Exercise 12 (Cross-Referencing)

Try modifying your code so that it has cross-references. Again, changes made from the previous exercise are illustrated **like this**:

Code ↑

```
\documentclass[12pt]{scrreprt}

\usepackage{datetime}

\title{A Simple Document}
\author{Me}

\begin{document}

\maketitle

\tableofcontents

\begin{abstract}
A brief document to illustrate how to use \LaTeX.
\end{abstract}

\chapter{Introduction}
```

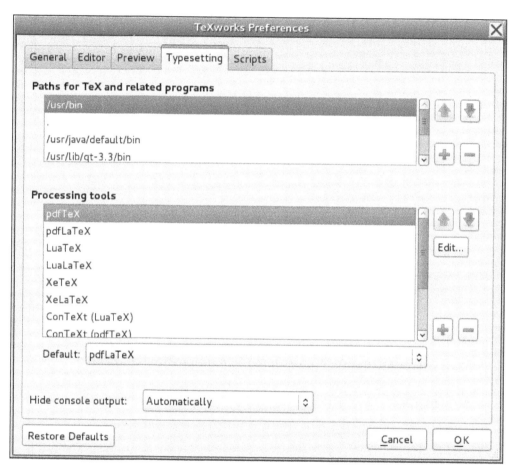

Figure 5.2. TeXWorks Preferences

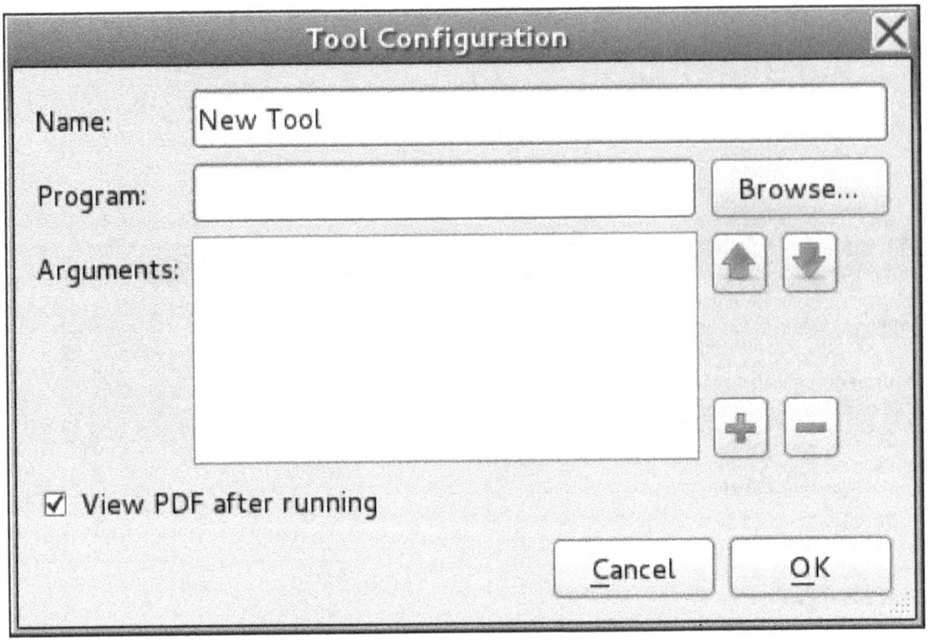

Figure 5.3. Tool Configuration Dialog

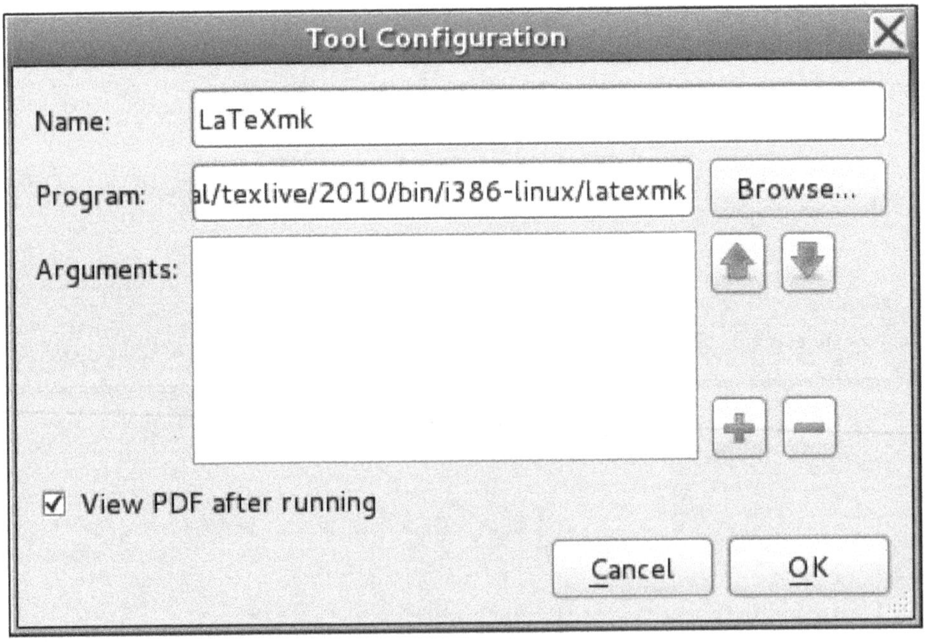

Figure 5.4. Tool Configuration Dialog: set the name and program location

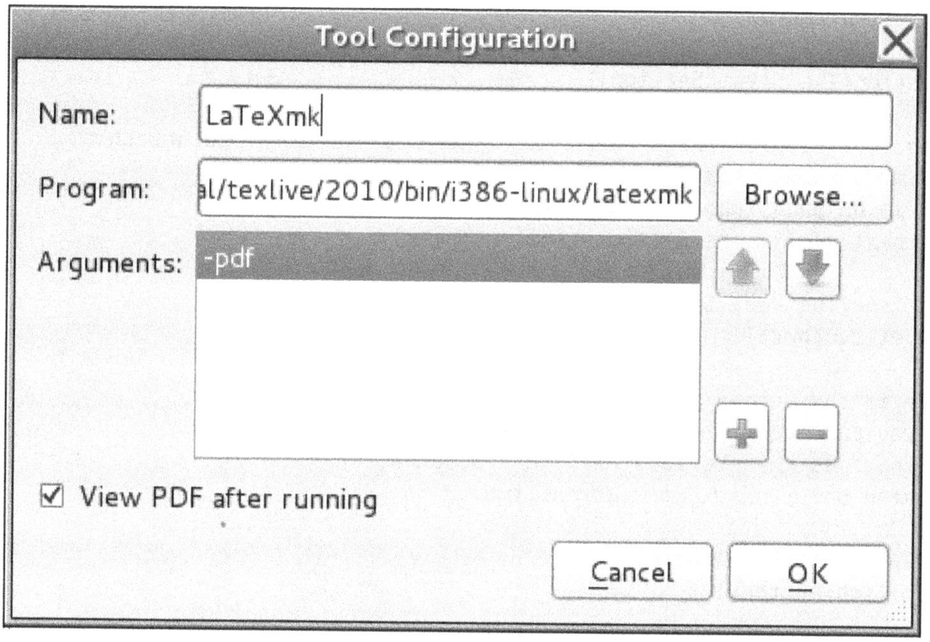

Figure 5.5. Tool Configuration Dialog: adding -pdf argument

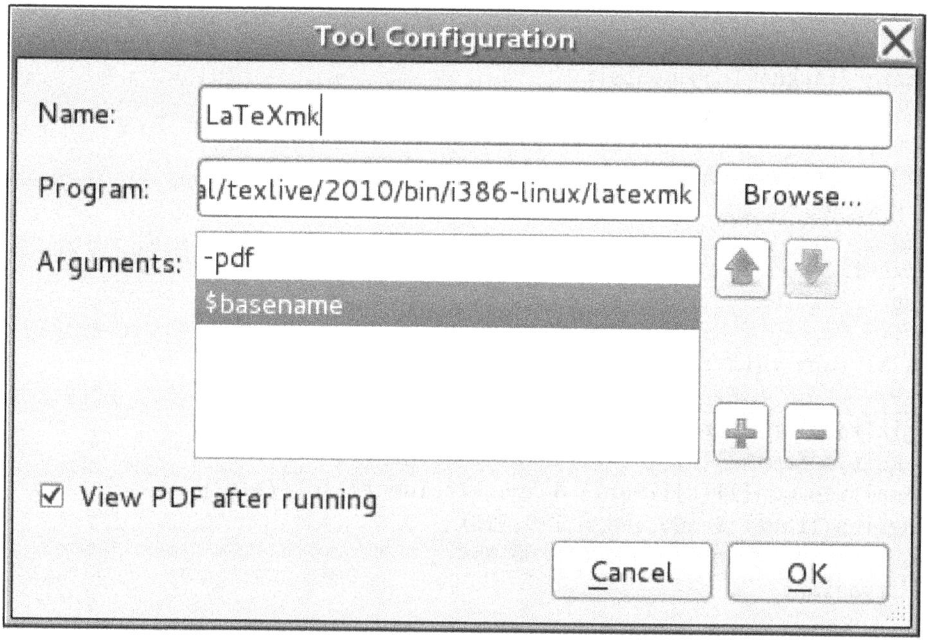

Figure 5.6. Tool Configuration Dialog: adding $basename argument

```
\label{ch:intro}

\section{The First Section}

This is a simple \LaTeX\ document.  Here is the first paragraph.
The next chapter is Chapter~\ref{ch:another}
and is on page~\pageref{ch:another}.
The next section is Section~\ref{sec:next}.

\section{The Next Section}
\label{sec:next}

Here is the second paragraph\footnote{with a footnote}.
As you can see it's a rather short paragraph, but not
as short as the previous one. This document was
created on: \today\ at \currenttime.

\chapter{Another Chapter}
\label{ch:another}

Here's another very interesting chapter.
We're going to put a picture here later.
See Chapter~\ref{ch:intro} for an
introduction.

\chapter*{Acknowledgements}

I would like to acknowledge all those
very helpful people who have assisted
me in my work.

\appendix
\chapter{Tables}

We will turn this tabular environment into a table later.

\begin{tabular}{lrr}
 & \multicolumn{2}{c}{\bfseries Expenditure}\\
 & \multicolumn{1}{c}{Year1} & \multicolumn{1}{c}{Year2}\\
\bfseries Travel & 100,000 & 110,000\\
\bfseries Equipment & 50,000 & 60,000
\end{tabular}

\end{document}
```

Code ↓

(You can download[5.6] a copy of this file.)

5.6. Creating a Bibliography

If you have a large number of citations in your document, it's best to use an external bibliographic application, such as bibtex or biber. However, that is beyond the scope of this book (see, instead, *A Guide to LaTeX* [7], *The LaTeX Companion* [3] or *Using LaTeX to Write a PhD Thesis* [13]). Therefore this section just gives a brief explanation of the thebibliography environment, which is usually automatically generated using bibtex or biber.

[FAQ: Creating a BibTeX bibliography file]

`\begin{thebibliography}{⟨widest tag⟩}`

Definition

This environment is very similar to the list making environments described in Section 4.4, but instead of `\item` use

`\bibitem[⟨tag⟩]{⟨key⟩}`

Definition

where ⟨key⟩ is a unique keyword that identifies this item. Your keyword can be anything you like, but as with `\label` I recommend that you use a short memorable keyword. I tend to use the first author's surname followed by the year of publication.

The bibliography heading depends on the class file you are using. Most of the article-style classes, such as scrreprt, use `\refname` (which produces "References") in an unnumbered section, whereas the report and book-styles, such as scrreprt and scrbook, use `\bibname` (which produces "Bibliography") in an unnumbered chapter. See Table 8.1 on page 149 for the list of the common textual label commands.

Most class files don't automatically add the bibliography to the table of contents. The KOMA-Script classes provide the bibliography option. This can be bibliography=totoc (an unnumbered unit added to the table of contents), for example,

`\documentclass[bibliography=totoc]{scrreprt}`

Input

or bibliography=totocnumbered (a numbered unit added to the table of contents), for example,

`\documentclass[bibliography=totocnumbered]{scrreprt}`

Input

If you're not using one of the KOMA-Script classes, consult the documentation for your class to see if there is an equivalent option. Failing that, you can use `\addcontentsline` (described in Section 5.4). For example (using a class that defines chapters):

[5.6]`http://www.dickimaw-books.com/latex/novices/html/exercises/crossref.tex`

Input ↑

```
\addcontentsline{toc}{chapter}{\bibname}
\begin{bibliography}{1}
```

Input ↓

EXAMPLE:
(This example uses the command \LaTeXe which produces the LaTeX 2_ε logo. This indicates the current version of LaTeX rather than the old 2.09 version.)[5.7] The class style in use is scrbook, so the title is given by \bibname ("Bibliography").

Input ↑

```
\begin{thebibliography}{3}
\bibitem{lamport94} ''\LaTeX: a document preparation system'', Leslie
Lamport, 2nd edition (updated for \LaTeXe), Addison-Wesley (1994).

\bibitem{kopka95} ''A Guide to \LaTeX: document preparation for beginners
and advanced users'', Helmut Kopka and Patrick W. Daly, Addison-Wesley
(1995).

\bibitem{goossens94} ''The \LaTeX\_Companion'', Michel Goossens, Frank
Mittelbach and Alexander Samarin, Addison-Wesley, (1994).
```

Input ↓

```
\end{thebibliography}
```

Output ↑

Bibliography

[1] "LaTeX: a document preparation system", Leslie Lamport, 2nd edition (updated for LaTeX 2_ε), Addison-Wesley (1994).

[2] "A Guide to LaTeX: document preparation for beginners and advanced users", Helmut Kopka and Patrick W. Daly, Addison-Wesley (1995).

[3] "The LaTeX Companion", Michel Goossens, Frank Mittelbach and Alexander Samarin, Addison-Wesley, (1994).

Output ↓

You can cite an item in your bibliography with the command

Definition   \cite[⟨*text*⟩]{⟨*key list*⟩}

[5.7] If a friend or colleague gives you a file containing \documentstyle instead of \documentclass they are nearly 20 years out of date.

EXAMPLE:

↑ Input

```
For more information about writing bibliographies see
Goossens \emph{et al.}~\cite{goossens94}.
```

↓ Input

Output:

For more information about writing bibliographies see Goossens *et al.* [3]. Output

If you want to cite multiple works, use a comma-separated list:

↑ Input

```
For more information about writing bibliographies
see~\cite{kopka95,goossens94}.
```

↓ Input

Output:

For more information about writing bibliographies see [2,3]. Output

The optional argument ⟨*text*⟩ to the \cite command can be used to add text to the citation.

EXAMPLE:

↑ Input

```
For more information about writing bibliographies see
Goossens \emph{et al.}~\cite[Chapter~13]{goossens94}.
```

↓ Input

Output:

↑ Output

For more information about writing bibliographies see Goossens *et al.* [3, Chapter 13].

↓ Output

The thebibliography environment has a mandatory argument:

\begin{thebibliography}{⟨*widest tag*⟩} Definition

The argument ⟨*widest tag*⟩ is the widest tag in the list of entries. This helps LaTeX to align the references correctly. In the example above, the tags appeared as: [1], [2] and [3], and [3] is the widest so that was used as the argument. These tags can be changed from the default numbers to something else using the optional argument to the \bibitem command.

EXAMPLE (TEXTUAL TAGS):
This example uses the optional argument of \bibitem to use textual rather than numerical tags. The widest tag is [Goossens 1994] so that is chosen to be the argument
of the thebibliography environment:

Input ↑

```
\begin{thebibliography}{Goossens 1994}

\bibitem[Lamport 1994]{lamport94} ''\LaTeX\ : a document preparation
system'', Leslie Lamport, 2nd edition (updated for \LaTeXe),
Addison-Wesley (1994).

\bibitem[Kopka 1995]{kopka95} ''A Guide to \LaTeX: document preparation
for beginners and advanced users'', Helmut Kopka and Patrick W. Daly,
Addison-Wesley (1995).

\bibitem[Goossens 1994]{goossens94} ''The \LaTeX\_Companion'', Michel
Goossens, Frank Mittelbach and Alexander Samarin, Addison-Wesley, (1994).
```

Input ↓
```
\end{thebibliography}
```

Output ↑

Bibliography

[Lamport 1994]   "LATEX : a document preparation system", Leslie Lamport, 2nd edition (updated for LATEX 2ε), Addison-Wesley (1994).

[Kopka 1995]   "A Guide to LATEX: document preparation for beginners and advanced users", Helmut Kopka and Patrick W. Daly, Addison-Wesley
(1995).

[Goossens 1994] "The LATEX Companion", Michel Goossens, Frank Mittelbach and
Alexander Samarin, Addison-Wesley, (1994).

Output ↓

Exercise 13 (Creating a Bibliography)

Try adding the following chapter to your document:

Input ↑

```
\chapter{Recommended Reading}
For a basic introduction to \LaTeX\_see Lamport~\cite{lamport94}. For
more detailed information about \LaTeX\_and associated applications,
consult Kopka and Daly~\cite{kopka95} or Goossens \emph{et
al}~\cite{goossens94}.
```

Input ↓

and also add the bibliography shown above to the end of your document. You can download[5.8] the solution, but have a go by yourself first. Remember that, as before, you will need to LaTeX the document twice to get the references up-to-date, unless you're using `latexmk` (as described in Section 5.5) in which case it will be done automatically.

5.7. Page Styles and Page Numbering

You may have noticed that the documents you have created have all had their page numbers automatically inserted at the foot of most of the pages. If you have created the document that has gradually been modified over the previous few sections, you may have noticed that the title page has no header or footer, the table of contents starts on page 1, the abstract page has no page number, and the pages after the abstract start on page 1 and continue incrementally onwards from that point. All the page numbers are Arabic numerals. This can be changed using the command:

[FAQ: Page numbering "⟨n⟩ of ⟨m⟩"]

`\pagenumbering{`⟨*style*⟩`}`

Definition

where ⟨*style*⟩ can be one of:

arabic Arabic numerals (1, 2, 3, ...)

roman Lower case Roman numerals (i, ii, iii, ...)

Roman Upper case Roman numerals (I, II, III, ...)

alph Lower case alphabetical characters (a, b, c, ...)

Alph Upper case alphabetical characters (A, B, C, ...)

Traditionally, the front matter (table of contents, list of figures etc) should have lower case Roman numeral page numbering, while the main matter should be in Arabic numerals.

[FAQ: Page numbering by chapter]

EXAMPLE:

⊤ Input

```
\author{Me}
\title{A Simple Document}
\maketitle

\pagenumbering{roman}
\tableofcontents

\begin{abstract}
```

[5.8]http://www.dickimaw-books.com/latex/novices/html/exercises/biblio.tex

```
This is the abstract.
\end{abstract}

\pagenumbering{arabic}
\chapter{Introduction}
```

Input ↓

The scrbook class provides:

Definition   `\frontmatter`

which switches to lower case Roman numeral page numbering, and

Definition   `\mainmatter`

which switches to Arabic numeral page numbering. These two declarations also change the way the sectioning units, such as `\chapter` and `\section`, appear. The former, `\frontmatter`, suppresses the numbering (regardless of whether or not you've used the starred version of the sectioning commands). The latter, `\mainmatter`, switches the numbering back on (unless otherwise suppressed by using the starred sectioning commands). In addition, scrbook provides

Definition   `\backmatter`

which doesn't affect the page numbering but, like `\frontmatter`, suppresses the sectional unit numbering.

NOTE:
The abstract environment isn't defined by the scrbook class, as a book summary is usually incorporated into an introductory section.

EXAMPLE:

Input ↑

```
\documentclass[12pt]{scrbook}

\title{A Simple Document}
\author{Me}

\begin{document}
\maketitle

\frontmatter
\tableofcontents

\chapter{Summary}
A brief document to
illustrate how to use \LaTeX.
```

```
\mainmatter

\chapter{Introduction}
\label{ch:intro}

\end{document}
```

↓ Input

The headers and footers can be changed using the command

\pagestyle{⟨*style*⟩}

Definition

Individual pages can be changed using

\thispagestyle{⟨*style*⟩}

Definition

Standard styles are:

empty   No header or footer.

plain   Header empty, page number in footer.

headings   Header contains page number and various information, footer empty.

myheadings   Header specified by user, footer empty.

If the myheadings style is used, the header information can be specified using:

\markboth{⟨*left head*⟩}{⟨*right head*⟩}

Definition

if the twoside option has been passed to the class file (default for scrbook), or

\markright{⟨*right head*⟩}

Definition

if the oneside option has been passed to the class file (default for scrartcl and scrreprt).

The scrreprt class file uses the empty style for the title and abstract pages and plain for the first page of each new chapter. By default the remaining pages are also plain, but these can be changed using the \pagestyle command. The scrbook class defaults to the headings style instead of plain.

The KOMA-Script bundle provides a way to define new page styles, but that's beyond the scope of this introductory tutorial. See the KOMA-Script documentation for further details if you are interested.

[FAQ: Alternative head- and footlines in LaTeX]

This book mostly[5.9] uses the headings page style and the scrbook class with the twoside option, so the odd and even page headers are different, whereas the A4 PDF version (available from http://www.dickimaw-books.com/) uses the oneside option, so the odd and even page headers are the same. The on-screen PDF version of

---

[5.9]I made some modifications to the page style for the footers in the summary and index.

this book uses a page style I defined myself that incorporates a navigation bar in the footer.

Exercise 14 (Page Styles and Page Numbering)

Try modifying your code so that it uses the scrbook class, \frontmatter and \mainmatter. Replace the abstract environment with an unnumbered chapter, as shown below. Again, changes made from the previous document are illustrated **like this**:

Code ↑

```
\documentclass[12pt]{scrbook}

\usepackage{datetime}

\pagestyle{headings}

\title{A Simple Document}
\author{Me}

\begin{document}

\maketitle

\frontmatter
\tableofcontents

\chapter{Summary}
A brief document to
illustrate how to use \LaTeX.

\mainmatter

\chapter{Introduction}
\label{ch:intro}

\section{The First Section}

This is a simple \LaTeX\ document.
Here is the first paragraph.
The next chapter is Chapter~\ref{ch:another}
and is on page~\pageref{ch:another}.
The next section is Section~\ref{sec:next}.

% Rest of document unchanged but
```

```
% omitted for brevity.
\end{document}
```

↓ Code

(You can download[5.10] the edited document.)

5.8. Multi-Lingual Support: using the babel package

You may have noticed that the \tableofcontents and \chapter commands have produced English words like "Contents" and "Chapter". If you are writing in another language, this is not appropriate. In this case, you can use the babel package, and specify which language you will be using, either as an option to the babel package, or as an option to the class file. If you are writing in more than one language, list all the languages that you will be using where the last named language is the default language. For example:

[FAQ: How to change LaTeX's "fixed names"]

[FAQ: Using a new language with Babel]

[FAQ: Parallel setting of text]

\usepackage[english,french]{babel}

or

\documentclass[english,french]{scrreprt}
\usepackage{babel}

You can then switch between the named languages either using the declaration:

\selectlanguage{⟨*language*⟩}

Definition

or the otherlanguage environment:

\begin{otherlanguage}{⟨*language*⟩}

Definition

These will affect all translations, including the date format and predefined names like "Chapter". This also changes the hyphenation patterns. (See Section 2.14.)

If you only want to set a short section of text in a different language, without affecting the date format or predefined names, then you can either use the command:

\foreignlanguage{⟨*language*⟩}{⟨*text*⟩}

Definition

or the starred version of the otherlanguage environment:

\begin{otherlanguage*}{⟨*language*⟩}

Definition

You can test to see if a given language is currently selected using:

\iflanguage{⟨*language*⟩}{⟨*true text*⟩}{⟨*false text*⟩}

Definition

[5.10]http://www.dickimaw-books.com/latex/novices/html/exercises/pagestyle.tex

EXAMPLE:

Input ⊤

```
\documentclass[UKenglish,USenglish,french]{scrartcl}
% french is the last named option, so that's the current language

\usepackage[T1]{fontenc}
\usepackage[utf8]{inputenc}
\usepackage{babel}

\begin{document}
Ce texte est en fran\c{c}ais. La date aujourd'hui est: \today.

\selectlanguage{USenglish}
This text is in US English. Today's date is: \today.

\selectlanguage{UKenglish}
This text is in UK English. Today's date is: \today.
\end{document}
```

Input ↓

Result:

Output ⊤

Ce texte est en français. La date aujourd'hui est : 25 septembre 2012.
This text is in US English. Today's date is: September 25, 2012.
This text is in UK English. Today's date is: 25th September 2012.

Output ↓

NOTE:

If you are using the french option, the colon character (:) is made active (that is, it's turned into a special character) so if you are writing in French it's best not to use a colon in labels (so where I've used, say, ch:def you may need to change the colon to something else).

CHAPTER 6

THE graphicx PACKAGE

It is possible to generate images using LaTeX commands (See the pgf/tikz package or *The LaTeX Graphics Companion* [5]) however most people find it easier to create a picture in some other application, and include that file into their LaTeX document.

[FAQ: Drawing with TeX]

PDFLaTeX can insert PDF, PNG and JPG image files into your document. If your image file is in a different format, you may be able to find an application to convert it. Modern TeX-distributions can automatically convert EPS files to PDF during the LaTeX run using the Perl script `epstopdf`. If your TeX-distribution doesn't support this, you can convert your EPS file using `epstopdf` explicitly. For example, if you have an EPS image called, say, `sample-image.eps`, you can convert it to a PDF image called `sample-image.pdf`, by using the following command in a terminal or command prompt:

[FAQ: Spawning programs from (La)TeX: \write18]

```
epstopdf sample-image.eps
```

or (full path name may be required)

```
perl epstopdf sample-image.eps
```

To insert an image file into your document, you first need to specify that you want to use the graphicx package. So the following must go in the preamble:

```
\usepackage{graphicx}
```

Input

The image can then be included in your document using the command

```
\includegraphics[⟨key-val options⟩]{⟨filename⟩}
```

Definition

where ⟨*filename*⟩ is the name of your image file *without the file extension*, and ⟨*key-val options*⟩ is a comma-separated list of options that can be used to change the way the image is displayed. Note that if you have an image where the file name contain spaces or multiple dots, you need to use the grffile package:

[FAQ: "Modern" graphics file names]

```
\usepackage{graphicx,grffile}
```

Input

EXAMPLE:

Suppose you had a file called `shapes.pdf`, then to include it in your document you would do:

```
\includegraphics{shapes}
```

Input

which would produce:

You can specify a full or relative pathname, but you must use a forward slash /
as the directory divider, even if you are using Windows. For example:

`\includegraphics{pictures/shapes}`

means the file `pictures/shapes.pdf` on Unix-type systems, and it means the file
`pictures\shapes.pdf` on Windows.[6.1] This is mainly because the backslash character is a LATEX special character indicating a command, but it also helps portability
between platforms.

You can specify the order of the file types to look for with the command

`\DeclareGraphicsExtensions{⟨ext-list⟩}`

where ⟨*ext-list*⟩ is a comma-separated list of extensions. For example, you might
want to search first for PDF files, then for PNG files, then for JPG files and finally
for EPS files:

`\DeclareGraphicsExtensions{.pdf,.png,.jpg,.eps}`

The default for PDFLATEX is:

`.png,.pdf,.jpg,.mps,.jpeg,.jbig2,.jb2,.PNG,.PDF,.JPG,.JPEG,.JBIG2,.JB2,`
`.eps`

The optional argument ⟨*key-val options*⟩ should be a comma-separated list of
⟨*key*⟩=⟨*value*⟩ pairs. Common options are:

`angle=⟨x⟩`   rotate the image by $x°$ anticlockwise.

`width=⟨length⟩`   scale the image so that the width is ⟨*length*⟩. (Remember to
                     specify the units.)

`height=⟨length⟩`   scale the image so that the height is ⟨*length*⟩. (Remember to
                     specify the units.)

`scale=⟨value⟩`   Scale the image by ⟨*value*⟩

`trim=⟨l⟩ ⟨b⟩ ⟨r⟩ ⟨t⟩` Specifies the amount to remove from each side. For example

`\includegraphics[trim=1 2 3 4]{shapes}`

[6.1]Or `shapes.png` or `shapes.jpg` or `shapes.eps`. The example assumes a PDF image file.

crops the image by 1bp from the left, 2bp from the bottom, 3bp from the right and 4bp from the top. (Recall the bp unit from Table 2.1 on page 25.)

draft   Don't actually print the image, just draw a box of the same size and print the filename inside it.

EXAMPLE:

This example first rotates the image by 45° anticlockwise, then scales it so that the width is 1 inch.

`\includegraphics[angle=45,width=1in]{shapes}` Input

Output

Note that this isn't the same as scaling and then rotating:

`\includegraphics[width=1in,angle=45]{shapes}` Input

Output

You can also scale an image relative to the text area using the length registers `\textwidth` and `\textheight`. For example, to scale a portrait image so that its height is three-quarters of the text area height, you can do:

`\includegraphics[height=0.75\textheight]{shapes}` Input

or to scale a landscape image so that its width is half the text area width, you can do:

`\includegraphics[height=0.5\textwidth]{shapes}` Input

NOTE:

The `\includegraphics` command is another form of box (see Section 4.7), and can be used in the middle of a line of text, just like the tabular environment. See Section 7.1 to find out how to put the image in a figure with a caption.

EXAMPLE:

Recall the **ex** unit of measure from Table 2.1 on page 25. This can be used to scale an image relative to the font size:

```
An image can be inserted into a line of text like this:
\includegraphics[height=2ex]{shapes}
```

Output   An image can be inserted into a line of text like this:

6.1. Graphical Transformations

The graphicx package also provides commands to rotate, resize, reflect and scale text. They are as follows:

Definition   `\rotatebox[`⟨*option list*⟩`]{`⟨*angle*⟩`}{`⟨*text*⟩`}`

Rotates ⟨*text*⟩ by ⟨*angle*⟩ (degrees anti-clockwise by default). The optional argument ⟨*option list*⟩ is a comma-separated list of any of the following options:

- `units=`⟨*number*⟩

  The number of units in one full anti-clockwise rotation. So `units=-360` means that ⟨*angle*⟩ specifies degrees clockwise whereas `units=6.283185` means that ⟨*angle*⟩ is in radians.

- `origin=`⟨*label*⟩

  The point of rotation. The value ⟨*label*⟩ may contain one from either or both of the two lists: `lrc` (left, right, centre) and `tbB` (top, bottom, baseline). Alternatively the origin may be specified using the following two keys:

- `x=`⟨*dimen*⟩

- `y=`⟨*dimen*⟩

EXAMPLE:

```
base line
\rotatebox{45}{Some text}
\rotatebox[units=-360]{45}{Some text}
\rotatebox[units=-360,origin=rB]{45}{Some text}
\rotatebox[x=3em,y=3em]{45}{Some text}
base line
```

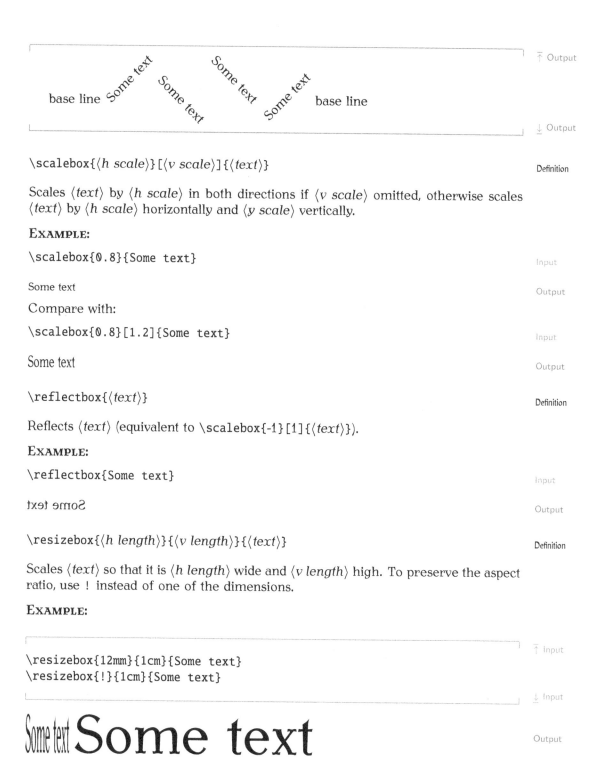

`\scalebox{⟨h scale⟩}[⟨v scale⟩]{⟨text⟩}` Definition

Scales ⟨text⟩ by ⟨h scale⟩ in both directions if ⟨v scale⟩ omitted, otherwise scales ⟨text⟩ by ⟨h scale⟩ horizontally and ⟨y scale⟩ vertically.

EXAMPLE:

`\scalebox{0.8}{Some text}` Input

Some text Output

Compare with:

`\scalebox{0.8}[1.2]{Some text}` Input

Some text Output

`\reflectbox{⟨text⟩}` Definition

Reflects ⟨text⟩ (equivalent to `\scalebox{-1}[1]{⟨text⟩}`).

EXAMPLE:

`\reflectbox{Some text}` Input

ʇxǝʇ ǝɯoƧ Output

`\resizebox{⟨h length⟩}}{⟨v length⟩}{⟨text⟩}` Definition

Scales ⟨text⟩ so that it is ⟨h length⟩ wide and ⟨v length⟩ high. To preserve the aspect ratio, use ! instead of one of the dimensions.

EXAMPLE:

`\resizebox{12mm}{1cm}{Some text}`
`\resizebox{!}{1cm}{Some text}`

Some text Some text Output

6.2. Package Options

The graphicx package can have the following options passed to it:

draft Don't actually display the images, just print the filename in a box of the correct size. This is useful if you want to print out a draft copy of a document to check the text rather than the images.

final Opposite of draft (default).

hiderotate Don't show rotated text.

hidescale Don't show scaled text.

Remember that relevant options passed to the class file also affect packages.

EXAMPLE (DRAFT MODE):
Draft mode helps to speed up compilation of a large document when you are editing the text. In the preamble:

Input `\usepackage[draft]{graphicx}`

or

Input ⊤

`\documentclass[draft]{scrbook}`

`\usepackage{graphicx}`

Input ↓

Later in the document:

Input `\includegraphics[width=1in,angle=45]{pictures/shapes}`

Output

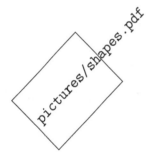

Exercise 15 (Using the graphicx Package)

Download the image file shapes.pdf from http://www.dickimaw-books.com/latex/novices/html/exercises/ (or create your own image), and include it into your document. (You can download[6.2] an example solution.)

[6.2]http://www.dickimaw-books.com/latex/novices/html/exercises/graphic.tex

For more information on the graphicx package see *The LaTeX Graphics Companion* [5] or the graphicx documentation.

RELATED UK FAQ [19] TOPICS:

- How to import graphics into (La)TeX documents

- Imported graphics in PDFLaTeX

- Imported graphics in dvips

- Imported graphics in dvipdfm

- Importing graphics from "somewhere else"

- Portable imported graphics

- Repeated graphics in a document

- Limit the width of imported graphics

- Top-aligning imported graphics

- Labelling graphics

- Graphics division by zero

CHAPTER 7

FLOATS

Figures and tables are referred to as "floats" because they are *floated* to the nearest location. This prevents ugly large spaces appearing on the page if there isn't enough room for the figure or table before the page break. Floats have a caption and associated number. It is customary for captions to appear at the bottom of figures but at the top of tables [18, 11].

[FAQ: The style of captions]

For both figures and tables, the caption is generated using the command:

`\caption[`⟨*short caption*⟩`]{`⟨*text*⟩`}`

Definition

Note that the `\caption` command has a moving argument, so fragile commands will need to be protected using `\protect`. The optional argument ⟨*short caption*⟩ is used to provide an alternative shorter caption for the list of figures or list of tables, akin to the optional argument to the sectioning commands described in Section 5.3.

[FAQ: Footnotes in captions]

NOTE:

Although the `\caption` command can have an optional short title, in general, captions should be brief. They should not contain lots of description or background detail [18]. That type of information should be placed in the main text not the caption.

POSITIONING:

Both the figure and table environments have an optional argument ⟨*placement specifiers*⟩, which indicates permissible locations for the float. This may be a combination of h ("here"), t (top), b (bottom) and p (page of floats.) Note that this only gives a general guideline as to where the float will end up. The final location is governed by other factors, such as space left on the page and the proportion of text to floats on the page. If you omit one or more of the placement specifiers, then you are prohibiting the float from being placed in that location. A common mistake is to do

[FAQ: Wide figures in two-column documents]

`\begin{figure}[h]`

✗

which says "I want the figure here and it can't go anywhere else!" If the figure *can't* be placed exactly here (for example, there may not be enough room on the page), then you have given it no alternative location, which can result in this and all subsequent figures being dumped at the end of the chapter or document, or can result in a fatal error when running LaTeX. You may be able to manage with only one of the other options, for example,

[FAQ: "Too many unprocessed floats"]

`\begin{figure}[t]`

(In fact, modern TₑX distributions now replace [h] with [t] if the float can't be placed.) However, if you have a large number of floats it is advisable to provide as many options as possible:

\begin{figure}[htbp]

Similarly for tables.

If you are absolutely adamant that an image must go "right here", then it's not a float, and you shouldn't be using the figure environment. It's just a horizontal box, like the example on page 117. Similarly for tabulated material.

It's worth bearing in mind what the Oxford Style Manual [11] has to say:

> "Text must not be read into it so as to give [the figure] an explicit and fixed introduction, for example 'in the following figure': the final placement is determined by page breaks, which cannot be anticipated before setting, and this makes rewording the text necessary if the illustration does not fit the make-up of the page."

Turabian [18] gives the same advice (and reiterates it for figures):

> "All text references to a table should be by a number, not by an introductory phrase such as 'in the following table'."

7.1. Figures

Figures are created using the figure environment.

Definition   \begin{figure}[⟨*placement specifiers*⟩]

This environment may contain one or more captions (specified, as described above, with the \caption command) but page breaks are not allowed in the contents of a figure environment. The optional argument ⟨*placement specifiers*⟩ is as described above.

Recall from Chapter 6 (The graphicx Package) that we can include an image in our document with the command \includegraphics defined in the graphicx package. We can put our shapes.pdf image into a figure as follows:

Input ↑
```
\begin{figure}[htbp]
  \includegraphics{shapes}
  \caption{Some Shapes}
\end{figure}
```
Input ↓

So far so good, but our picture needs to be centred. This can be done using the \centering declaration mentioned in Section 2.12:

```
\begin{figure}[htbp]
  \centering
  \includegraphics{shapes}
  \caption{Some Shapes}
\end{figure}
```
↑ Input

↓ Input

The \caption command generates a number, just like \section, so we can cross-reference it with \ref and \label. First, let's label the figure:

```
\begin{figure}[htbp]
  \centering
  \includegraphics{shapes}
  \caption{Some Shapes}
  \label{fig:shapes}
\end{figure}
```
↑ Input

↓ Input

Now we can reference it:

```
Figure~\ref{fig:shapes} shows some shapes.
```
Input

(As before we use ~ to make an unbreakable space.) This produces the following output in the text:

Figure 7.1 shows some shapes.
Output

and produces Figure 7.1.

Figure 7.1. Some Shapes

IMPORTANT NOTE:
If you want to change the caption font, ***don't*** do, e.g.:

```
\caption{\bfseries Some Shapes}
```

Recall \addtokomafont from Section 5.3. This can also be used to change the fonts used by the caption.

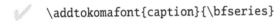 `\addtokomafont{caption}{\bfseries}`

Similarly for the caption label. For example:

Input   `\addtokomafont{captionlabel}{\scshape}`

LIST OF FIGURES

Just as we were able to generate a table of contents using `\tableofcontents`, we can also generate a list of figures using the command

Definition   `\listoffigures`

This creates a file with the extension `.lof` (see Section 2.4). As with `\tableofcontents` you will need to LaTeX your document twice to get the list of figures up-to-date, unless you're using `latexmk` (as described in Section 5.5) in which case it will be done automatically.

Exercise 16 (Creating Figures)

If you did Exercise 15 (page 120), you should have a document with an image in it. You now need to put this image into a figure environment. Remember to centre the image, and give the figure a caption. Next, try labelling the figure and referencing it in the text. You could also put in a list of figures after the table of contents. You can download[7.1] an example.

7.1.1. Side-By-Side Figures

Recall at the start of Section 7.1, I mentioned that the figure environment may contain one or more captions. In most cases, you'll just have a single caption per figure environment, but sometimes you may want to have two figures side-by-side, in which case you'll need two captions within the same figure environment in order to keep the figures together.

To do this, we can use the minipage environment, which was covered in Section 4.7. Recall that the minipage environment creates a horizontal box, which means that two mini-pages can be placed side-by-side on the same line. All you need to do now, is place one image and caption in one mini-page, and the other image and caption in the neighbouring mini-page. (Do you remember what effect is obtained by placing a percent symbol at the end of a line?)[7.2]

[7.1]`http://www.dickimaw-books.com/latex/novices/html/exercises/figures.tex`
[7.2]See page 8.

```
\begin{figure}[htbp]
 \begin{minipage}{0.5\linewidth}
  \centering
  \includegraphics{circle}
  \caption{A Circle}
  \label{fig:circle}
 \end{minipage}%
 \begin{minipage}{0.5\linewidth}
  \centering
  \includegraphics{rectangle}
  \caption{A Rectangle}
  \label{fig:rectangle}
 \end{minipage}
\end{figure}
```

The above code produces Figures 7.2 and 7.3 on the following page. Note that each mini-page uses \centering to centre its contents, and the label is also placed in the same mini-page, after the \caption command. If the \label was not in the same scope as the \caption, the cross-reference would be incorrect.

A common mistake when trying to create side-by-side figures is to do:

```
\begin{figure}[htbp]
 \begin{minipage}{0.5\linewidth}
  \centering
  \includegraphics{circle}
  \caption{A Circle}
  \label{fig:circle}
 \end{minipage}

 \begin{minipage}{0.5\linewidth}
  \centering
  \includegraphics{rectangle}
  \caption{A Rectangle}
  \label{fig:rectangle}
 \end{minipage}
\end{figure}
```

This produces one figure on top of the other, instead of side-by-side. This is because the blank line indicates a paragraph break, so each minipage is in a separate paragraph, so it's not possible for them to be on the same line.

If you want a bit of spacing in your code to make it more readable, use % to comment out the paragraph break. For example:

```
\end{minipage}%
%
\begin{minipage}{0.5\linewidth}
```

Figure 7.2. A Circle

Figure 7.3. A Rectangle

7.2. Tables

Tables are produced in much the same way as figures, except that the table environment is used instead.

Definition \begin{table}[⟨*placement specifiers*⟩]

Where the optional argument ⟨*placement specifiers*⟩ is as described on page 123.

As mentioned at the start of this chapter, tables typically have the caption at the top of the table [18]. With the KOMA-Script classes, such as scrartcl, scrreprt and scrbook, use the class option captions=tableabove to ensure that the vertical spacing appears correctly between the caption and the table content and put \caption at the start of *[FAQ: Tables* the table environment. Page breaks are not permitted in the table environment. (The *longer than* longtable package can be used for that instead. See the longtable documentation for *a single* further details.)
page]

EXAMPLE:
In the preamble:

Input   \documentclass[captions=tableabove]{scrbook}

Later in the document:

Input ⊼

```
\begin{table}[htbp]
 \caption{A Sample Table}
 \label{tab:sample}
 \centering
 \begin{tabular}{lr}
 Item  & Cost\\
 Video & 8.99\\
 CD    & 9.99\\
 DVD   & 15.00
 \end{tabular}
\end{table}
```

Input ↓

This produces Table 7.1 on the facing page.

Table 7.1. A Sample Table

Item	Cost
Video	8.99
CD	9.99
DVD	15.00

Again, the \centering declaration is used to centre the tabular environment. As with figures, you can create a list of tables using the command

\listoftables

Definition

This creates a file with the extension .lot (see Section 2.4). As with the table of contents and list of figures, you will need to LaTeX your document twice to get the list of tables up-to-date, unless you're using latexmk (as described in Section 5.5) in which case it will be done automatically.

Exercise 17 (Creating Tables)

If you did Exercise 7 (page 76), you should have a tabular environment in your document. Try turning this into a table, and add Table 7.1. You could also try adding a list of tables. As before, you can download[7.3] the solution.

7.2.1. Side-by-Side Tables

You can create side-by-side tables using an analogous method to the side-by-side figures approach described above.

EXAMPLE:
This example is similar to the one in Section 7.1.1. Again, take care to ensure that there is no paragraph break between the two minipage environments.

↑ Input

```
\begin{table}
 \begin{minipage}{0.5\linewidth}
  \caption{Prices for 2011}
  \label{tab:prices2011}
  \centering
  \begin{tabular}{lr}
   Item & Price (£)\\
   Widgets & 10.99\\
   Whatsits & 5.99
  \end{tabular}
```

[7.3]http://www.dickimaw-books.com/latex/novices/html/exercises/tables.tex

```
 \end{minipage}%
%
 \begin{minipage}{0.5\linewidth}
  \caption{Prices for 2012}
  \label{tab:prices2012}
  \centering
  \begin{tabular}{lr}
   Item & Price (\pounds)\\
   Widgets & 11.99\\
   Whatsits & 6.99
  \end{tabular}
 \end{minipage}%
\end{table}
```

Input ↓

This produces Tables 7.2 and 7.3.

Table 7.2. Prices for 2011			Table 7.3. Prices for 2012	
Item	Price (£)		Item	Price (£)
Widgets	10.99		Widgets	11.99
Whatsits	5.99		Whatsits	6.99

7.3. Sideways Floats

The rotating package provides the sidewaysfigure environment:

Definition   `\begin{sidewaysfigure}`

and the sidewaystable environment:

Definition   `\begin{sidewaystable}`

which are like figure and table, respectively, but rotate the entire float (including caption) sideways. This sideways float is always placed on a page of its own.

If you have used the twoside class option (or you are using a class like scrbook, which defaults to that option) then the sideways floats will be rotated clockwise or anti-clockwise, depending on whether they fall on an even (verso) or odd (recto) numbered page. (Requires a second LaTeX run to get it correct.)

EXAMPLE:

Input ↑

```
\begin{sidewaysfigure}
 \centering
```

```
 \includegraphics[width=0.75\textheight]{shapes}
 \caption{A Sideways Figure}
 \label{fig:sideways}
\end{sidewaysfigure}
```
↓ Input

The above code produces Figure 7.4 on the next page.

7.4. Sub-Floats

Some floats have sub-floats within them. For example, a figure may contain several sub-figures, each of which requires a caption. The simplest way to do this is to use the subcaption package that provides the subfigure and subtable environments:

\begin{subfigure}[⟨*pos*⟩]{⟨*width*⟩}
Definition

\begin{subtable}[⟨*pos*⟩]{⟨*width*⟩}
Definition

Within these environments, you can use \caption to create a sub-caption. (In addition to the main \caption for the containing figure or table environment.)

NOTE:
The subcaption package requires the caption package, but doesn't automatically load it, so you'll need to load both:

\usepackage{caption,subcaption}
Input

EXAMPLE:
This is very similar to the side-by-side figures example from Section 7.1.1.

↑ Input
```
\begin{figure}[htbp]
\begin{subfigure}[b]{0.5\linewidth}
 \centering
 \includegraphics{rectangle}
 \caption{Rectangle}\label{fig:rectangle}
\end{subfigure}%
%
\begin{subfigure}[b]{0.5\linewidth}
 \centering
 \includegraphics{circle}
 \caption{Circle}\label{fig:circle}
\end{subfigure}%
\caption{Two Shapes}
\label{fig:shape}
\end{figure}
```
↓ Input

Figure 7.4. A Sideways Figure

This produces Figure 7.5. Elsewhere in the document, the figure and its components can be referenced:

```
Figure~\ref{fig:shapes2} shows some shapes. Figure~\ref{fig:rectangle}
shows a rectangle and Figure~\ref{fig:circle} shows a circle.
```
↑ Input
↓ Input

which produces the following text:

Figure 7.5 shows some shapes. Figure 7.5a shows a rectangle and Figure 7.5b shows a circle.
↑ Output
↓ Output

You can also reference just the sub-float using

```
\subref{⟨label⟩}
```
Definition

which is analogous to \ref, but only displays the sub-float number without the number associated with its containing float.

EXAMPLE:

```
Figure~\ref{fig:shapes2} shows: (\subref{fig:rectangle}) a rectangle and
(\subref{fig:circle}) a circle.
```
↑ Input
↓ Input

produces

Figure 7.5 shows: (a) a rectangle and (b) a circle.
Output

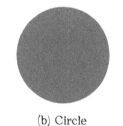

(a) Rectangle   (b) Circle

Figure 7.5. Two Shapes

NOTE:
The subfigure labels (a, b, etc) should typically be in italic [18]. This can be achieved with the caption package using:

```
\DeclareCaptionLabelFormat{⟨format-name⟩}{⟨code⟩}
```
Definition

where ⟨*format-name*⟩ is the name for this new format and ⟨*code*⟩ is the code used to format the label where #2 gets replaced by the reference number.

Once you have defined a new format, you can then use

Definition   `\captionsetup[⟨type⟩]{⟨options⟩}`

to switch to that new format. For subfloats, ⟨*type*⟩ needs to be set to sub. The second argument ⟨*options*⟩ is a ⟨*key*⟩=⟨*value*⟩ comma-separated list. The key that sets the format is labelformat. (For further details about both `\DeclareCaptionLabelFormat` and `\captionsetup`, see the caption package documentation.)

For example, to create a format called em-noparens that displays the number in an emphasized font without parentheses:

Input   `\DeclareCaptionLabelFormat{em-noparens}{\emph{#2}}`

Now switch to that new format:

Input   `\captionsetup[sub]{labelformat=em-noparens}`

Note that this only changes the caption label format. It doesn't affect the font used by `\ref` or `\subref`. For `\ref`, you can use the fncylab package, which provides the command:

Definition   `\labelformat{⟨ctr⟩}{⟨defn⟩}`

Within ⟨*defn*⟩, use #1 to represent the subfigure value and use `\thefigure` for the encapsulating figure number. For example:

Input   `\labelformat{subfigure}{\thefigure\emph{#1}}`

Now

Input   `\ref{fig:circle}`

will produce

Output   7.5*a*

Unfortunately, this doesn't work for `\subref`. Instead you will have to do, for example, the following in the text:

Input   `\emph{\subref{fig:circle}}`

If you want to add parentheses, the above can be modified to:

Input ↑
```
\DeclareCaptionLabelFormat{em-parens}{(\emph{#2})}
\captionsetup[sub]{labelformat=em-parens}
```
Input ↓
```
\labelformat{subfigure}{\thefigure(\emph{#1})}
```

For `\subref`, you will have to do, for example, the following in the text:

Input   `(\emph{\subref{fig:circle}})`

Exercise 18 (Creating Sub-Figures)

Download the image files `rectangle.pdf` and `circle.pdf` from `http://www.dickimaw-books.com/latex/novices/html/exercises/` (or create your own images) and add Figure 7.5 on page 133 to your document. You can download[7.4] the solution.

[7.4] `http://www.dickimaw-books.com/latex/novices/html/exercises/subfloats.tex`

CHAPTER 8

DEFINING COMMANDS

It's possible to define your own commands or redefine existing ones. Be very careful about redefining existing commands; don't redefine a command simply because you want to use the name, only redefine it if you are making a modification. For example, if you want to change the format of the current date, you would redefine \today, but if you want to define a command to display a specific date, you should define a new command with a different name.

There are several reasons why you might want to define a new command:

1. Reduce typing:

   Suppose you have a series of commands or text that you find yourself frequently using, then you could define a command to do all these other commands for you.

   EXAMPLE:

   Suppose you want a lot of large bold slanted sans-serif portions of text within your document. Every time you type those portions of text, you will have to do something like:

   `\textsf{\large\bfseries\slshape Some text}` Input

   It would be much easier if you could use just one command to do all that, called, say, \largeboldsfsl:

   `\largeboldsfsl{Some text}` Input

   or you could call it, say, \lbsfsl which is shorter, but slightly less memorable:

   `\lbsfsl{Some text}` Input

2. Ensure consistency:

   You may find that you want to format an object a certain way.

   EXAMPLE:

   Recall near the end of Section 7.4, I suggested the following to reference a subfigure (when using \subref instead of \ref):

   `(\emph{\subref{fig:circle}})` Input

   For consistency, you might want to define a command, say,

`\formattedsubref{`⟨*label*⟩`}`

that was the same as (`\emph{\subref{`⟨*label*⟩`}}`).

ANOTHER EXAMPLE

Suppose your document has a lot of keywords in it, and you want to format these keywords in a different font, say sans-serif, so that they stand out. You could just do:

Input

`A \textsf{command} usually begins with a backslash.`

however, it is better to define a new command called, say, `\keyword` that will typeset its argument in a sans-serif font. That way it becomes a lot easier to change the format at some later date. For example, you may decide to splash out and have your keywords typed in a particular colour. In which case, all you need to do is simply change the definition of the command `\keyword`, otherwise you'll have to go through your entire document looking for keywords and changing each one which could be very time consuming if you have a large document. You might also decide at some later date to make an index for your document. Indexing all the keywords then becomes much simpler, as again all you'll need to do is modify the `\keyword` command.

New commands are defined using the command:

Definition   `\newcommand{`⟨*cmd*⟩`}[`⟨*n-args*⟩`][`⟨*default*⟩`]{`⟨*text*⟩`}`

The first mandatory argument ⟨*cmd*⟩ is the name of your new command, which must start with a backslash. The optional argument ⟨*n-args*⟩ specifies how many arguments your new command must take. The next optional argument ⟨*default*⟩ will be discussed later. The final mandatory argument ⟨*text*⟩ specifies what LaTeX should do every time it encounters this command.

EXAMPLE (NO PARAMETERS):

Let's begin with a trivial example. Suppose I wanted to write a document about a particular course, say "Programming — Languages and Software Construction", and I had to keep writing the course title, then I might decide to define a command that prints the course title rather than having to laboriously type it out every time. Let's call our new command `\coursetitle`. We want the following code:

Input   `The course \emph{\coursetitle} is an undergraduate course.`

to produce the following output:

Output ↑

The course *Programming — Languages and Software Construction* is an undergraduate course.

Output ↓

Clearly this command doesn't need any arguments, so we don't need to worry about the optional argument ⟨*n-args*⟩ to \newcommand, and the only thing our new command needs to do is print:

Programming --- Languages and Software Construction

so we would define our new command as follows:

```
\newcommand{\coursetitle}{Programming --- Languages and Software
Construction}
```

↑ Input
↓ Input

Commands must always be defined before they are used. The best place to define commands is in the preamble:

↑ Input

```
\documentclass{scrartcl}

\newcommand{\coursetitle}{Programming --- Languages
and Software Construction}

\begin{document}

\section{\coursetitle}

The course \emph{\coursetitle} is an undergraduate course.

\end{document}
```

↓ Input

EXAMPLE (ONE MANDATORY ARGUMENT):

Now let's try defining a command that takes an argument (or parameter). Let's go back to our \keyword example on the facing page. This command needs to take one argument that is the keyword. Let's suppose we want keywords to come out in sans-serif, then we could do:

```
\newcommand{\keyword}[1]{\textsf{#1}}
```

Input

In this case we have used the optional argument ⟨*n-args*⟩ to \newcommand. We want our command \keyword to have one argument, so we have [1]. In \textsf{#1} the #1 represents the first argument. (If we had more than one argument, #2 would represent the second argument, #3 would represent the third argument etc. up to a maximum of 9.) So

```
\keyword{commands}
```

[FAQ: How to break the 9-argument limit]

will be equivalent to

```
\textsf{commands}
```

and

`\keyword{environment}`

will be equivalent to

`\textsf{environment}`

and so on. Again, it's best to put the command definition in the preamble to ensure the command won't be used before it's defined.

Input ↑

```
\documentclass{scrartcl}

\newcommand{\keyword}[1]{\textsf{#1}}

\begin{document}

A \keyword{command} usually begins with a backslash.

\end{document}
```

Input ↓

Now if we want to change the way the keywords are formatted, we can simply change the definition of \keyword. Let's modify our code so that the keyword is now in a slanted sans-serif font:

Input ↑

```
\documentclass{scrartcl}

\newcommand{\keyword}[1]{\textsf{\slshape #1}}

\begin{document}

A \keyword{command} usually begins with a backslash.

\end{document}
```

Input ↓

Let's go one stage further. The color package provides the declaration:

Definition   `\color{⟨col-name⟩}`

which switches the foreground colour to ⟨col-name⟩. It also provides the text-block command:

Definition   `\textcolor{⟨col-name⟩}{⟨text⟩}`

which sets ⟨text⟩ in the colour given by ⟨col-name⟩.

So let's use the color package to make our keywords blue:

```
\documentclass{scrartcl}

\usepackage{color}

\newcommand{\keyword}[1]{\textsf{\slshape\color{blue}#1}}

\begin{document}

A \keyword{command} usually begins with a backslash.

\end{document}
```

Or we could index the keywords. To do this we need the makeidx package and the commands \makeindex, \index{⟨*text*⟩} and \printindex:

```
\documentclass{scrartcl}

\usepackage{makeidx}

\makeindex

\newcommand{\keyword}[1]{\textsf{\slshape #1}\index{#1}}

\begin{document}

A \keyword{command} usually begins with a backslash.

\printindex

\end{document}
```

For further information about how to create an index, see *A Guide to LaTeX* [7] or *The LaTeX Companion* [3]. Alternatively, if you want a brief overview, try *Using LaTeX to Write a PhD Thesis* [13].

Since it is unlikely that the keyword will contain a paragraph break, we should indicate that this is a short command using the starred form:

```
\newcommand*{\keyword}[1]{\textsf{\slshape #1}\index{#1}}
```

Now if you forget to add the closing brace, for example, \keyword{command, then TeX's error checking mechanism will pick up the error sooner. This will give an error message that looks like:

```
! Paragraph ended before \keyword was complete.
<to be read again>
                        \par
1.604
```

This at least gives you the line number (604 in this example) of the end of the paragraph where the error has occurred.

If you don't used the starred form of \newcommand, then you will get the somewhat less than helpful error:

```
! File ended while scanning use of \keyword.
```

If you have a very large document, it may take a while to track down where exactly you have missed a brace.

Exercise 19 (Defining a New Command)

Try typing up the following code:

Code ⊤

```
\documentclass{scrartcl}

\newcommand*{\keyword}[1]{\textsf{#1}}

\begin{document}

A \keyword{command} usually begins with a backslash.

Segments of code may be \keyword{grouped}.

Some \keyword{commands} take one or more \keyword{arguments}.
\end{document}
```

Code ↓

Then modify your code so that the keywords are in a slanted sans-serif font or modify your code so that the keywords come out in blue (using the color package as in the example earlier). Again you can download[8.1] the result.

FOR THE MORE ADVENTUROUS:
If you want to create an index as in the previous example, you will need to use the application makeindex. If you used latexmk back in Section 5.5, you can just carry on using that as before. If not you need to do the following in TeXworks:

1. Create the PDF as described in Section 3.1.

[8.1]http://www.dickimaw-books.com/latex/novices/html/exercises/newcom.tex

2. Select MakeIndex from the drop-down list next to the build (typeset) button (see Figure 8.1 on the next page).

3. Click on the build button. If all goes well, you won't see anything different. If you see something like the following:

```
Couldn't find input index file exercise19  nor exercise19.idx.
```

then you probably forgot to add the command \makeindex to the preamble. Add it in and go back to Step 1.

4. Select pdfLaTeX from the drop-down list and build the PDF file again. Move to the last page of the PDF, and you should see the index.

8.1. Defining Commands with an Optional Argument

As mentioned earlier, the \newcommand command has a second optional argument ⟨default⟩. This allows you to define a command with an optional argument. For example, suppose we want a command called, say, \price. Suppose we want the following code:

[FAQ: More than one optional argument]

Input

```
\price{100}
```

to produce the following output:

£100 excl VAT @ 17.5%

Output

and let's suppose we want an optional argument so that we can change the VAT. That is, we would want the following code:

```
\price[20]{30}
```

Input

to produce the following output:

£30 excl VAT @ 20%

Output

Therefore we want to define a command such that if the optional argument is absent we will have 17.5, and if it is present the optional argument will be substituted instead. This command can be defined as follows:

```
\newcommand{\price}[2][17.5]{\pounds #2 excl VAT @ #1\%}
```

Input

Here, #1 represents the optional argument (by default 17.5) and #2 represents the mandatory argument (the second argument if the optional argument is present, or the only argument if the optional argument is absent.)

As before, since the argument is unlikely to contain a paragraph break, we should indicate that it is a short command using the starred form:

```
\newcommand*{\price}[2][17.5]{\pounds #2 excl VAT @ #1\%}
```

Input

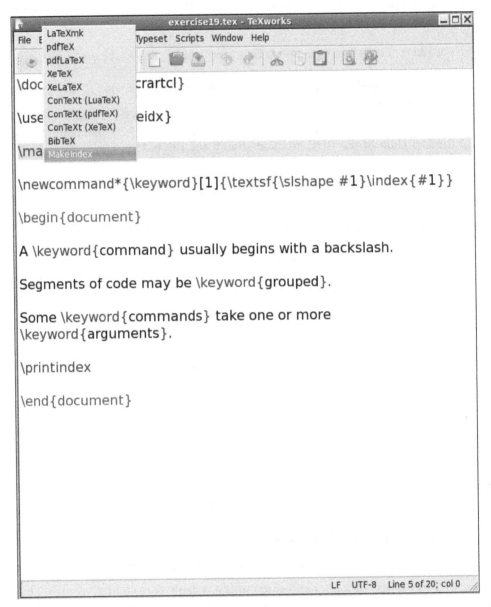

Figure 8.1. Selecting MakeIndex in TeXWorks

Exercise 20 (Defining Commands with an Optional Argument)

In this exercise, you will need to define a slightly modified version of the above example. Try defining a command called, say, \cost. It should take one optional argument and one mandatory argument. Without the optional argument, it behaves in the same way as the \price example above, so that, say,

\cost{50}   Input

will produce

£50 excl VAT @ 17.5%   Output

but with the optional argument, you can change the excl VAT @ 17.5\% bit. So that, say,

\cost[inc VAT]{50}   Input

will produce

£50 inc VAT   Output

You can download[8.2] the solution.

FOR THE MORE ADVENTUROUS:
If you did Exercise 19 (page 142) and you modified \keyword so that it indexed the keyword, you may have noticed that

\keyword{command}   Input

and

\keyword{commands}   Input

produced separate entries in the index. It would be better to have an optional argument to override the indexing mechanism. For example,

\keyword{command}   Input

should print and index the word "command", whereas

\keyword[command]{commands}   Input

should print "commands" and index "command". In other words, we need an optional argument that defaults to the mandatory argument if it is not present. This is how to achieve that type of effect:[8.3]

```
\newcommand*{\keyword}[2][\keywordentry]{%     ↑ Input
  \def\keywordentry{#2}%
  \textsf{#2}%
  \index{#1}%
}                                               ↓ Input
```

[8.2]http://www.dickimaw-books.com/latex/novices/html/exercises/newcomopt.tex
[8.3]Recall from Chapter 2 (Some Definitions) the percent symbol discards the space resulting from the end of line character.

In this example, the default value for the optional argument is set to the command \keywordentry. At the start of \keyword this is defined to be the mandatory argument (as specified by #2) using TeX's \def command:[8.4]

\def\keywordentry{#2}

Then typeset the keyword (given in the mandatory argument #2) in a sans-serif font:

\textsf{#2}

Now index the term using the optional argument (#1):

\index{#1}

If an optional argument is specified, #1 will be the given argument, but if the optional argument is missing, #1 will be \keywordentry, which has earlier been set to the mandatory argument #2.

8.2. Redefining Commands

Commands can be redefined using the command:

Definition \renewcommand{⟨*cmd*⟩}[⟨*n-args*⟩][⟨*default*⟩]{⟨*text*⟩}

This has exactly the same format as \newcommand but is used for redefining existing commands. Again there is a starred version to indicate that the command is a short command.

CAVEAT:
Never redefine a command whose existing function is unknown to you or just because you want to use a particular command name, regardless of its previous function. By way of illustration: as a production editor, I have to combine articles by different authors into a single book. Each author supplies the LaTeX code for their own article. Every so often, I get code that redefines a command for the convenience of the author. Later on another author tries to use the same command, on the assumption that the command behaves according to its original definition. This tends to involve the accent commands as they are short and that saves the author typing. It usually goes along these lines: author A redefines \c (the cedilla accent command) to display a maths bold "**c**" to indicate a vector. Later, author B, uses the cedilla accent, say, in the name François:

Fran\c{c}ois

Author A's hack turns this into Franccois.

Example (Redefining List Labels):

Recall the itemize environment discussed in Section 4.4.1. You may have up to four nested itemize environments, the labels for the outer environment are specified by the command \labelitemi, the labels for the second level are specified by \labelitemii, the third by \labelitemiii and the fourth by \labelitemiv. By default, \labelitemi is a bullet point (•), \labelitemii is an en dash (–), \labelitemiii is an asterisk (∗) and \labelitemiv is a centred dot (·). These can be changed by redefining \labelitemi etc.

Recall from Table 4.2 on page 48 that the command \dag produces a dagger symbol, we can use this symbol instead of a bullet point:

```
\renewcommand*{\labelitemi}{\dag}
\begin{itemize}

\item Animal

\item Mineral

\item Vegetable

\end{itemize}
```

↑ Input

↓ Input

Output:

↑ Output

† Animal

† Mineral

† Vegetable

↓ Output

Here's another example, it uses the PostScript font ZapfDingbats via the pifont package:

```
\renewcommand*{\labelitemi}{\ding{43}}
\begin{itemize}

\item Animal

\item Mineral

\item Vegetable

\end{itemize}
```

↑ Input

↓ Input

Output:

☞ Animal

☞ Mineral

☞ Vegetable

In the above example, it would actually be easier to use the dinglist environment defined in the pifont package:

```
\begin{dinglist}{43}

\item Animal

\item Mineral

\item Vegetable

\end{dinglist}
```

EXAMPLE (REDEFINING THE DEFAULT FONT):

Recall from Section 4.5.3 that the default font family is usually the serif (Roman) family. So what happens if you need to write your entire document in, say, Helvetica? The default font family name is stored in:

`\familydefault`

This command is usually defined to be just `\rmdefault`, which in turn stores the name of the default serif font (initially cmr, Computer Modern Roman). If you want the default font to be sans-serif, all you need do is add the following line to the preamble:

`\renewcommand{\familydefault}{\sfdefault}`

`\sfdefault` stores the name of the default sans-serif font (initially cmss, Computer Modern Sans-Serif) and the helvet package redefines `\sfdefault` to phv, which is the identifier for the Helvetica font. So the following document will be in Helvetica:

```
\documentclass{scrartcl}

\usepackage{helvet}
\renewcommand{\familydefault}{\sfdefault}
```

```
\begin{document}
This is a sample document.
\end{document}
```

Similarly, if you want the default font to be monospaced (typewriter) then you'd need to do:

```
\renewcommand{\familydefault}{\ttdefault}
```
Input

Incidentally, you may have noticed in Section 4.5.3 that although I said I'd used the anttor and libris packages to set the serif and sans-serif families for this book, I didn't mention anything about the typewriter (monospaced) font. I used the TXTT font, but that doesn't have a corresponding package. You just redefine \ttdefault to txtt:

```
\renewcommand*{\ttdefault}{txtt}
```
Input

EXAMPLE (REDEFINING FIXED NAMES):
You may have noticed that LaTeX automatically generates pieces of text such as "Chapter", "Figure", "Bibliography". These are generated by the commands shown in Table 8.1.

Table 8.1. Predefined Names ([†]Book and report style classes (such as scrreprt and scrbook), [‡]article-style classes (such as scrartcl), remainder book, report and article-style classes)

Command	Default Text
\contentsname	Contents
\listfigurename	List of Figures
\listtablename	List of Tables
\bibname[†]	Bibliography
\refname[‡]	References
\indexname	Index
\figurename	Figure
\tablename	Table
\partname	Part
\chaptername[†]	Chapter
\appendixname	Appendix
\abstractname	Abstract

You can change the defaults using \renewcommand. For example, suppose you want the table of contents to be labelled "Table of Contents", instead of the default "Contents", you would need to do:

```
\renewcommand*{\contentsname}{Table of Contents}
```
Input

In fact, the babel package (see Section 5.8) uses this method to redefine the com-

[FAQ: Changing the words babel uses]

mands in Table 8.1 on the preceding page whenever you switch language using \selectlanguage or within the contents of the otherlanguage environment. This unfortunately has the side-effect that means if you try to redefine these commands, babel will automatically overwrite your definition whenever there's a language change, which includes at the beginning of the document environment. Instead you need to use babel's \addto mechanism.

Definition \addto{⟨*command*⟩}{⟨*code*⟩}

This patches the definition of a command (specified in the first argument) adding ⟨*code*⟩ to the end of the command definition. Whenever babel switches the current language, it uses the command \captions⟨*language*⟩, which performs all the redefinitions of commands like those listed in Table 8.1 on the previous page. For example, if you are using babel with the english option and you want to change \contentsname so that it does "Table of Contents" instead of "Contents", you need to do:

Input ↑

```
\addto{\captionsenglish}{%
  \renewcommand{\contentsname}{Table of Contents}%
}
```

Input ↓

NOTES:

Take care if you want to patch an existing command. For example, suppose you want to append something to the action of a command. You might be tempted to do

```
\renewcommand*{\foo}{\foo Something else}
```

This will cause an infinite loop where \foo recursively calls itself. Instead you should use one of the commands provided by the etoolbox package (such as \appto, which has the same syntax as babel's \addto described above). For further details, read the etoolbox documentation.

Exercise 21 (Renewing Commands)

If you did Exercises 16 and 17, go back to that document and changed the figures and tables so that they are labelled "Fig" and "Tab" instead of "Figure" and "Table". Hint: you need to redefine \tablename and \figurename.

You can download[8.5] the solution.

─────────────

[8.5]http://www.dickimaw-books.com/latex/novices/html/exercises/renewcom.tex

Chapter 9

Mathematics

As mentioned in the introduction, LaTeX is particularly good at typesetting mathematics. In order to use any of the maths commands we need to be in one of the mathematics environments. There are two basic types of mathematics: *in-line maths* and *displayed maths*. In-line maths is mathematics that occurs within a line of text, for example:

The variable x is transformed by the function $f(x)$. Output

Displayed maths is mathematics that occurs on a line of its own. For example:

↑ Output

A polynomial is a function of the form

$$f(x) = \sum_{i=0}^{n} a_i x^i$$

↓ Output

The maths environments switch to LaTeX's "math mode", which uses specialist maths fonts and spacing rather than just using an italic font.

If you want to typeset any mathematics, I strongly advise using the amsmath package:

```
\usepackage{amsmath}
```

This patches some existing LaTeX commands and environments and also provides many useful additions.

This chapter is just an introduction to typesetting mathematics in LaTeX. If you want a comprehensive guide, I recommend you read *Math Mode* by Herbert Voß [21], which can be access via `texdoc` (see Section 1.1):

```
texdoc mathmode
```

9.1. In-Line Mathematics

In-line mathematics is created using the math environment. (Note U.S. spelling — "math" not "maths").

EXAMPLE:

```
The variable \begin{math}x\end{math} is transformed by the function
\begin{math}f(x)\end{math}.
```

It's somewhat cumbersome having to type \begin{math} and \end{math} and it also makes the source code a little difficult to read so there are shorthand notations that can be used instead: \(is equivalent to \begin{math} and \) is equivalent to \end{math}. So the example above can be rewritten:

```
The variable \(x\) is transformed by the function \(f(x)\).
```

There is an even shorter notation: The special character $ is equivalent to both \begin{math} and \end{math}:

```
The variable $x$ is transformed by the function $f(x)$.
```

This is considerably easier to type and to read, but you need to make sure that all your $ symbols have matching pairs. The above code will look like:

The variable x is transformed by the function $f(x)$.

The other advantage in using $ over \(and \) is that $ is a robust command, whereas \(and \) are fragile commands and will need to be protected if they occur in a moving argument. (See Section 2.9.)

Note: you should always make sure you are in maths mode to typeset any variables (such as x, y, z), as this will ensure that the correct maths fonts are used, as well as the appropriate spacing. Similarly, don't use $ as a short cut for an italic font.

```
Notice the $difference$ between $(x', y', z')$ and \textit{(x', y', z')}.
```

Notice the $difference$ between (x', y', z') and (x', y', z').

9.2. Displayed Mathematics

One-line unnumbered displayed mathematics can be created using:

\[⟨*maths*⟩\]

where ⟨*maths*⟩ is the mathematics to be displayed.

EXAMPLE:

```
A linear function is a function of the form
\[ y = mx + c \]
```

Output:

A linear function is a function of the form

$$y = mx + c$$

↑ Output

↓ Output

Don't use the displaymath environment or $$...$$ [16]. Use \[and \] with the amsmath package.

The equation environment provides something similar to \[\], except that the equation is numbered. Modifying the above example:

↑ Input

```
A linear function is a function of the form
\begin{equation}
y = mx + c
\end{equation}
```

↓ Input

results in the following output:

↑ Output

A linear function is a function of the form

$$y = mx + c \qquad (9.1)$$

↓ Output

Normal text can be inserted into the equation using

\text{⟨text⟩}

Definition

which is provided by the amsmath package.

EXAMPLE:

\[x = 2 \text{ and } y = -1 \]

Input

results in the following output:

↑ Output

$$x = 2 \text{ and } y = -1$$

↓ Output

Recall from Section 5.5 that we can cross-reference most things that LaTeX automatically numbers using \ref and \label. Equations can be cross-referenced in the same way:

[FAQ:
Re-using an
equation]

Input ↑

```
Equation~\ref{eqn:linear} is a linear function.
\begin{equation}
\label{eqn:linear}
f(x) = mx + c
\end{equation}
```

Input ↓

Output ↑

Equation 9.2 is a linear function.

$$f(x) = mx + c \qquad (9.2)$$

Output ↓

Equation numbers are usually given in parentheses, which can be done using:

Input   `Equation~(\ref{eqn:linear})`

The amsmath package provides a convenient short cut:

Definition   `\eqref{⟨label⟩}`

So the above can be written as:

Input   `Equation~\eqref{eqn:linear}`

Output   Equation (9.2)

NOTE:
Both the equation environment and \[...\] are only designed for one line of maths.
Therefore you must not have any line breaks or paragraph breaks within them. The
following will cause an error:

✗
✗

```
\begin{equation}

f(x) = mx + c

\end{equation}
```

Either remove the blank lines or comment them out:

```
\begin{equation}
%
f(x) = mx + c
%
\end{equation}
```

9.3. **Multiple Lines of Displayed Maths**

The amsmath package provides the align and align* environments for aligned equations. The starred version doesn't number the equations. These environments provide pairs of left- and right-aligned columns. As with the tabular environment, use & to separate columns and \\ to separate rows. Unlike the tabular environment, there is no argument as the column specifiers are predefined. Another difference is that no page breaks can occur in the tabular environment, but it's possible to allow a page break in align or align* using

`\displaybreak[⟨n⟩]`   *Definition*

immediately before the \\ where it is to take effect. The optional argument is a number from 0 to 4 indicating the desirability to break the page (from 0 the least to 4 the most).

If you want to mix numbered and unnumbered rows, you can use

`\notag`   *Definition*

to suppress the numbering for a particular row in the align environment. This command must go before \\ at the end of the row. The default equation numbering can be overridden for a particular row using:

`\tag{⟨tag⟩}`   *Definition*

where ⟨*tag*⟩ is the replacement for the equation number.

Don't use the eqnarray or eqnarray* environments. They're obsolete [16].

EXAMPLE (UNNUMBERED):

```
\begin{align*}
y &= 2x + 2\\
  &= 2(x+1)
\end{align*}
```
↑ Input

↓ Input

↑ Output

$$y = 2x + 2$$
$$= 2(x + 1)$$

↓ Output

Note that the equals sign is placed at the start of the second column, *after* the ampersand &. This ensures the correct amount of spacing on either side. If the first line of the above equation was changed to:

`y =& 2x + 2\\`

there wouldn't be enough space on the right of the equal sign:

$$y = 2x + 2$$

EXAMPLE (ONE ROW NUMBERED):

Input ↑
```
\begin{align}
y &= 2x + 2\notag\\
   &= 2(x+1)
\end{align}
```
Input ↓

Output ↑

$$y = 2x + 2$$
$$= 2(x + 1) \tag{9.3}$$

Output ↓

EXAMPLE (FOUR COLUMNS):

Input ↑
```
\begin{align*}
y &= 2x + 2 & z &= 6x + 3\\
   &= 2(x+1) &    &= 3(2x+1)
\end{align*}
```
Input ↓

Output ↑

$$y = 2x + 2 \qquad\qquad z = 6x + 3$$
$$= 2(x + 1) \qquad\qquad = 3(2x + 1)$$

Output ↓

As with equation, you can cross-reference individual rows of an align environment, but you must remember to put \label *before* the end of row \\ separator. You can reference a row in the align* environment if you have assigned it a tag with \tag, but don't try labelling a row in the align environment where the numbering has been suppressed with \notag.

EXAMPLE (CROSS-REFERENCED):
This example has two numbered equations in an align environment, both of which
are labelled and referenced:

```
The function $f(x)$ is given in Equation~\eqref{eq:fx}, and its
derivative $f'(x)$ is given in Equation~\eqref{eq:dfx}.
\begin{align}
f(x) &= 2x + 1 \label{eq:fx}\\
f'(x) &= 2 \label{eq:dfx}
\end{align}
```
↑ Input
↓ Input

↑ Output

The function $f(x)$ is given in Equation (9.4), and its derivative $f'(x)$ is given in
Equation (9.5).

$$f(x) = 2x + 1 \qquad (9.4)$$
$$f'(x) = 2 \qquad (9.5)$$

↓ Output

Recall the command \text{⟨*text*⟩} from the previous section. This can be used
within cells of the align and align* environments, but the amsmath package also provides

```
\intertext{⟨text⟩}
```
Definition

which can be used for a line of interjection between the rows. This command may
only go right after \\.

EXAMPLE

```
\begin{align*}
y &= 2x + 2\\
\intertext{Using the distributive law:}
&= 2(x+1)
\end{align*}
```
↑ Input
↓ Input

↑ Output

$$y = 2x + 2$$

Using the distributive law:

$$= 2(x + 1)$$

↓ Output

There are other environments for multiple-line displayed maths, but they are beyond the scope of this book. See the amsmath documentation for further details.

9.4. Mathematical Commands

Most of the commands described in this section may only be used in one of the mathematics environments. If you try to use a mathematics command outside a maths environment you will get a "Missing $ inserted" error message.

9.4.1. Maths Fonts

Just as we are able to change text fonts using the commands \textrm, \textbf etc, we can also use commands to change the maths font. Basic maths font changing commands are shown in Table 9.1.

Table 9.1. Maths Font Changing Commands

Command	Example Input	Corresponding Output (Computer Modern)
\mathrm{⟨*maths*⟩}	xyz	xyz
\mathsf{⟨*maths*⟩}	xyz	xyz
\mathtt{⟨*maths*⟩}	$\mathtt{xyz}$	xyz
\mathit{⟨*maths*⟩}	xyz	*xyz*
\mathbf{⟨*maths*⟩}	$\mathbf{xyz}$	**xyz**
\mathcal{⟨*maths*⟩}	$\mathcal{XYZ}$	𝒳𝒴𝒵

[FAQ: Better script fonts for maths]

The calligraphic fonts via \mathcal are only available for upper-case characters. Table 9.2 lists additional font commands supplied with the amsmath and amsfonts packages.

Table 9.2. The amsfonts[‡] and amsmath[†] Font Commands

Command	Example Input	Example Output
[‡]\mathbb{⟨*maths*⟩}	$\mathbb{A+B=C}$	$\mathbb{A} + \mathbb{B} = \mathbb{C}$
[‡]\mathfrak{⟨*maths*⟩}	$\mathfrak{A+B=C}$	$\mathfrak{A} + \mathfrak{B} = \mathfrak{C}$
[†]\boldsymbol{⟨*maths*⟩}	$\boldsymbol{A+B=C}$	$\boldsymbol{A + B = C}$
[†]\pmb{⟨*symbol*⟩}	$\pmb{+-=}$	**+ − =**

9.4.2. Greek Letters

Greek letters that differ from the corresponding Roman letters are obtained by placing a backslash in front of the name.[9.1] Lower case and upper case Greek letters are shown in Table 9.3 and Table 9.4, respectively. There are also some variants of certain symbols, such as \vartheta as opposed to \theta.

Table 9.3. Lower Case Greek Letters

\alpha	α	\beta	β	\gamma	γ
\delta	δ	\epsilon	ϵ	\varepsilon	ε
\zeta	ζ	\eta	η	\theta	θ
\vartheta	ϑ	\iota	ι	\kappa	κ
\lambda	λ	\mu	μ	\nu	ν
\xi	ξ	\pi	π	\varpi	ϖ
\rho	ρ	\varrho	ϱ	\sigma	σ
\varsigma	ς	\tau	τ	\upsilon	υ
\phi	ϕ	\varphi	φ	\chi	χ
\psi	ψ	\omega	ω		

Table 9.4. Upper Case Greek Letters

\Gamma	Γ	\Delta	Δ	\Theta	Θ
\Lambda	Λ	\Xi	Ξ	\Pi	Π
\Sigma	Σ	\Upsilon	Υ	\Phi	Φ
\Psi	Ψ	\Omega	Ω		

EXAMPLE:
The following code

\[x' = x + \Delta x \]

produces:

$$x' = x + \Delta x$$

9.4.3. Subscripts and Superscripts

Subscripts are obtained either by the command

\sb{⟨*maths*⟩}

or by the special character:

_{⟨*maths*⟩}

[9.1]So, for example, there is no omicron since it looks the same as a Roman o.

Superscripts are obtained either by the command

Definition   \sp{⟨*maths*⟩}

or by the special character:

Definition   ^{⟨*maths*⟩}

EXAMPLES:
1. This example uses \sb and \sp:

Input   \[y = x\sb{1}\sp{2} + x\sb{2}\sp{2}\]

2. This example uses _ and ^

Input   \[y = x_{1}^{2} + x_{2}^{2}\]

3. Recall from page 16 that mandatory arguments only consisting of one character don't need to be grouped, so the above code can also be written as:

Input   \[y = x_1^2 + x_2^2\]

This is simpler than the first two examples. However it's a good idea to be in the habit of always using braces in case you forgot them when they're needed.

All three of the above examples produce the same output:

Output $$y = x_1^2 + x_2^2$$

Notice how the subscript gets tucked under the slope of the Y in:

Input   \[Y_{1}^{2} \]

Output $$Y_1^2$$

Compare with

Input   \[Y{}_{1}^{2} \]

Output $$Y_1^2$$

EXAMPLE (NESTED)
Subscripts and superscripts can also be nested (note that it is now necessary to group the argument to the superscript command):

Input   \[f(x) = e^{x_1} \]

which produces

Output $$f(x) = e^{x_1}$$

This example isn't quite right as e isn't actually a variable and shouldn't be typeset in italic. The correct way to do this is:

\[f(x) = \mathrm{e}^{x_1} \]   Input

which results in:

$$f(x) = \mathrm{e}^{x_1}$$ Output

If you are going to use e a lot, it will be simpler to define a new command to do this. The definition should go in the preamble:

\newcommand{\e}{\mathrm{e}}   Input

Then in the document:

\[f(x_1, x_2) = \e^{x_1^2} + \e^{x_2^2} \]   Input

$$f(x_1, x_2) = \mathrm{e}^{x_1^2} + \mathrm{e}^{x_2^2}$$ Output

Take care when nesting subscripts or superscripts. The following

x_1_2   ✖

will give a ! Double subscript error.

9.4.4. Functional Names

Functions such as log and tan can't simply be typed in as log or tan otherwise they will come out looking like the variables l times o times g (*log*) or t times a times n (*tan*). Instead you should use one of the commands listed in Table 9.5. The functions denoted with [†] can have limits by using the subscript command _ or the superscript command ^. In addition, the modulo commands listed in Table 9.6 on the next page are also available.

[FAQ: Sub- and superscript positioning for operators]

Table 9.5. Function Names ([†]indicates command may have limits, [‡]defined by amsmath).

\arccos	arccos	\arcsin	arcsin	\arctan	arctan
\arg	arg	\cos	cos	\cosh	cosh
\cot	cot	\coth	coth	\csc	csc
\deg	deg	\det[†]	det	\dim	dim
\exp	exp	\gcd[†]	gcd	\hom	hom
\inf[†]	inf	\injlim[†‡]	inj lim	\ker	ker
\lg	lg	\lim[†]	lim	\liminf[†]	lim inf
\limsup[†]	lim sup	\ln	ln	\log	log
\max[†]	max	\min[†]	min	\Pr[†]	Pr
\projlim[†‡]	proj lim	\sec	sec	\sin	sin
\sinh	sinh	\sup[†]	sup	\tan	tan
\tanh	tanh	\varinjlim[†‡]	$\varinjlim$	\varliminf[†‡]	$\varliminf$
\varlimsup[†‡]	$\varlimsup$	\varprojlim[†‡]	$\varprojlim$		

Table 9.6. Modulo Commands (‡defined by amsmath package)

Command	Example Input	Example Output
\bmod	$m \bmod n$	$m \bmod n$
\pmod{⟨*maths*⟩}	$m \pmod{n}$	$m \pmod n$
\mod{⟨*maths*⟩}‡	$m \mod{n}$	$m \bmod n$
\pod{⟨*maths*⟩}‡	$m \pod{n}$	$m \ (n)$

EXAMPLE (TRIGONOMETRIC FUNCTIONS):
This example uses the cos and sin functions and also the Greek letter theta.

Input   `\[ z = r(\cos\theta + i\sin\theta) \]`

Output
$$z = r(\cos\theta + i\sin\theta)$$

EXAMPLE (LIMIT):
The command \infty is the infinity symbol ∞, and the command \to displays an arrow pointing to the right. Note the use of _ since the limit is a subscript.

Input   `\[ \lim_{x\to\infty} f(x) \]`

Output
$$\lim_{x\to\infty} f(x)$$

The operators with limits behave differently depending on whether they are in displayed or in-line maths. Notice the difference when the same code appears in-line:

Input   `In a line of text $\lim_{x\to\infty} f(x)$`

which now displays as:

Output   In a line of text $\lim_{x\to\infty} f(x)$

EXAMPLE (WITH SUBSCRIPT):
This is another example of a functional name using a subscript:

Input   `\[ \min_x f(x) \]`

Output
$$\min_x f(x)$$

Again, notice the difference when it is used in-line:

Input   `In a line of text $\min_x f(x)$`

Output   In a line of text $\min_x f(x)$

Defining New Functional Operators

It may be that you want a function that isn't specified in Table 9.5 on page 161. In this case, the amsmath provides the **preamble only** command

`\DeclareMathOperator{⟨cmd⟩}{⟨operator name⟩}`   Definition

or its starred variant

`\DeclareMathOperator*{⟨cmd⟩}{⟨operator name⟩}`   Definition

Both versions define a command called ⟨cmd⟩, which must start with a backslash, that typesets ⟨operator name⟩ as a function name. The starred version is for function names that can take limits (like \lim and \min described above).

[FAQ: Defining a new log-like function in LaTeX]

EXAMPLE (OPERATOR WITHOUT LIMITS):
Suppose I want a function called card, which represents the cardinality of a set S. First I need to define the new operator command (which I'm going to call \card) *in the preamble*:

`\DeclareMathOperator{\card}{card}`   Input

This operator doesn't take any limits, so I have used the unstarred version.
    Later in the document, I can use this new operator command:

`\[ n = \card(\mathcal{S}) \]`   Input

$$n = \mathrm{card}(S)$$ Output

In this example \mathcal is used as sets are typically represented in a calligraphic font.

EXAMPLE (OPERATOR WITH LIMITS):
Suppose I now want a function called mode, which represents the mode of a set of numbers. First, I define the operator command in the preamble:

`\DeclareMathOperator*{\mode}{mode}`   Input

This operator needs to be able to have a subscript, so I have used the starred version.
    Later in the document, I can use this new operator command:

`\[ x_m = \mode_{x \in \mathcal{S}}(x) \]`   Input

$$x_m = \operatorname*{mode}_{x \in S}(x)$$ Output

9.4.5. Fractions

Fractions are created using the command

Definition   \frac{⟨*numerator*⟩}{⟨*denominator*⟩}

The amsmath package also provides the command

Definition   \cfrac[⟨*pos*⟩]{⟨*numerator*⟩}{⟨*denominator*⟩}

which is designed for continued fractions. The optional argument pos can be used for left (l) or right (r) placement of any of the numerators. (The default is centred.)

EXAMPLE:
A simple fraction:

Input   \[\frac{1}{1+x} \]

Produces:

Output
$$\frac{1}{1+x}$$

Compare with:

Input   In-line: $ \frac{1}{1+x} $

which produces:

Output   In-line: $\frac{1}{1+x}$

EXAMPLE (NESTED):

Input   \[\frac{1+\frac{1}{x}}{1+x+x^2} \]

Output
$$\frac{1+\frac{1}{x}}{1+x+x^2}$$

EXAMPLE (CONTINUED FRACTION);
A continued fraction (example taken from amsmath documentation and uses \sqrt, described in Section 9.4.6, and \dotsb, described in Section 9.4.7):

Input ↑
```
\[
\cfrac{1}{\sqrt{2}+
\cfrac{1}{\sqrt{2}+
\cfrac{1}{\sqrt{2}+\dotsb
}}}
\]
```
Input ↓

$$\cfrac{1}{\sqrt{2} + \cfrac{1}{\sqrt{2} + \cfrac{1}{\sqrt{2} + \cdots}}}$$

↑ Output
↓ Output

EXAMPLE (A DERIVATIVE):

```
\[ f'(x) = \frac{df}{dx} \]
```
Input

$$f'(x) = \frac{df}{dx}$$
Output

As with "e", the differential operator "d" should be in an upright font as it is not a variable:

```
\[
  f'(x) = \frac{\mathrm{d}f}{\mathrm{d}x}
\]
```
↑ Input
↓ Input

$$f'(x) = \frac{\mathrm{d}f}{\mathrm{d}x}$$
Output

The above example is rather cumbersome, particularly if you have a lot of derivatives, so it might be easier to define a new command (see Chapter 8 (Defining Commands)). In the preamble define:

```
\newcommand{\deriv}[2]{\frac{\mathrm{d}#1}{\mathrm{d}#2}}
```
Input

Then in the document:

```
\[ f'(x) = \deriv{f}{x} \]
```
Input

$$f'(x) = \frac{\mathrm{d}f}{\mathrm{d}x}$$
Output

EXAMPLE (PARTIAL DERIVATIVE):

Partial derivatives can be obtained similarly using the command \partial to display the partial derivative symbol. As in the previous example, first define a new command to format a partial derivative in the preamble:

```
\newcommand{\pderiv}[2]{\frac{\partial #1}{\partial #2}}
```
Input

Then in the document:

```
\[ f_x = \pderiv{f}{x} \]
```
Input

$$f_x = \frac{\partial f}{\partial x}$$
Output

EXAMPLE (DOUBLE PARTIAL DERIVATIVE):

Input ⊤

```
\[
  f_{xy} = \frac{\partial^2 f}{\partial x \partial y}
\]
```

Input ↓

Output

$$f_{xy} = \frac{\partial^2 f}{\partial x \, \partial y}$$

EXAMPLE (FIRST PRINCIPLES):

Input ⊤

```
\[
    f'(x) = \lim_{\Delta x \to 0}
    \frac{f(x + \Delta x)-f(x)}{\Delta x}
\]
```

Input ↓

Output

$$f'(x) = \lim_{\Delta x \to 0} \frac{f(x + \Delta x) - f(x)}{\Delta x}$$

9.4.6. Roots

Roots are obtained using the command

Definition   \sqrt[⟨*order*⟩]{⟨*maths*⟩}

without the optional argument ⟨*order*⟩ it will produce a simple square root. Cubic roots etc can be obtained using the optional argument.

EXAMPLES:

1. A square root:

Input   \[\sqrt{a+b} \]

Output $\sqrt{a + b}$

2. A cubic root:

Input   \[\sqrt[3]{a+b} \]

Output $\sqrt[3]{a + b}$

3. An nth root:

Input   \[\sqrt[n]{a+b} \]

Output $\sqrt[n]{a + b}$

9.4.7. Mathematical Symbols

Relational symbols are shown in Table 9.7. If you want a negation that is not shown, you can obtain it by preceding the symbol with the command \not. For example: \not\subset produces the symbol $\not\subset$.

[FAQ: Where can I find the symbol for …]

Table 9.7. Relational Symbols

\approx	$\approx$	\asymp	$\asymp$	\bowtie	$\bowtie$
\cong	$\cong$	\dashv	$\dashv$	\doteq	$\doteq$
\equiv	$\equiv$	\frown	$\frown$	\ge or \geq	$\geq$
\gg	$\gg$	\in	$\in$	\le or \leq	$\leq$
\ll	$\ll$	\mid or |	$\mid$	\models	$\models$
\neq	$\neq$	\ni	$\ni$	\notin	$\notin$
\parallel	$\parallel$	\prec	$\prec$	\preceq	$\preceq$
\perp	$\perp$	\propto	$\propto$	\sim	$\sim$
\simeq	$\simeq$	\smile	$\smile$	\sqsubseteq	$\sqsubseteq$
\sqsupseteq	$\sqsupseteq$	\subset	$\subset$	\subseteq	$\subseteq$
\succ	$\succ$	\succeq	$\succeq$	\supset	$\supset$
\supseteq	$\supseteq$	\vdash	$\vdash$		

Binary operator symbols are shown in Table 9.8 on the following page, and arrow symbols are shown in Table 9.9. There are also over and under arrows (Table 9.10) that have an argument. The over arrows put an extendible arrow over their argument, and the under arrows put an extendible arrow under their argument. In addition, the amsmath package provides extensible arrows that take a superscript and, optionally, a subscript:

\xleftarrow[⟨*subscript*⟩]{⟨*superscript*⟩}

Definition

\xrightarrow[⟨*subscript*⟩]{⟨*superscript*⟩}

Definition

EXAMPLE:

```
\[
    A \xleftarrow{n+m-p} B \xrightarrow[X]{n+p} C
\]
```

↑ Input

↓ Input

$$A \xleftarrow{n+m-p} B \xrightarrow[X]{n+p} C$$

↑ Output

↓ Output

Table 9.8. Binary Operator Symbols

\amalg	⨿	\ast	∗	\bullet	•
\bigcirc	◯	\bigtriangledown	▽	\bigtriangleup	△
\cap	∩	\cdot	·	\circ	∘
\cup	∪	\dagger	†	\ddagger	‡
\diamond	⋄	\div	÷	\mp	∓
\odot	⊙	\ominus	⊖	\oplus	⊕
\oslash	⊘	\otimes	⊗	\pm	±
\setminus	\	\sqcap	⊓	\sqcup	⊔
\star	⋆	\times	×	\triangleleft	◁
\triangleright	▷	\uplus	⊎	\vee	∨
\wedge	∧	\wr	≀		

Table 9.9. Arrow Symbols

\downarrow	↓	\Downarrow	⇓
\hookleftarrow	↩	\hookrightarrow	↪
\leftarrow or \gets	←	\Leftarrow	⇐
\leftharpoondown	↽	\leftharpoonup	↼
\leftrightarrow	↔	\Leftrightarrow	⇔
\longleftarrow	⟵	\Longleftarrow	⟸
\longleftrightarrow	⟷	\Longleftrightarrow	⟺
\longmapsto	⟼	\longrightarrow	⟶
\Longrightarrow	⟹	\mapsto	↦
\nearrow	↗	\nwarrow	↖
\rightarrow or \to	→	\Rightarrow	⇒
\rightharpoondown	⇁	\rightharpoonup	⇀
\rightleftharpoons	⇌	\searrow	↘
\swarrow	↙	\uparrow	↑
\Uparrow	⇑	\updownarrow	↕
\Updownarrow	⇕		

Table 9.10. Over and Under Arrows ([†]defined by amsmath)

Definition	Example	
\overleftarrow{⟨*maths*⟩}	\overleftarrow{ABC}	$\overleftarrow{ABC}$
\overrightarrow{⟨*maths*⟩}	\overrightarrow{ABC}	$\overrightarrow{ABC}$
\overleftrightarrow{⟨*maths*⟩}[†]	\overleftrightarrow{ABC}	$\overleftrightarrow{ABC}$
\underleftarrow{⟨*maths*⟩}[†]	\underleftarrow{ABC}	$\underleftarrow{ABC}$
\underrightarrow{⟨*maths*⟩}[†]	\underrightarrow{ABC}	$\underrightarrow{ABC}$
\underleftrightarrow{⟨*maths*⟩}[†]	\underleftrightarrow{ABC}	$\underleftrightarrow{ABC}$

Table 9.11. Symbols with Limits

\sum	$\sum$	\int	$\int$	\oint	$\oint$
\prod	$\prod$	\coprod	$\coprod$	\bigcap	$\bigcap$
\bigcup	$\bigcup$	\bigsqcup	$\bigsqcup$	\bigvee	$\bigvee$
\bigwedge	$\bigwedge$	\bigodot	$\bigodot$	\bigotimes	$\bigotimes$
\bigoplus	$\bigoplus$	\biguplus	$\biguplus$		

Symbols that can have limits are shown in Table 9.11. The size of these symbols depends on whether they are in displayed maths or in-line maths.

EXAMPLE (DISPLAYED SUMMATION AND PRODUCT):
The limits of summations and products are placed above and below the symbol in displayed maths:

↑ Input

```
\[
  f(x) = \sum_{i=1}^{n} x_i + \prod_{i=1}^{n} x_i
\]
```

↓ Input

$$f(x) = \sum_{i=1}^{n} x_i + \prod_{i=1}^{n} x_i$$

Output

EXAMPLE (IN-LINE SUMMATION AND PRODUCT):
The limits of summations and products are placed to the right of the symbol in in-line maths:

↑ Input

```
In a line of text:
\begin{math}
  f(x) = \sum_{i=1}^{n} x_i + \prod_{i=1}^{n} x_i
\end{math}
```

↓ Input

In a line of text: $f(x) = \sum_{i=1}^{n} x_i + \prod_{i=1}^{n} x_i$

Output

MULTILINE SUB- OR SUPERSCRIPTS
The amsmath package provides the command:

\substack{⟨*maths*⟩}

Definition

which can be used for multiline sub- or superscripts. Within the argument ⟨*maths*⟩ use \\ to separate rows. For example:

Input ↑
```
\[
\sum_{
 \substack
 {
   i \in \mathcal{I}\\
   i \neq 0
 }
 }
 x_i
\]
```
Input ↓

Output ↑

$$\sum_{\substack{i \in \mathcal{I} \\ i \neq 0}} x_i$$

Output ↓

9.4.8. Ellipses

Ellipsis (omission mark) commands are shown in Table 9.12. The amsmath package also provides: \dotsc for dots with commas, \dotsb for dots with binary operators/relations, \dotsm for multiplication dots, \dotsi for dots with integrals and \dotso for other dots, which can be used as replacements for \ldots and \cdots.

Table 9.12. Ellipses ([†] provided by amsmath package)

\vdots	⋮	\cdots	⋯	\dotsb[†]	⋯	\dotsi[†]	⋯	\dotsm[†]	⋯
\ddots	⋱	\ldots	...	\dotsc[†]	...	\dotso[†]	...		

EXAMPLE (LOW ELLIPSIS):
This example uses the command \forall to produce the "for all" symbol ∀, and it also uses \␣ (backslash space) to make a space before the for all symbol. The amsmath "dots with commas" ellipsis \dotsc is used rather than the standard \ldots:

Input ↑
```
\[
a_ix_i = b_i\ \forall i = 1,\dotsc, n
\]
```
Input ↓

Output $$a_i x_i = b_i \ \forall i = 1, \ldots, n$$

EXAMPLE (CENTRED ELLIPSIS):
This example uses the amsmath "dots with binary operators/relations" \dotsb instead of the standard \cdots:

```
\[
y = a_1 + a_2 + \dotsb + a_n
\]
```

↑ Input

↓ Input

$$y = a_1 + a_2 + \cdots + a_n$$

Output

Exercise 22 (Maths: Fractions and Symbols)

This exercise uses a fraction, a square root, subscripts, superscripts and symbols. Try to reproduce the following output:

↑ Output

The quadratic equation

$$\sum_{i=0}^{2} a_i x^i = 0$$

has solutions given by

$$x = \frac{-a_1 \pm \sqrt{a_1^2 - 4a_2 a_0}}{2a_2}$$

↓ Output

Again you can download[9.2] the solution.

9.4.9. Delimiters

Placing brackets around a tall object in maths mode, such as fractions, does not look right if you use normal sized brackets. For example:

```
\[
   (\frac{1}{1+x})
\]
```

↑ Input

↓ Input

results in:

$$(\frac{1}{1+x})$$

Output

[9.2]http://www.dickimaw-books.com/latex/novices/html/exercises/mathssym.tex

Instead, you can automatically resize the delimiters using the commands:

Definition \left⟨*delimiter*⟩

and

Definition \right⟨*delimiter*⟩

Rewriting the above example:

Input ↑
```
\[
  \left( \frac{1}{1+x} \right)
\]
```
Input ↓

produces:

Output
$$\left(\frac{1}{1+x} \right)$$

Note that you must always have matching \left and \right commands, although the delimiters used may be different. If you want one of the delimiters to be invisible, use a . (full stop) as the delimiter. Available delimiters are shown in Table 9.13. (Note for a vertical bar delimiter it's best to use amsmath's \lvert command instead of | and \lVert instead of \|.) Sometimes using \left and \right doesn't produce the optimal sized delimiters. In which case you can use additional commands provided by the amsmath package shown in Table 9.14 on the facing page.

Table 9.13. Delimiters ([†]defined by amsmath)

(	(	)	)	[	[	]	]
\{	{	\}	}	\lvert[†]	|	\rvert[†]	|
\lVert[†]	‖	\rVert[†]	‖	\langle	⟨	\rangle	⟩
\lfloor	⌊	\rfloor	⌋	\lceil	⌈	\rceil	⌉
\uparrow	↑	\downarrow	↓	\Uparrow	⇑	\Downarrow	⇓
\updownarrow	↕	\Updownarrow	⇕	/	/	\backslash	\

EXAMPLE (VERTICAL BAR DELIMITERS):

Input ↑
```
\[
\left\lvert
\frac{1}{1+x}
\right\rvert
\]
```
Input ↓

Output
$$\left\lvert \frac{1}{1+x} \right\rvert$$

Table 9.14. Additional Commands Provided by amsmath for Delimiter Sizing

Definitions		Example	
Default Size		`$( X )$`	(X)
`\bigl`⟨*delim*⟩	`\bigr`⟨*delim*⟩	`$\bigl( X \bigr)$`	$\bigl(X \bigr)$
`\Bigl`⟨*delim*⟩	`\Bigr`⟨*delim*⟩	`$\Bigl( X \Bigr)$`	$\Bigl(X \Bigr)$
`\biggl`⟨*delim*⟩	`\biggr`⟨*delim*⟩	`$\bigl( X \biggr)$`	$\biggl(X \biggr)$
`\Biggl`⟨*delim*⟩	`\Biggr`⟨*delim*⟩	`$\Biggl( X \Biggr)$`	$\Biggl(X \Biggr)$

EXAMPLE (DELIMITER WITH SUBSCRIPT):
Delimiters can take limits:

```
\[
\left\lvert
\frac{1}{1+x}
\right\rvert_{x=0}
\]
```
↑ Input

↓ Input

$$\left\lvert \frac{1}{1+x} \right\rvert_{x=0}$$
Output

EXAMPLE (MISMATCH):
The left and right delimiters don't have to match:

```
\[
\left[\frac{1}{1+x}\right\rangle
\]
```
↑ Input

↓ Input

$$\left[\frac{1}{1+x}\right\rangle$$
Output

EXAMPLE (AN INVISIBLE DELIMITER):
Every `\right` must have a matching `\left` (and vice versa), so use a . (full stop) for an invisible delimiter.

Input ⊤

```
\[
 \left.
  \frac{\partial f}{\partial x}
 \right\rvert_{x=0}
\]
```

Input ↓

Output

$$\left. \frac{\partial f}{\partial x} \right|_{x=0}$$

We have now covered enough to reproduce the equation shown in Chapter 1 (Introduction):

Input ⊤

```
\newcommand*{\pderiv}[2]{\frac{\partial #1}{\partial #2}}
\newcommand*{\e}{\mathrm{e}}

\[
\pderiv{^2\mathcal{L}}{{z_i^\rho}^2} =
-\pderiv{\rho_i}{z_i^\rho}
\left(
  \pderiv{v_i}{\rho_i} \frac{\e^{v_i}}{1-\e^{v_i}}
  + v_i \frac{\e^{v_i}\pderiv{v_i}{\rho_i}(1-\e^{v_i})
          +\e^{2v_i}\pderiv{v_i}{\rho_i}}{(1-\e^{v_i})^2}
\right)
\]
```

Input ↓

Output ⊤

$$\frac{\partial^2 \mathcal{L}}{\partial z_i^{\rho^2}} = -\frac{\partial \rho_i}{\partial z_i^{\rho}} \left(\frac{\partial v_i}{\partial \rho_i} \frac{\mathrm{e}^{v_i}}{1 - \mathrm{e}^{v_i}} + v_i \frac{\mathrm{e}^{v_i} \frac{\partial v_i}{\partial \rho_i}(1 - \mathrm{e}^{v_i}) + \mathrm{e}^{2v_i} \frac{\partial v_i}{\partial \rho_i}}{(1 - \mathrm{e}^{v_i})^2} \right)$$

Output ↓

NOTE:

The above code looks a bit complicated, and there are so many braces that it can be easy to lose track, so here are some ways of making it a little easier to type:

1. Whenever you start a new environment type in the \begin and \end bits first, and then insert whatever goes inside the environment. This ensures that you always have a matching \begin and \end. The same goes for \[and \].

2. Whenever you type any braces, always type the opening and closing braces first, and then insert whatever goes in between. This will ensure that your braces always match up.

So keeping these notes in mind, let's try typing in the code in a methodical manner:

1. Start and end the displayed maths mode:

```
\[
\]
```
↑ Input
↓ Input

2. We now need a partial derivative. (The command `\pderiv` is defined as described earlier on page 165. Make sure you remember to define it, preferably in the preamble.)

```
\[
\pderiv{}{}
\]
```
↑ Input
↓ Input

3. Let's do the first argument. This partial derivative is actually a double derivative, which means we need a squared bit on the top along with a calligraphic L:

```
\[
\pderiv{^2 \mathcal{L}}{}
\]
```
↑ Input
↓ Input

4. The second argument is the z_i^{ρ} squared bit. This is a nested superscript `{z_i^\rho}^2`:

```
\[
\pderiv{^2 \mathcal{L}}{{z_i^\rho}^2}
\]
```
↑ Input
↓ Input

5. We can do the next partial derivative in the same way. This one is slightly easier to do:

Input ⊤

```
\[
\pderiv{^2 \mathcalL}{{z_i^\rho}^2} =
-\pderiv{\rho_i}{z_i^\rho}
\]
```

Input ↓

6. Delimiters also need to occur in pairs, like curly braces and \begin and \end, so let's do them next:

Input ⊤

```
\[
\pderiv{^2 \mathcal{L}}{{z_i^\rho}^2} =
-\pderiv{\rho_i}{z_i^\rho}
  \left(
  \right)
\]
```

Input ↓

7. Now we need to do the bits inside the brackets. First of all we have yet another partial derivative:

Input ⊤

```
\[
\pderiv{^2 \mathcal{L}}{{z_i^\rho}^2} =
-\pderiv{\rho_i}{z_i^\rho}
  \left(
    \pderiv{v_i}{\rho_i}
  \right)
\]
```

Input ↓

8. Now we have a fraction following the partial derivative from the previous step. (Make sure you use braces for the exponential bit: \e^{v_i} (e^{v_i}) is not the same as \e^v_i (e^v_i). The command \e is defined as described earlier in Section 9.4.3. Make sure you define it, preferably in the preamble.)

Input ⊤

```
\[
\pderiv{^2 \mathcal{L}}{{z_i^\rho}^2} =
-\pderiv{\rho_i}{z_i^\rho}
  \left(
    \pderiv{v_i}{\rho_i} \frac{\e^{v_i}}{1-\e^{v_i}}
  \right)
\]
```

Input ↓

9. This is followed by v_i times another fraction:

```
\[
\pderiv{^2 \mathcal{L}}{{z_i^\rho}^2} =
-\pderiv{\rho_i}{z_i^\rho}
  \left(
    \pderiv{v_i}{\rho_i} \frac{\e^{v_i}}{1-\e^{v_i}}
    + v_i \frac{}{}
  \right)
\]
```

10. The bottom part of the fraction (the denominator) is easier than the top, so let's do that first:

```
\[
\pderiv{^2 \mathcal{L}}{{z_i^\rho}^2} =
-\pderiv{\rho_i}{z_i^\rho}
  \left(
    \pderiv{v_i}{\rho_i} \frac{\e^{v_i}}{1-\e^{v_i}}
    + v_i \frac{}{(1-\e^{v_i})^2}
  \right)
\]
```

11. Now for the top part of the fraction (the numerator). To refresh your memory, it should look like:

$$e^{v_i} \frac{\partial v_i}{\partial \rho_i}(1 - e^{v_i}) + e^{2v_i} \frac{\partial v_i}{\partial \rho_i}$$

That's a bit complicated, so let's break it down:

a) The first term is:

`\e^{v_i}`

b) The next term is another partial derivative:

`\pderiv{v_i}{\rho_i}`

c) Then we have:

`(1-\e^{v_i})`

d) Next we have to add on:

`+\e^{2v_i}`

e) And finally we have:

```
\pderiv{v_i}{\rho_i}
```

So the numerator is:

Input ⤒

```
\e^{v_i}\pderiv{v_i}{\rho_i}(1-\e^{v_i})
  + \e^{2v_i}\pderiv{v_i}{\rho_i}
```

Input ↓

Inserting this into our code:

Input ⤒

```
\[
\pderiv{^2\mathcal{L}}{{z_i^\rho}^2} =
-\pderiv{\rho_i}{z_i^\rho}
\left(
  \pderiv{v_i}{\rho_i} \frac{\e^{v_i}}{1-\e^{v_i}}
  + v_i \frac{\e^{v_i}\pderiv{v_i}{\rho_i}(1-\e^{v_i})
            +\e^{2v_i}\pderiv{v_i}{\rho_i}}{(1-\e^{v_i})^2}
\right)
\]
```

Input ↓

9.4.10. Arrays

Mathematical structures such as matrices and vectors require elements to be arranged in rows and columns. Just as we can align material in rows and columns in text mode using the tabular environment (Section 4.6), we can do the same in maths mode using the array environment. The array environment has the same format as the tabular environment, however it must be in maths mode. The column half-gaps are given by the length register \arraycolsep (analogous to \tabcolsep).

EXAMPLE:

Input ⤒

```
\[
\begin{array}{rrr}
0 & 1 & 19\\
-6 & 10 & 200
\end{array}
\]
```

Input ↓

$$
\begin{array}{rrr}
0 & 1 & 19\\
-6 & 10 & 200
\end{array}
$$

↑ Output

↓ Output

EXAMPLE (ADDING DELIMITERS):

↑ Input

```
\[
\left(
 \begin{array}{rrr}
   0 & 1 & 19\\
   -6 & 10 & 200
 \end{array}
\right)
\]
```

↓ Input

$$
\left(
\begin{array}{rrr}
0 & 1 & 19\\
-6 & 10 & 200
\end{array}
\right)
$$

Output

ADDING A VERTICAL RULE:

A vertical rule can be added using | in the column specifier. For example:

↑ Input

```
\[
\left(
 \begin{array}{rr|r}
   0 & 1 & 19\\
   -6 & 10 & 200
 \end{array}
\right)
\]
```

↓ Input

$$
\left(
\begin{array}{rr|r}
0 & 1 & 19\\
-6 & 10 & 200
\end{array}
\right)
$$

Output

EXAMPLE (CASES):

This example uses an invisible delimiter:

↑ Input

Input ↓

```
\[
f(x) =
\left\{
  \begin{array}{rl}
  -1 & x < 0\\
   0 & x = 0\\
  +1 & x > 0
  \end{array}
\right.
\]
```

Output

$$f(x) = \left\{ \begin{array}{rl} -1 & x < 0 \\ 0 & x = 0 \\ +1 & x > 0 \end{array} \right.$$

This can be rewritten more compactly using the amsmath cases environment:

Input ↑

```
\[
f(x) =
\begin{cases}
 -1 & x < 0\\
  0 & x = 0\\
 +1 & x > 0
\end{cases}
\]
```

Input ↓

Output

$$f(x) = \begin{cases} -1 & x < 0 \\ 0 & x = 0 \\ +1 & x > 0 \end{cases}$$

The amsmath package provides some convenient environments to typeset matrices: pmatrix, bmatrix, Bmatrix, vmatrix and Vmatrix. These are similar to the array environment except there is no argument, and they add (respectively) ( ), [ ], { }, | | and ‖ ‖ delimiters. There is also the matrix environment that doesn't have any delimiters.

EXAMPLE:

Input ↑

```
\begin{equation}
 \begin{pmatrix}
  a & b\\
  c & d
 \end{pmatrix}
\end{equation}
```

Input ↓

$$\begin{pmatrix} a & b \\ c & d \end{pmatrix} \tag{9.6}$$

↑ Output

↓ Output

The amsmath package also provides the environment smallmatrix designed for in-line use. You need to add any delimiters explicitly.

EXAMPLE:

```
Here is a small matrix
\begin{math}
 \left(
  \begin{smallmatrix}
  a & b\\
  c & d
  \end{smallmatrix}
 \right)
\end{math}
in a line of text.
```

↑ Input

↓ Input

Here is a small matrix $\left(\begin{smallmatrix} a & b \\ c & d \end{smallmatrix}\right)$ in a line of text.

Output

9.4.11. Vectors

A variable representing a vector can be typeset using the command:

```
\vec{⟨variable⟩}
```

Definition

EXAMPLE:

```
\[ \vec{x} \]
```

Input

$$\vec{x}$$

Output

Vectors are often typeset in bold. This can be done by redefining the \vec command (see Section 8.2). You could use \mathbf, for example:

```
\renewcommand{\vec}[1]{\mathbf{#1}}

\[
  \vec{x}\cdot\vec{\xi} = z
\]
```

↑ Input

↓ Input

Output $$\mathbf{x} \cdot \xi = z$$

However, as you may have noticed, the Greek letter ξ has not come out in bold. Here's an alternative (using \boldsymbol defined in the amsfonts package):

Input ⊤
```
\renewcommand{\vec}[1]{\boldsymbol{#1}}
\[
  \vec{x}\cdot\vec{\xi} = z
```
Input ↓
```
\]
```

Output $$\boldsymbol{x} \cdot \boldsymbol{\xi} = z$$

Located (or position) vectors, on the other hand, are usually typeset with a right arrow, but the default definition of \vec produces an arrow that is too small:

Input $$\[\vec{OP} \]$$

Output $$\vec{OP}$$

Instead, use \overrightarrow (Table 9.10 on page 168):

Input $$\[\overrightarrow{OP} \]$$

Output $$\overrightarrow{OP}$$

You might prefer to define separate commands for a located vector and a vector variable.

EXAMPLE:
In the preamble, define \lvec for a located vector and \bvec for a vector variable:

Input ⊤
```
\newcommand*{\lvec}[1]{\overrightarrow{#1}}
\newcommand*{\bvec}[1]{\boldsymbol{#1}}
```
Input ↓

Later in the document:

Input ⊤
```
Let $\bvec{u}=(x, y)$ represent $\lvec{OP}$, then
\[
  \lVert \bvec{u} \rVert = \sqrt{x^2 + y^2}
```
Input ↓
```
\]
```

Output ⊤

Let $\boldsymbol{u} = (x, y)$ represent $\overrightarrow{OP}$, then

$$\|\boldsymbol{u}\| = \sqrt{x^2 + y^2}$$

Output ↓

Exercise 23 (Maths: Vectors and Arrays)

Try to produce the following:

↑ Output

$$A\boldsymbol{x} = \begin{pmatrix} 0 & 1 \\ 2 & 3 \end{pmatrix} \begin{pmatrix} 1 \\ 2 \end{pmatrix} = \begin{pmatrix} 2 \\ 8 \end{pmatrix} = \boldsymbol{y}$$

↓ Output

As before, you can download[9.3] the solution.

9.4.12. Mathematical Spacing

LaTeX deals with mathematical spacing fairly well, but sometimes you may find you want to adjust the spacing yourself. Available spacing commands are listed in Table 9.15.

Table 9.15. Mathematical Spacing Commands ([†]provided by amsmath)

Command	Example Input	Example Output
	`$AB$`	AB
`\thinspace` or `\,`	`$A\,B$`	$A\,B$
`\medspace`[†] or `\:`	`$A\:B$`	$A\:B$
`\thickspace`[†] or `\;`	`$A\;B$`	$A\;B$
`\quad`	`$A\quad B$`	$A\quad B$
`\qquad`	`$A\qquad B$`	$A\qquad B$
`\negthinspace` or `\!`	`$A\!B$`	AB
`\negmedspace`[†]	`$A\negmedspace B$`	AB
`\negthickspace`[†]	`$A\negthickspace B$`	AB

Exercise 24 (More Mathematics)

This exercise uses the spacing command `\qquad`. In addition, it has a function name, diag, and it uses the `\forall` and ellipses symbols. It also redefines the `\vec` command, as was done in the previous section, uses the bmatrix environment (see Section 9.4.10), and has subscripts and superscripts.

Try to reproduce the following output:

The set of linear equations:

$$a_i x_i = b_i \qquad \forall i = 1, \ldots, n$$

can be written as a matrix equation:

$$\text{diag}(\boldsymbol{a})\boldsymbol{x} = \boldsymbol{b}$$

where $\boldsymbol{x} = (x_1, \ldots, x_n)^T$, $\boldsymbol{b} = (b_1, \ldots, b_n)^T$ and

$$\text{diag}(\boldsymbol{a}) = \begin{bmatrix} a_1 & 0 & \cdots & 0 \\ 0 & a_2 & \ddots & \vdots \\ \vdots & \ddots & \ddots & 0 \\ 0 & \cdots & 0 & a_n \end{bmatrix}$$

Again, you can download[9.4] the solution.

[9.4]http://www.dickimaw-books.com/latex/novices/html/exercises/moremaths.tex

CHAPTER 10

DEFINING ENVIRONMENTS

Just as you can define new commands, you can also define new environments. The command

Definition

`\newenvironment{`⟨*env-name*⟩`}[`⟨*n-args*⟩`][`⟨*default*⟩`]{`⟨*begin-code*⟩`}{`⟨*end-code*⟩`}`

is used to define a new environment. As with new commands, you can use the optional argument ⟨*n-args*⟩ to define an environment with arguments, and ⟨*default*⟩ to define an environment with an optional argument.

The first argument ⟨*env-name*⟩ is the name of your new environment. Remember that the environment name must not have a backslash. The mandatory arguments ⟨*begin-code*⟩ and ⟨*end-code*⟩ indicate what LATEX should do at the beginning and end of the environment. Note that although ⟨*begin-code*⟩ can reference the arguments using #1 etc, the ⟨*end-code*⟩ part can't.

EXAMPLE (AN EXERCISE ENVIRONMENT):

Let's first consider an example of an environment without any arguments. Let's make an environment called, say, exercise that prints **Exercise** in bold and typesets the contents of the environment in italic, with a gap between the title and the contents. In other words, we want the following code:

```
\begin{exercise}
This is a sample.
\end{exercise}
```

to produce the following output:

Exercise

This is a sample.

(In the next chapter we will add numbering.)

Let's first consider what we want this environment to do: we can get the word "Exercise" in bold using `\textbf`, and the italic font can be obtained by using the itshape environment (recall Section 4.5). So, at the start of our new environment we need

```
\textbf{Exercise}\begin{itshape}
```

and at the end of our new environment we need to end the itshape environment:

Input

```
\end{itshape}
```

Putting the above together into the new environment definition:

Input ↑
Input ↓

```
\newenvironment{exercise}% environment name
{% begin code
  \textbf{Exercise}\begin{itshape}%
}%
{\end{itshape}}% end code
```

Let's try it out:

Input ↑
Input ↓

```
\begin{exercise}
This is a sample.
\end{exercise}
```

Output

Exercise *This is a sample.*

Not quite right. Let's put a paragraph break after **Exercise**, and put one before it as well. The command \par can be used to make a paragraph break and the extra bit of vertical spacing can be produced using \vspace. The length \baselineskip is the interline spacing. Modifications are shown in bold **like this**.

Input ↑
Input ↓

```
\newenvironment{exercise}% environment name
{% begin code
  \par\vspace{\baselineskip}%
  \textbf{Exercise}\begin{itshape}%
  \par\vspace{\baselineskip}%
}%
{\end{itshape}}% end code
```

Let's have a look at the output now:

Output ↑
Output ↓

Exercise

This is a sample.

[FAQ: There's a space added after my environment]

The indent at the start of each line is caused by the normal paragraph indentation. This can be suppressed using \noindent. It's also a good idea to suppress any spaces immediately following \begin{exercise} and \end{exercise}, which can be done using \ignorespaces and \ignorespacesafterend. Modifications are again shown in bold **like this**.

```
\newenvironment{exercise}% environment name
{% begin code
  \par\vspace{\baselineskip}\noindent
  \textbf{Exercise}\begin{itshape}%
  \par\vspace{\baselineskip}\noindent\ignorespaces
}%
{% end code
  \end{itshape}\ignorespacesafterend
}
```
↑ Input

↓ Input

The exercise environment now appears as:

↑ Output

Exercise

This is a sample.

↓ Output

Now let's modify our code so that the environment takes an argument. The argument should indicate the exercise topic. For example, the following code:

↑ Input

```
\begin{exercise}{An Example}
This is a sample.
\end{exercise}
```

↓ Input

should produce the following result:

↑ Output

Exercise (An Example)

This is a sample.

↓ Output

As with \newcommand, #1 is used to indicate the first argument. We can now modify the code as follows:

↑ Input

```
\newenvironment{exercise}[1]% environment name
{% begin code
  \par\vspace{\baselineskip}\noindent
  \textbf{Exercise (#1)}\begin{itshape}%
  \par\vspace{\baselineskip}\noindent\ignorespaces
}%
```

```
{% end code
  \end{itshape}\ignorespacesafterend
}
```

Input ↓

10.1. Redefining Environments

It is also possible to redefine an environment using:

Definition

\renewenvironment{⟨*env-name*⟩}[⟨*n-args*⟩][⟨*default*⟩]{⟨*begin-code*⟩}{⟨*end-code*⟩}

As with \renewcommand, only redefine an existing environment if you want a modified version of that environment rather than because you like the environment name.

Exercise 25 (Defining a New Environment)

If you did any of the exercises from Exercise 10 (page 90) to Exercise 17 (page 129), go back to the document you created and define the exercise environment as in the example above. Then try creating some exercises using this environment. You could, maybe, put an exercise in the first chapter, and then another one in the second chapter. Again you can download[10.1] an example.

———————

[10.1] http://www.dickimaw-books.com/latex/novices/html/exercises/newenv.tex

CHAPTER 11

COUNTERS

As we have seen, LaTeX automatically generates numbers for chapters, sections, equations etc. These numbers are stored in *counters*. The names of these counters are usually the same as the name of the object with which it is associated but without any backslash. For example, the \chapter command has an associated counter called chapter, the \footnote command has an associated counter called footnote, the equation environment has an associated counter called equation, the figure environment has an associated counter called figure and the table environment has an associated counter called table. There is also a counter called page that keeps track of the current page number.

The value of a counter can be displayed using the command

\the⟨counter⟩

Definition

where ⟨counter⟩ is the name of the associated counter. Note that ⟨counter⟩ does not go in curly braces and adjoins \the (for example, \thepage, \thesection or \thechapter). In fact, we have already encountered \thefigure in Section 7.4.

[FAQ: Page number is wrong at start of page]

EXAMPLE:

```
This page is Page~\thepage.
The current chapter is Chapter~\thechapter.
```

↑ Input

↓ Input

This page is Page 189. The current chapter is Chapter 11.

Output

New counters can be created using the command:

\newcounter{⟨counter-name⟩}[⟨outer-counter⟩]

Definition

The mandatory argument ⟨counter-name⟩ is the name of your new counter (no backslash in the name). For example, let's define a counter called exercise to keep track of each exercise. (Recall the exercise example from Chapter 10 (Defining Environments).)

\newcounter{exercise}

Input

We can now display the value of the counter using the command \theexercise. At the moment the counter has the value zero, the value can be changed using one of the following commands:

`\stepcounter{⟨counter⟩}`   Increments ⟨counter⟩ by 1

`\refstepcounter{⟨counter⟩}`   As above, but allows you to cross-reference the
                                            counter using `\label` and `\ref`

`\setcounter{⟨counter⟩}{⟨num⟩}`   Sets the counter to ⟨num⟩

`\addtocounter{⟨counter⟩}{⟨num⟩}` Adds ⟨num⟩ to ⟨counter⟩

A couple of the commands above take a number ⟨num⟩ as one of the arguments.
If you want to use another counter for this argument, you need to use

Definition `\value{⟨counter⟩}`

For example, if you want to set our new exercise counter to the same value as the
page counter, you would do

Input `\setcounter{exercise}{\value{page}}`

Let's go back to the exercise environment you created in Exercise 25 (page 188). The
exercises really ought to have an associated number, and this number should be
incremented each time we use the exercise environment. So let's modify our code
to do this. Modifications are illustrated in bold **like this:**

Input ↑

```
\newcounter{exercise}

\newenvironment{exercise}[1]% environment name
{% begin code
  \par\vspace{\baselineskip}\noindent
  \refstepcounter{exercise}%
  \textbf{Exercise \theexercise\␣(#1)}%
  \begin{itshape}%
  \par\vspace{\baselineskip}%
  \noindent\ignorespaces
}%
{% end code
  \end{itshape}%
  \par\vspace{\baselineskip}%
  \noindent\ignorespacesafterend
}
```

Input ↓

Note that the counter needs to be incremented before it is used. I've also added an
extra `\vspace` at the end of the environment and a paragraph break. Since we've
used `\refstepcounter` instead of `\stepcounter` we can cross-reference our *exercise*
environment:

⊤ Input

```
Exercise~\ref{ex:simple} is a simple exercise.

\begin{exercise}{Simple Exercise}
\label{ex:simple}%
This is a simple exercise.
\end{exercise}
```

↓ Input

This produces the following output:

⊤ Output

Exercise 1 is a simple exercise.

Exercise 1 (Simple Exercise)

This is a simple exercise.

↓ Output

The counter representation can be changed by redefining \theexercise using the \renewcommand command described in Section 8.2. The following commands can be used to display the counter:

[FAQ: Redefining counters' \the-commands]

\arabic{⟨*counter*⟩}	Arabic numeral (1, 2, 3, …)
\Roman{⟨*counter*⟩}	Upper case Roman numeral (I, II, III, …)
\roman{⟨*counter*⟩}	Lower case Roman numeral (i, ii, iii, …)
\alph{⟨*counter*⟩}	Lower case letter (a, b, c, …, z)
\Alph{⟨*counter*⟩}	Upper case letter (A, B, C, …, Z)
\fnsymbol{⟨*counter*⟩}	A footnote symbol (∗ † ‡ § ¶ ‖ ∗∗ †† ‡‡)

EXAMPLE:

To make the chapter numbers appear as upper case Roman numerals you would do:

```
\renewcommand{\thechapter}{\Roman{chapter}}
```

Input

You may have noticed that \newcounter has an optional argument ⟨*outer-counter*⟩. This is for use if you require the new counter to be reset every time ⟨*outer-counter*⟩ is incremented. For example, the section numbers in the scrbook class are dependent on the chapter numbers. Each time a new chapter is started, the section numbers are reset. Suppose we want our exercise counter to be dependent on the chapter counter, we would do

[FAQ: Master and slave counters]

```
\newcounter{exercise}[chapter]
```

Input

Note that if you make a counter dependent on another counter like this, the default action of \the⟨*counter*⟩ remains the same, so \theexercise won't print the chapter number. To make the chapter number appear as well, we need to redefine \theexercise (recall Section 8.2):

Input   \renewcommand{\theexercise}{\thechapter.\arabic{exercise}}

Notice the use of \thechapter instead of, say, \arabic{chapter}. This way we don't need to keep track of the chapter counter format.

EXAMPLE (FOOTNOTE MARKERS):
The footnote counter is reset at the start of each chapter but by default the chapter number isn't displayed in \thefootnote. In this book \thefootnote was redefined so that it displays the chapter number:

Input   \renewcommand{\thefootnote}{\thechapter.\arabic{footnote}}

Exercise 26 (Using Counters)

Modify the document from Exercise 25 (page 188) so that the exercise environment has a counter. Make the counter dependent on the chapter. You can download[11.1] an example.

[11.1] http://www.dickimaw-books.com/latex/novices/html/exercises/counters.tex

APPENDIX A

DOWNLOADING AND INSTALLING PACKAGES

New LaTeX packages are being created all the time, so you may find that there are some packages that you don't have on your installation. In this case, if you don't have the package you want, you can download it from CTAN [1]. Before discussing installing new packages, it is a good idea for you to understand the TeX Directory Structure (TDS).

All the files that make up the TeX distribution are stored in a standard hierarchical structure. The root directory of the main distribution is usually called texmf or texmf-dist. Its location depends on your system. For example, if you are using TeX Live 2012 on UNIX/Linux, it will probably be located in /usr/local/texlive/2012/texmf-dist or if you are using MiKTeX it may be located in c:\texmf or c:\Program Files\texmf. Whichever system you are using, I shall refer to this directory as ⟨TEXMF⟩. So, if you are using TeX Live 2012, ⟨TEXMF⟩/doc refers to the directory /usr/local/texlive/2012/texmf-dist/doc, or if you are using MiKTeX, ⟨TEXMF⟩\doc refers to the folder c:\texmf\doc or c:\Program Files\texmf\doc. In general, you should not make any modifications to the ⟨TEXMF⟩ directory tree as it will get overridden whenever you update your TeX distribution.

You should also have a local texmf tree. Again, the location of the local texmf tree depends on your system. If you are using TeX Live, it may be /usr/local/texlive/texmf-local. If you are using MiKTeX, it may be c:\localtexmf or c:\Program Files\localtexmf. Whichever system you are using, I shall refer to this directory as ⟨TEXMF-LOCAL⟩. There is also the ⟨TEXMF-HOME⟩ directory. On UNIX-like systems this is usually ~/texmf. On Windows it's usually in your user folder. This is the one where you typically install any new classes or packages.

These directories must all have the same structure. The principle sub-directories relating to LaTeX are illustrated in Figure A.1 on the next page. It may be that your ⟨TEXMF-HOME⟩ directory doesn't exist or doesn't contain some of these sub-directories, if so, you will need to create them.

You can use the kpsewhich application to find out the locations of ⟨TEXMF-LOCAL⟩ and ⟨TEXMF-HOME⟩. Since kpsewhich is a command-line application, you will need a command prompt or terminal open (see Section 2.5). At the command prompt, type

```
kpsewhich -var-value=TEXMFHOME
```

to display the location of ⟨TEXMF-HOME⟩ or

```
kpsewhich -var-value=TEXMFLOCAL
```

[FAQ: Installing things on a (La)TeX system]
[FAQ: Installation using MiKTeX package manager]
[FAQ: What is the TDS?]

to display the location of ⟨*TEXMF-LOCAL*⟩. (Remember to press the enter ↵ key at the end of the line.)

The documentation for LaTeX classes and packages can be found in the doc/latex sub-directories: ⟨*TEXMF*⟩/doc/latex, ⟨*TEXMF-LOCAL*⟩/doc/latex and ⟨*TEXMF-HOME*⟩/doc/latex.

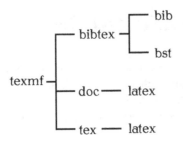

Figure A.1. The TeX Directory Structure (TDS) Showing the Main LaTeX-Related Sub-Directories.

Some packages are supplied in this format.[A.1] For example, the package sample-package may be distributed in a compressed file sample-package.tds.zip, which contains the files

```
doc/latex/sample-package/sample-package.pdf
tex/latex/sample-package/sample-package.sty
tex/latex/sample-package/sample-foo.sty
tex/latex/sample-package/sample-bar.sty
```

In this case all you need to do is decompress the contents of the archive into the ⟨*TEXMF-LOCAL*⟩ or ⟨*TEXMF-HOME*⟩ directory.

On older TeX-distributions, you would then need to refresh the TeX database (described in Section A.2 on page 196). With new distributions, you don't need to do this if you are installing a new package into your ⟨*TEXMF-HOME*⟩ directory.

EXAMPLE (UNIX-LIKE):
To install sample-package.tds.zip (assuming you're in the same directory as that file):

```
unzip -d ~/texmf sample-package.tds.zip
```

A.1. DTX and INS Files

[FAQ: Documented LaTeX sources (.dtx files)]

Not all packages are provided in the TDS [14] format. Instead (or additionally) many are supplied with the code and documentation all bundled together in one file. This file usually has the extension .dtx, and it usually comes with an installation script that has the extension .ins. Once you have downloaded the .dtx and .ins files,

---

[A.1]Complete list at http://mirror.ctan.org/install/macros/latex/contrib/.

you will then have to extract the code before you can use it. Let's go back to the previous example. The package sample-package is now distributed in a DTX file, so the `sample-package.zip` archive contains the files

`sample-package.dtx sample-package.ins`

(with hopefully a `README` or `INSTALL` file). Note that this archive, unlike the TDS one, doesn't contain any `.sty` files. The documentation source and the package code (`sample-package.sty`, `sample-foo.sty` and `sample-bar.sty`) are all contained in the file `sample-package.dtx`. This is how to extract them:

1. Extract the contents of `sample-package.zip` to a temporary directory.

2. Run LATEX on the file `sample-package.ins`. If you are using a terminal, you can type the following at the command prompt:

   `latex sample-package.ins`

   If you are using a front-end, such as TeXWorks, open the `.ins` file (for example `sample-package.ins`), and click on the build/typeset button.

   This will create the files containing the package code. In this example it will create the main package file `sample-package.sty` and supplementary packages `sample-foo.sty` and `sample-bar.sty`.

3. Make a sub-directory of ⟨*TEXMF-LOCAL*⟩/`tex/latex`[A.2] in which to place these files. In this example, the package is called "sample-package", so make a sub-directory called `sample-package`.

4. Move the files created in Step 2 into the new sub-directory you created in the previous step.

5. Run PDFLATEX on the file `sample-package.dtx`. (The same as in Step 2, but use the file `sample-package.dtx` instead of `sample-package.ins`.) This will create a file called `sample-package.pdf`. You may need to repeat this step to ensure that the cross references are up-to-date. Check the `README` file or `INSTALL` file to see if there is anything else you need to do. (If you have downloaded the package from CTAN, it's possible that the documentation has already been supplied, as package authors are encouraged to supply a PDF version of the documentation for on-line viewing. If so, you can omit this step.)

6. Make a sub-directory of ⟨*TEXMF-LOCAL*⟩/`doc/latex`[A.3] in which to place the documentation. In this example, the package is called "sample-package", so make a sub-directory called `sample-package`.

7. Move the files created in Step 5 into the new sub-directory you created in the previous step.

[A.2] or ⟨*TEXMF-LOCAL*⟩\`tex\latex` on Windows
[A.3] or ⟨*TEXMF-LOCAL*⟩\`doc\latex` on Windows

As mentioned above, on older TEX-distributions, you would then need to refresh the TEX database, but this isn't required for ⟨*TEXMF-HOME*⟩ installs on new distributions.

A.2. Refreshing the TEX Database

On older TEX distributions you had to refresh the TEX database whenever you installed new classes or packages. With newer installations you don't need to do this if you install them in your ⟨*TEXMF-HOME*⟩ directory, except under certain circumstances (for example, you're using using a networked drive). If it turns out that TEX can't find a new class or package you have installed in ⟨*TEXMF-HOME*⟩ you will need to update the database using the `texhash` (or `mktexlsr`) application. This is a command-line application, so you need a terminal or command prompt (see Section 2.5).

For example, on UNIX/Linux, to update ⟨*TEXMF-HOME*⟩ (the directory ~/texmf) you need to type the following at the command prompt:

```
texhash ~/texmf
```

If you are using a modern TEX distribution, such as MiKTeX, TeX Live or MacTeX there should be a package manager that has a package installation and refresh facility. For example, TeX Live comes with the TeX Live Manager (`tlmgr` or `mactlmgr`) and recent versions of MiKTeX have an application called MiKTeX Update Wizard which can automatically download and install known packages.

If you experience any problems, contact your system administrator for help or try one of the resources listed in Appendix C (Need More Help?).

RELATED UK FAQ [19] TOPICS:
- Installing things on a (La)TeX system

- Installing files "where (La)TeX can find them"

- Installation using MiKTeX package manager

- "Temporary" installation of (La)TeX files

- "Private" installations of files

APPENDIX B

COMMON ERRORS

- If you're running LaTeX from a terminal and the only message that gets displayed is:

```
latex: Command not found.
```

or

```
Bad command or file name
```

then you have either mistyped the command name, or you don't have LaTeX installed on your computer, or your path hasn't been set up correctly. First check that you have typed the command correctly, then check to see if you have TeX installed. Failing that, contact your system administrator for help or try one of the resources listed in Appendix C (Need More Help?).

- If you're running LaTeX from a terminal and you get the message (or something similar):

```
This is TeX, Version 3.14159 (Web2C 7.3.1)
! I can't find file 'sample'.
<*> sample
```

```
Please type another input file name:
```

then you have either misspelt the filename or you are in the wrong directory. If you have misspelt the filename, simply type in the correct name at the prompt. If you are in the wrong directory or you want to quit, type X followed by the return character ⏎. To check you are in the right directory, on a Unix-like system you can type:

```
ls
```

This will list the contents of the directory. If you are certain that you have spelt the filename correctly and that you are in the right directory, there may be something wrong with your path, in which case contact your system administrator.

- Error messages will usually look something like:

```
! Undefined control sequence.
1.1 \docmentclass
                    [12pt]{scrartcl}
?
```

The first line is the error message. In this example I have misspelt the command \documentclass. The next line begins with 1. followed by a number. This is the line number in the source code where the error occurred. In this case the error occurred on line 1. Following the line number is the input line LaTeX has processed so far, and staggered on the next line is the remainder of the input line.

Here's another example. Suppose line 8 of my source code looks like:

```
The date today is: \toady, which is nice to know.
```

The error in this case is the misspelling of the command \today. The error message will appear as follows:

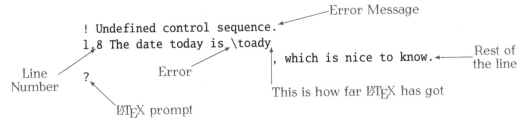

At the LaTeX prompt, you can either type h for a help message, or type x to exit LaTeX and go back to your source code and fix the problem.

There follows below a list of common error messages. If your problem isn't listed there, try the UK FAQ [19].

B.1. * (No message, just an asterisk prompt!)

You've gone into TeX! This is probably because you've forgotten the \end{document}. The asterisk is the TeX prompt. At this point the best thing to do is to abort the TeX run.

B.2. Argument of \cline has an extra }

If this error occurred on the first line in your tabular environment, you may have forgotten the argument to the tabular environment.

B.3. Argument of \multicolumn has an extra }

If this error occurred on the first line in your tabular environment, you may have forgotten the argument to the tabular environment.

B.4. \begin{...} ended by \end{...}

The beginning of your environment doesn't have a matching end.

- Check to make sure you have spelt the name of the environment correctly. You will get this error message if you do, say,

  \end{docment}

  instead of

  \end{document}

- Check that for every \begin you have a corresponding \end with the same name.

B.5. Bad math environment delimiter

Only a certain type of character may be used as a delimiter (for example, ( ) [ ]), check which one you have specified. This error may also occur if you have forgotten a \right or not used it in the same scope. (Remember to use a . if you want an invisible delimiter) or you may have forgotten to end your array environment with \end{array}.

B.6. Can only be used in preamble.

Some commands, such as \usepackage may only appear in the preamble. Check to see where you have put it. For example, this error will be caused by doing:

\documentclass{scrartcl}

\begin{document}

\usepackage{graphicx}

instead of

\documentclass{scrartcl}

\usepackage{graphicx}

\begin{document}

B.7. Command ... already defined

You have tried to define a command which already exists. Try giving it a different name. Remember never to redefine a command if you don't know what the command originally does.

Alternatively, you have tried to define an environment which already exists. Give the new environment a different name. Again, never redefine an environment where you don't know what the original environment does.

B.8. Display math should end with $$

You may have a dollar sign ($) in a displayed maths environment, such as the equation environment. Remember that $ is short hand for \begin{math} or \end{math}, so you can't end one of the other environments with a $. (This error message is in fact a bit confusing, as it seems to be suggesting that you end a displayed maths environment with $$ which you also shouldn't do.)

[FAQ: Why use \[...\] in place of $$...$$]

B.9. Environment ... undefined

LaTeX doesn't recognise the environment you have specified.

- Check you have spelt the environment name correctly.

  You will get this error if you do, say,

  ✗

  \begin{docment}

  instead of

  ✓

  \begin{document}

- If it's your own environment, check you have defined the environment before using it.

- If the environment is defined in a package, check you have included the package using the \usepackage command.

B.10. Extra alignment tab has been changed to \cr

You have too many ampersands (&) in one row. The most probable cause is that you have forgotten the end of row command \\ on the previous row. Remember also that if you have a \multicolumn command to span more than one column, you should have fewer &s in that row. This error can also occur from a confusion over the two meanings of \\: a line break within a paragraph cell and a row break. In which case, you need to use \tabularnewline instead of \\.

B.11. Extra \right

There are a number of possible causes. The most probable is that you have a \right that doesn't have a matching \left. (Remember left comes before right.) Another possible cause is that you have missed out \end{array}. (Remember that environments provide implicit grouping, and \left and its matching \right must appear within the same group level.)

B.12. File ended while scanning use of ...

The most usual cause of this error is a missing closing brace.

You will get this error if you do, say,

\end{document

instead of

\end{document}

B.13. File not found

LaTeX can't find the file you have specified. You will be given the opportunity to type in the correct filename at the prompt. If you want to quit, simply type X followed by the return character ↵ .

- Make sure that you have spelt the filename correctly.

  This error will be caused by, say,

  \documentclass{scrarticle}

  instead of

  \documentclass{scrartcl}

  If this is the case, simply type in the correct name at the prompt (followed by the return character ↵) then go back and fix the spelling in the source code.

- Make sure that the file is in the same directory as your document or in the LaTeX path. If the file is in another directory (not in the LaTeX path), you will need to specify the pathname, but remember that when using LaTeX under Windows, you need to use a forward slash (/) as the directory divider, as a backslash would be interpreted as a command. For example, if you have a file called shapes.pdf in the subdirectory pictures then you would get a "file not found" error message if you did

  \includegraphics{shapes}

instead of

`\includegraphics{pictures/shapes}`

- If the file is a package or class file, it's possible that you don't have that file installed on your computer. If this is the case you will need to download and install it as described in Appendix A (Downloading and Installing Packages). Remember that you need to refresh the database after installing a new package or class file.

B.14. Illegal character in array arg

You have used a character in the argument of a tabular or array environment that is not allowed. The standard available characters are: r (right justified), l (left justified), c (centred) and p, as well as @{⟨*inter-col text*⟩}. Remember that if you want to use the >{⟨*decl*⟩} or <{⟨*decl*⟩} specifiers, you must include the array package.

This error will also occur if you have forgotten the argument to the tabular or array environment.

B.15. Illegal parameter number in definition

You have referred to a parameter (argument) number that is greater than the number of parameters you have specified. For example, suppose you defined the command to have only one parameter, then you can't use #2 which refers to the second, non-existent, parameter. Remember that you need to specify how many parameters you want in the optional argument to \newcommand, otherwise it will be assumed that the command has no arguments.

B.16. Illegal unit of measure (pt inserted)

You have either not specified a unit when giving a length (even zero lengths must have a unit) or you have specified an invalid unit or you have misspelt the unit. Available units are listed in Table 2.1 on page 25.

B.17. Lonely \item

The command \item may only appear in one of the list making environments (such as itemize). Make sure you haven't forgotten your environment.

B.18. Misplaced alignment tab character &

You have used the special character & where you shouldn't have. Recall from Section 4.3 that if you want an & sign to appear you need to do \& not just &.

You would have got this error message if you had done, say,

```
& our equipment
```

instead of

```
\& our equipment
```

B.19. Missing } inserted

You have missed a closing curly brace, or you may have missed out an argument.

EXAMPLE:
If the following line occurs in a tabular environment:

```
& \multicolumn{2}{c}\\
```

this will produce the error. (The third argument to \multicolumn has been omitted.)

B.20. Missing $ inserted

This message can be caused by a number of errors:

- You might have missed the beginning of one of the mathematics environments (that is, you've used a command that must only appear in maths mode).

- You may have typed $ instead of \$ (you actually want a dollar symbol to appear). Recall from Section 4.3 that if you want a $ sign to appear you need to do \$ not just $.

  You would have got this error message if you had done, say,

  ```
  expenditure came to $2000.00
  ```

  instead of

  ```
  expenditure came to \$2000.00
  ```

- You may have missed the end of a mathematics environment, or you may have a paragraph break within an in-line or displayed maths environment, where it is not permitted. Make sure you don't have any blank lines within the environment. If you want a blank line in your code to make it easier to edit, try having a percent sign at the start of an empty line to ensure that the line is ignored by LATEX. For example:

```
\begin{equation}
%
E = mc^2
%
\end{equation}
```

B.21. Missing \begin{document}

You have put some text outside of the document environment. Check the following:

- You have remembered \begin{document}
  This error would be caused by, say,

  ✗
  ```
  \documentclass{scrartcl}

  This is a simple document
  ```

  instead of

  ✔
  ```
  \documentclass{scrartcl}

  \begin{document}
  This is a simple document.
  ```

- You haven't placed any text before \begin{document}. For example:

  ✗
  ```
  \documentclass{scrartcl}

  This is a simple document
  \begin{document}
  ```

  instead of

  ✔
  ```
  \documentclass{scrartcl}

  \begin{document}
  This is a simple document
  ```

- You haven't missed out the backslash at the start of either \documentclass or \begin{document}
  This error would be caused by, say,

  ✗
  ```
  documentclass{scrartcl}
  ```

  instead of

  ✔
  ```
  \documentclass{scrartcl}
  ```

B.22. Missing delimiter

You have forgotten to specify the type of delimiter you want (for example, ( ) [ ] \{ \}). (Remember to use a . if you want an invisible delimiter, and remember that if you want a curly brace, you must have a backslash followed by the curly brace.)

EXAMPLE:
This error will occur if you do, say,

```
f(x) = \left{
\begin{array}{ll}
0 & x \leq 0\\
1 & x > 1
\end{array}
\right.
```

instead of

```
f(x) = \left\{
\begin{array}{ll}
0 & x \leq 0\\
1 & x > 1
\end{array}
\right.
```

B.23. Missing \endcsname inserted

This is a TeX error rather than a LaTeX error which makes it harder to determine the cause, however it can be caused by placing a backslash in front of the name of an environment. (Remember that environment names do not contain a backslash.)
 This error will be caused by, say,

```
\begin{\sffamily}
```

instead of

```
\begin{sffamily}
```

B.24. Missing \endgroup inserted

A number of things could have caused this. You may have missed out the end of an environment, or you may have an environment inside of another environment it's not allowed to be in. For example, this error can be caused by placing an eqnarray environment inside a displaymath environment, which is not allowed. (But, of course, you haven't used either of those obsolete environments [16], have you?)

B.25. Missing number, treated as zero

LaTeX is expecting a number. If your command takes more than one argument, check to make sure the arguments are in the correct order. For example, if you are using a minipage environment, you might have omitted the mandatory argument which specifies the width of the minipage, or you may have the optional arguments the wrong way round. The placement specifier should come first, followed by the height.

If you are using \addtocounter or \setcounter remember that the second argument must be a number, so if you want the value of a counter as the argument you must use \value. This error can be caused by, say,

✗   \setcounter{exercise}{chapter}

instead of

✓   \setcounter{exercise}{\value{chapter}}

B.26. Paragraph ended before \begin was complete

You've probably missed a closing brace at the end of the argument to \begin. This error will be caused by, say,

✗   \begin{document

instead of

✓   \begin{document}

B.27. Runaway argument

There are a number of possible causes of this error:

- Paragraph breaks are not permitted in the arguments of short commands. If there is a corresponding environment then you should use that instead. For example, this error message will be generated by doing, say,

  ✗
  \textbf{This is a simple document.
  Here is the first paragraph.

  Here is the second paragraph.}

  instead of

```
\begin{bfseries}
This is a simple document.
Here is the first paragraph.

Here is the second paragraph.
\end{bfseries}
```

- The closing brace of a mandatory argument is missing: This error will be caused by, say,

```
\title{A Simple Document
```

✗

instead of

```
\title{A Simple Document}
```

- This error can also be caused by omitting the mandatory argument of an environment. For example, this error will occur if you do, say,

```
\begin{thebibliography}
\bibitem{kopka95} A Guide to \LaTeXe
```

✗

instead of

```
\begin{thebibliography}{1}
\bibitem{kopka95} A Guide to \LaTeXe
```

B.28. Something's wrong–perhaps a missing \item

You may have missed an \item command. The first object in a list environment must either be an \item command, or another list environment.

This error will be caused by, say,

```
\begin{itemize}
Animal
\item Vegetable
\item Mineral
\end{itemize}
```

✗

instead of

```
\begin{itemize}
\item Animal
\item Vegetable
\item Mineral
\end{itemize}
```

This error can also be caused by a missing \bibitem in the bibliography. For example, the error will occur if you do, say,

✗
```
\begin{thebibliography}{1}
A Guide to \LaTeXe
```

instead of

✓
```
\begin{thebibliography}{1}
\bibitem{kopka95} A Guide to \LaTeXe
```

See also UK FAQ [19] entry: Perhaps a missing \item?.

B.29. There's no line here to end

You have placed a line breaking command (such as \\, \newline or \linebreak) where it doesn't make sense to have one.

B.30. Undefined control sequence

LATEX doesn't understand the command you have used.

- Check to see if you have misspelt the command name (remember that all LATEX command names are case-sensitive.)

  You will get this error if you do, say,

✗
```
This is a simple \Latex\␣document
```

  instead of

✓
```
This is a simple \LaTeX\␣document
```

- Check that you have remembered the space when typing \␣ (backslash space). For example, this error will occur if you do, say,

✗
```
This is a \LaTeX\sample document.
```

  instead of

✓
```
This is a \LaTeX\␣sample document
```

- If you are using a command that is defined in a package make sure you have included the package using \usepackage.

- Check that your command name hasn't run into the next piece of text. For example, you can do

```
man\oe{}uvre
```

or

```
man\oe uvre
```

or (not recommended)

```
man{\oe}uvre
```

but not

```
man\oeuvre
```                                                                          ✗

- Check if you have used a backslash instead of a forward slash as a directory divider. (Remember that when using LaTeX under Windows, you need to use a forward slash (/) as the directory divider, as a backslash would be interpreted as a command.)

  For example, suppose you have a file called shapes.pdf in a subdirectory called pictures, then you would get an error if you did

  ```
  \includegraphics{pictures\shapes}
  ```                                                                      ✗

  instead of

  ```
  \includegraphics{pictures/shapes}
  ```

B.31. You can't use 'macro parameter character #' in horizontal mode

You have used the special character # where you shouldn't have. Recall from Section 4.3 that if you want a # sign to appear you need to do \# not just #.

This error message will be caused by doing, say,

```
Item #1
```                                                                          ✗

instead of

```
Item \#1
```

Appendix C

Need More Help?

First, try to find your query in the UK FAQ [19]. TUG [17] also has a list of useful resources at http://tug.org/interest.html. If you're still stuck, you can post your question on a (La)TeX forum, newsgroup or mailing list, such as those listed below. If you do post a question, remember you're asking people who only have an altruistic interest in helping. No one is paying them to help you. Most of the class files and packages were written for free by people who had a need to solve a particular problem and decided to make their work publicly available. So no matter how frustrated you're feeling, stick to being polite. If you can't work out how to use a particular class or package, don't start by heaping offensive, unconstructive criticism on it as there's a chance the author will read the message. There's no sense in alienating the person most qualified to answer your question. In your message, stick to the following guidelines:

1. Cut to the chase. In other words, be concise about the nature of the problem. Don't write lots of long-winded paragraphs.

2. Provide a minimal example[C.1] that illustrates the problem.

EXAMPLE:
```
I'm trying to use the \foo command in the "bar" package,
but I'm getting the following error message:
! Undefined control sequence.
l.4 \foo

Here's a minimal example:
\documentclass{scrartcl}
\usepackage{bar}
\begin{document}
\foo{Blah}
\end{document}

I'm using bar version 1.0 (2012/06/30).
```

[C.1]see http://www.dickimaw-books.com/latex/minexample/

ANOTHER EXAMPLE:
I'm using the \foo command in the "bar" package. According
to the documentation, this command should display its argument
in a bold font, but it's coming out in italic instead.
Anyone know why?

Here's a minimal example:
\documentclass{scrartcl}
\usepackage{bar}
\begin{document}
\foo{Blah}
\end{document}

I'm using bar version 1.1 (2012/07/30).

There's no guarantee that you will get an answer, but if you follow the above
guidelines, you will increase your chances.

RESOURCES
- The LaTeX Community (http://www.latex-community.org/).

- TeX/LaTeX on StackExchange (http://tex.stackexchange.com/).

- comp.text.tex newsgroup (use a newsreader rather than the Google interface
  if you want to avoid the spam).

- texhax archives [15].

I strongly recommend that you also have a look at the On-Line Catalogue [22]. It's
also a good idea to look at the documentation that was installed with your TeX/LaTeX
distribution (see Section 1.1). If you are using MiKTeX you can access the on-line help
via the Start Menu:

Start→ Programs → MiKTeX → Help

(Please don't send your problems to me, unless you want to hire a consultant.
I read both the LaTeX Community Forum and comp.text.tex and answer relevant
questions if I have time, but it clogs up my inbox if people keep sending attachments
that are in the order of several megabytes in size.) Besides, you'll reach a wide group
of experts if you post to a newsgroup, forum or mailing list, rather than a single busy
individual.

BIBLIOGRAPHY

[1] The comprehensive TeX archive network. http://mirror.ctan.org/.

[2] The LaTeX font catalogue. http://www.tug.dk/FontCatalogue/.

[3] Michel Goossens, Frank Mittelbach, and Alexander Samarin. *The LaTeX companion*. Addison-Wesley, 1994.

[4] Michel Goossens, Sebastian Rahtz, et al. *The LaTeX web companion*. Addison-Wesley, 1999.

[5] Michel Goossens, Sebastian Rahtz, and Frank Mittelbach. *The LaTeX graphics companion*. Addison-Wesley, 1997.

[6] Donald Ervin Knuth. *The TeXbook*. Addison-Wesley, 1986.

[7] Helmut Kopka and Patrick W. Daly. *A guide to LaTeX 2_ε: document preparation for beginners and advanced users*. Addison-Wesley, 1995.

[8] Stefan Kottwitz. *LaTeX Beginner's Guide*. Packt Publishing, 2011.

[9] Leslie Lamport. *LaTeX : a document preparation system*. Addison-Wesley, 2nd edition, 1994.

[10] Scott Pakin. The comprehensive LaTeX symbol list. 2009. http://mirror.ctan.org/info/symbols/comprehensive or texdoc symbols.

[11] R. M. Ritter. *Oxford Style Manual*. Oxford University Press, 2003.

[12] Murray Sargent III. High-quality editing and display of mathematical text in office 2007, September 2006. http://blogs.msdn.com/b/murrays/archive/2006/09/13/752206.aspx.

[13] Nicola L. C. Talbot. *Using LaTeX to Write a Ph.D. Thesis*, volume 2 of *The Dickimaw LaTeX Series*. Dickmaw Books, 2012. http://www.dickimaw-books.com/latex/thesis/.

[14] What is the TDS? http://www.tex.ac.uk/cgi-bin/texfaq2html?label=tds.

[15] The texhax archives. http://tug.org/pipermail/texhax/.

[16] Mark Trettin and Jürgen Fenn. An essential guide to LaTeX 2_ε usage: obsolete commands and packages. 2007. http://mirror.ctan.org/info/l2tabu/english or texdoc l2tabu-en.

[17] The TeX user group. http://tug.org/.

[18] Kate L. Turabian. *A Manual for Writers of Term Papers, Theses, and Disser- tations*. The University of Chicago Press, sixth edition, 1996.

[19] UK list of TeX frequently asked questions. `http://www.tex.ac.uk/faq`.

[20] Marc van Dongen. *LaTeX and Friends*. Springer, 2012.

[21] Herbert Voß. Math mode, 2010. `http://mirror.ctan.org/info/math/voss/ mathmode/Mathmode.pdf` or `texdoc mathmode`.

[22] Graham Williams. TeX catalogue. `http://mirror.ctan.org/help/Catalogue/`.

Acronyms

CTAN The Comprehensive TEX Archive Network. http://mirror.ctan.org/.

GUI Graphical User Interface.

TDS TEX Directory Structure.

TUG TEX User Group. http://tug.org/.

UK FAQ UK List of TEX Frequently Asked Questions. http://www.tex.ac.uk/faq.

UK TUG UK TEX User Group. http://uk.tug.org/.

SUMMARY

Commands or environments defined in the LATEX kernel are always available.

Symbols

!

1) Used in \resizebox to maintain aspect ratio [§6.1]; 2) Exclamation symbol (end of sentence marker) [§2.13].

!`

Defined in: LATEX Kernel.

Upside-down exclamation mark ¡ symbol. See also \textexclamdown. [§4.3]

␣

A visual indication of a space in the code. When you type up the code, replace all instances of this symbol with a space via the space bar on your keyboard. [§2.0]

#⟨digit⟩

Defined in: LATEX Kernel.

Replacement text for argument ⟨digit⟩. [§8.0]

$

Defined in: LATEX Kernel.

Switches in and out of in-line math mode. [§9.1]

%

Defined in: LATEX Kernel.

Comment character used to ignore everything up to and including the newline character in the source code. [§2.0]

&

Defined in: LATEX Kernel.

Alignment tab. [§4.6]

'

Defined in: LATEX Kernel.

Closing quote or apostrophe ' symbol in text mode or prime symbol ' in math mode. See also \textquoteright. [§4.3]

''

Defined in: LATEX Kernel.

Closing double quote " symbol in text mode or double prime ″ in math mode. See also \textquotedblright. [§4.3]

(

Defined in: LATEX Kernel.

Opening parenthesis in text mode or left round bracket delimiter in math mode. [§9.4]

)

Defined in: LATEX Kernel.

Closing parenthesis in text mode or right round bracket delimiter in math mode. [§9.4]

-

Defined in: LATEX Kernel.

Hyphen - in text mode or minus sign − in math mode. [§4.3]

--

Defined in: LATEX Kernel.

En-dash – symbol. (Normally used for number ranges.) See also \textendash. [§4.3]

Defined in: LATEX Kernel.

Em-dash — symbol. (Normally used to indicate omissions or interruptions or to highlight a parenthetical element.) See also \textemdash. [§4.3]

.

Defined in: LATEX Kernel.

1) invisible delimiter [§9.4]; 2) period (full stop) or decimal point [§2.13].

/

1) Forward slash delimiter (math mode) [§9.4]; 2) Directory divider [§6.0]; 3) Forward slash symbol (see also \slash) [§2.0].

<

Defined in: LATEX Kernel (Math Mode).

Less than symbol. (Use \textless in text mode.) [§4.3]

<{⟨decl⟩}

Defined in: array package.

Used in tabular or array column specifiers after l, r, c, p, m or b to insert ⟨decl⟩ directly after the entry for that column. [§4.6]

>

Defined in: LATEX Kernel (Math Mode).

Greater than symbol. (Use \textgreater in text mode.) [§4.3]

>{⟨decl⟩}

Defined in: array package.

Used in tabular or array column specifiers before l, r, c, p, m or b to

insert ⟨decl⟩ directly in front of the entry for that column. [§4.6]

?

Question mark (end of sentence marker). [§2.13]

?‘

Defined in: LATEX Kernel.

Upside-down question mark ¿ symbol. See also \textquestiondown. [§4.3]

@{⟨text⟩}

Defined in: LATEX Kernel.

Used in the argument of tabular or array like environments to specify text to insert between columns. [§4.6]

[

Defined in: LATEX Kernel.

1) Left square bracket delimiter in math mode [§9.4]; 2) Open delimiter of an optional argument [§2.8]; 3) Open square bracket in text mode [§4.4].

\&

Defined in: LATEX Kernel.

Ampersand & symbol [§4.3]

\

Defined in: LATEX Kernel.

Escape character (indicates a command). [§2.6]

\$

Defined in: LATEX Kernel.

Dollar $ symbol. [§4.3]

\#

Defined in: LATEX Kernel.

Hash # symbol. [§4.3]

SUMMARY

\%

Defined in: LaTeX Kernel.

Percent % symbol [§4.3]

\!

Defined in: LaTeX Kernel (Math Mode).

Negative thin space. [§9.4]

\"{⟨c⟩}

Defined in: LaTeX Kernel.

Umlaut over ⟨c⟩. Example: \"{o}
produces ö. [§4.3]

\'{⟨c⟩}

Defined in: LaTeX Kernel.

Acute accent over ⟨c⟩. Example: \'{o}
produces ó. [§4.3]

\(

Defined in: LaTeX Kernel.

Equivalent to \begin{math}. [§9.1]

\)

Defined in: LaTeX Kernel.

Equivalent to \end{math}. [§9.1]

\,

Defined in: LaTeX Kernel.

Thin space. [§9.4]

\-

Defined in: LaTeX Kernel.

Insert discretionary hyphen. [§2.14]

\.{⟨c⟩}

Defined in: LaTeX Kernel.

Dot over ⟨c⟩. Example: \.{o} produces
ȯ. [§4.3]

\/

Defined in: LaTeX Kernel.

Italic correction. [§4.5]

\:

Defined in: LaTeX Kernel (Math Mode).

Medium space. [§9.4]

\;

Defined in: LaTeX Kernel (Math Mode).

Thick space. [§9.4]

\={⟨c⟩}

Defined in: LaTeX Kernel.

Macron accent over ⟨c⟩. Example:
\={o} produces ō. [§4.3]

\@

Defined in: LaTeX Kernel.

Used when a sentence ends with a
capital letter. This command should be
placed after the letter and before the
punctuation mark. [§2.13]

\[

Defined in: LaTeX Kernel
(inconsistency corrected in amsmath).

Starts an unnumbered single-line of
displayed maths. [§9.2]

\\[⟨height⟩]

Defined in: LaTeX Kernel.

1) Breaks a line without justification
(starred form forbids a page break)
[§2.8]; 2) Starts a new row in
tabular-style environments [§4.6].

\␣

Defined in: LaTeX Kernel.

(Backslash followed by space
character.) Horizontal spacing
command. [§2.13]

\]

Defined in: LaTeX Kernel
(inconsistency corrected in amsmath).

\]

Ends an unnumbered single-line of displayed maths. [§9.2]

\^{⟨c⟩}

Defined in: LaTeX Kernel.

Circumflex accent over ⟨c⟩. Example: \^{o} produces ô. [§4.3]

_

Defined in: LaTeX Kernel.

Underscore _ symbol (see also \textunderscore). [§4.3]

\`{⟨c⟩}

Defined in: LaTeX Kernel.

Grave accent over ⟨c⟩. Example: \`{o} produces ò. [§4.3]

\{

Defined in: LaTeX Kernel.

Left brace { character. In math mode may be used as a delimiter. [§4.3]

\|

Defined in: LaTeX Kernel (Math Mode).

Double vertical bar ‖ delimiter [§9.4]

\}

Defined in: LaTeX Kernel.

Right brace { character. In math mode may be used as a delimiter. [§4.3]

\~{⟨c⟩}

Defined in: LaTeX Kernel.

Tilde accent over ⟨c⟩. Example: \~{o} produces õ. [§4.3]

]

Defined in: LaTeX Kernel.

1) Right square bracket delimiter in math mode [§9.4]; 2) Closing delimiter of an optional argument [§2.8]; 3)

\^

Closing square bracket in text mode [§4.4].

^{⟨maths⟩}

Defined in: LaTeX Kernel (Math Mode).

Displays its argument as a superscript. [§9.4]

_{⟨maths⟩}

Defined in: LaTeX Kernel (Math Mode).

Displays its argument as a subscript. [§9.4]

‘

Defined in: LaTeX Kernel.

Open quote ‘ symbol. See also \textquoteleft. [§4.3]

‘‘

Defined in: LaTeX Kernel.

Open double quote " symbol. See also \textquotedblleft. [§4.3]

{

Defined in: LaTeX Kernel.

Marks the beginning of a group. [§2.7]

|

Defined in: LaTeX Kernel.

1) Vertical rule specifier (tabular or array) [§9.4]; 2) Delimiter. (Math mode only. Use \textbar in text mode.) [§9.4].

}

Defined in: LaTeX Kernel.

Marks the end of a group. [§2.7]

~

Defined in: LaTeX Kernel.

Unbreakable space. [§4.5]

A

\AA

Defined in: LaTeX Kernel.

Upper case A-ring Å character. [§4.3]

\aa

Defined in: LaTeX Kernel.

Lower case a-ring å character. [§4.3]

\begin{abstract}

Defined in: Most article- or report-style classes, such as scrartcl or screprt. Not usually defined in book-style classes, such as scrbook, but is defined in memoir.

Displays its contents as an abstract. [§5.2]

\abstractname

Defined in: Classes or packages that define an abstract environment.

Text used in abstract heading. [§8.2]

\addcontentsline{⟨*toc*⟩}{⟨*section unit*⟩}{⟨*text*⟩}

Defined in: LaTeX Kernel.

Adds a sectional unit header to the contents list. [§5.4]

\addto{⟨*command*⟩}{⟨*code*⟩}

Defined in: babel package.

Adds ⟨*code*⟩ to the definition of ⟨*command*⟩. (See also \appto.) [§8.2]

\addtocounter{⟨*counter*⟩}{⟨*increment*⟩}

Defined in: LaTeX Kernel.

Increments the value of a counter by the given amount. [§11.0]

\addtokomafont{⟨*element name*⟩}{⟨*commands*⟩}

Defined in: scrartcl, screprt and scrbook classes.

Sets the font characteristics for the given KOMA-Script element. [§5.3]

\addtolength{⟨*register*⟩}{⟨*dimension*⟩}

Defined in: LaTeX Kernel.

Adds ⟨*dimension*⟩ to the value of the given length register. [§2.17]

\AE

Defined in: LaTeX Kernel.

Æ ligature. [§4.3]

\ae

Defined in: LaTeX Kernel.

æ ligature. [§4.3]

\begin{align}

Defined in: amsmath package.

Used for numbered aligned equations. [§9.3]

\begin{align*}

Defined in: amsmath package.

Used for unnumbered aligned equations. [§9.3]

\Alph{⟨*counter*⟩}

Defined in: LaTeX Kernel.

Displays counter value as an upper case letter. (A, B, C, ..., Z) [§11.0]

\alph{⟨*counter*⟩}

Defined in: LaTeX Kernel.

Displays counter value as a lower case letter. (a, b, c, ..., z) [§11.0]

\alpha

Defined in: LaTeX Kernel (Math Mode).

Greek lower case alpha α. [§9.4]

\amalg

Defined in: LaTeX Kernel (Math Mode).

Binary operator II symbol. [§9.4]

\and

Defined in: LaTeX Kernel.

Used to separate authors in \author [§5.1]

\appendix

Defined in: Most classes that have the concept of document structure.

Indicates (but doesn't print anything) that the document is switching to the appendices. If chapters exist, the chapter numbering is reset and switched to a different format (usually upper case letters) otherwise the section numbering is reset and switched to a different format. [§5.3]

\appendixname

Defined in: Classes or packages that define chapters.

Number prefix used in appendix headings. [§8.2]

\approx

Defined in: LaTeX Kernel (Math Mode).

Relational $\approx$ symbol. [§9.4]

\appto{⟨command⟩}{⟨code⟩}

Defined in: etoolbox package.

Adds ⟨code⟩ to the definition of ⟨command⟩. [§8.2]

\arabic{⟨counter⟩}

Defined in: LaTeX Kernel.

Displays counter value as an Arabic number. (1, 2, 3, ...) [§11.0]

\arccos

Defined in: LaTeX Kernel (Math Mode).

Typesets arccos function name. [§9.4]

\arcsin

Defined in: LaTeX Kernel (Math Mode).

Typesets arcsin function name. [§9.4]

\arctan

Defined in: LaTeX Kernel (Math Mode).

Typesets arctan function name. [§9.4]

\arg

Defined in: LaTeX Kernel (Math Mode).

Typesets arg function name. [§9.4]

\begin{array}[⟨v-pos⟩]{⟨column specifiers⟩}

Defined in: LaTeX Kernel (Math Mode).

Environment for lining things up in rows and columns. Use tabular for text mode. [§9.4]

\arraycolsep

Defined in: LaTeX Kernel.

Length register specifying half the gap between columns in an array environment. [§9.4]

\ast

Defined in: LaTeX Kernel (Math Mode).

Binary operator $*$ symbol. [§9.4]

\asymp

Defined in: LaTeX Kernel (Math Mode).

Relational $\asymp$ symbol. [§9.4]

\author{⟨name⟩}

Defined in: Most classes that have the concept of a title page.

Specifies the document author (or authors). This command doesn't display any text so may be used in the preamble, but if it's not in the preamble it must be placed before \maketitle. [§5.1]

SUMMARY

B

`\b{⟨c⟩}`

Defined in: LaTeX Kernel.

Bar under ⟨c⟩. Example: `\b{r}` produces r̲. [§4.3]

`\backmatter`

Defined in: Most book-style classes, such as scrbook.

Suppresses chapter and section numbering, but still adds unstarred sectional units to the table of contents. (See also `\frontmatter` and `\mainmatter`.) [§5.7]

`\backslash`

Defined in: LaTeX Kernel (Math Mode).

Backslash \ symbol, which may be used as a delimiter. (Use `\textbackslash` for text mode.) [§9.4]

`\baselineskip`

Defined in: LaTeX Kernel.

A length register that stores the current interline spacing. This is recalculated whenever the font changes. [§10.0]

`\begin{⟨env-name⟩}[⟨env-option⟩]{⟨env-arg-1⟩}...{⟨env-arg-n⟩}`

Defined in: LaTeX Kernel.

Starts an environment. (Must have a matching `\end`.) [§2.15]

`\beta`

Defined in: LaTeX Kernel (Math Mode).

Greek lower case beta β. [§9.4]

`\bfseries`

Defined in: LaTeX Kernel.

Switches to the bold weight in the current font family. [§4.5]

`\begin{bfseries}`

Defined in: LaTeX Kernel.

Typesets the environment contents in a bold font. [§2.15]

`\bibitem[⟨tag⟩]{⟨key⟩}`

Defined in: LaTeX Kernel.

Indicates the start of a new reference in the bibliography. May only be used inside the contents of thebibliography environment [§5.6]

`\bibname`

Defined in: Report or book style classes that define a bibliography chapter.

Text used for bibliography chapter heading. (See also `\refname`.) [§8.2]

`\bigcap`

Defined in: LaTeX Kernel (Math Mode).

Collection intersection ⋂ symbol (may take limits). [§9.4]

`\bigcirc`

Defined in: LaTeX Kernel (Math Mode).

Binary operator ◯ symbol. [§9.4]

`\bigcup`

Defined in: LaTeX Kernel (Math Mode).

Collection union ⋃ symbol (may take limits). [§9.4]

`\Biggl⟨delimiter⟩`

Defined in: amsmath package (Math Mode).

Left delimiter sizing. [§9.4]

`\biggl⟨delimiter⟩`

Defined in: amsmath package (Math Mode).

Left delimiter sizing. [§9.4]

SUMMARY

\biggl

`\Biggr`⟨*delimiter*⟩

Defined in: amsmath package (Math Mode).

Right delimiter sizing. [§9.4]

`\biggr`⟨*delimiter*⟩

Defined in: amsmath package (Math Mode).

Right delimiter sizing. [§9.4]

`\Bigl`⟨*delimiter*⟩

Defined in: amsmath package (Math Mode).

Left delimiter sizing. [§9.4]

`\bigl`⟨*delimiter*⟩

Defined in: amsmath package (Math Mode).

Left delimiter sizing. [§9.4]

`\bigodot`

Defined in: LaTeX Kernel (Math Mode).

Big operator $\odot$ (may take limits). [§9.4]

`\bigoplus`

Defined in: LaTeX Kernel (Math Mode).

Big operator $\oplus$ (may take limits). [§9.4]

`\bigotimes`

Defined in: LaTeX Kernel (Math Mode).

Big operator $\otimes$ (may take limits). [§9.4]

`\Bigr`⟨*delimiter*⟩

Defined in: amsmath package (Math Mode).

Right delimiter sizing. [§9.4]

`\bigr`⟨*delimiter*⟩

Defined in: amsmath package (Math Mode).

Right delimiter sizing. [§9.4]

`\bigsqcup`

Defined in: LaTeX Kernel (Math Mode).

Big operator $\bigsqcup$ (may take limits). [§9.4]

`\bigtriangledown`

Defined in: LaTeX Kernel (Math Mode).

Binary operator $\bigtriangledown$ symbol. [§9.4]

`\bigtriangleup`

Defined in: LaTeX Kernel (Math Mode).

Binary operator $\triangle$ symbol. [§9.4]

`\biguplus`

Defined in: LaTeX Kernel (Math Mode).

Big operator $\biguplus$ (may take limits). [§9.4]

`\bigvee`

Defined in: LaTeX Kernel (Math Mode).

Big operator $\bigvee$ (may take limits). [§9.4]

`\bigwedge`

Defined in: LaTeX Kernel (Math Mode).

Big operator $\bigwedge$ (may take limits). [§9.4]

`\begin{Bmatrix}`

Defined in: amsmath package (Math Mode).

Like the array environment, but doesn't have an argument and adds curly brace delimiters. [§9.4]

`\begin{bmatrix}`

Defined in: amsmath package (Math Mode).

Like the array environment, but doesn't have an argument and adds square bracket delimiters. [§9.4]

`\bmod`

Defined in: LaTeX Kernel (Math Mode).

Modulo operator. [§9.4]

SUMMARY

`\boldsymbol{⟨symbol⟩}`

Defined in: amsmath package (Math Mode).

Like `\mathbf` but also works for numbers and many nonalphabetical symbols. (See also `\pmb`.) [§9.4]

`\bottomrule[⟨wd⟩]`

Defined in: booktabs package.

Horizontal rule for the bottom of a tabular environment. [§4.6]

`\bowtie`

Defined in: LaTeX Kernel (Math Mode).

Relational ⋈ symbol. [§9.4]

`\bullet`

Defined in: LaTeX Kernel (Math Mode).

Binary operator • symbol. [§9.4]

C

`\c{⟨c⟩}`

Defined in: LaTeX Kernel.

Cedilla under ⟨c⟩. Example: `\c{o}` produces ǫ. [§4.3]

`\cap`

Defined in: LaTeX Kernel (Math Mode).

Binary operator ∩ symbol. [§9.4]

`\caption[⟨short caption⟩]{⟨caption text⟩}`

Defined in: LaTeX Kernel.

Inserts the caption for a float such as a figure or table. **This command has a moving argument.** [§7.0]

`\captionsetup[⟨float type⟩]{⟨options⟩}`

Defined in: caption package.

Used to set up the options affecting float captions. [§7.4]

`\begin{cases}`

Defined in: amsmath package (Math Mode).

Like the array environment, but adds a left brace start delimiter and an invisible end delimiter. [§9.4]

`\cdot`

Defined in: LaTeX Kernel (Math Mode).

Centred dot · symbol. [§9.4]

`\cdots`

Defined in: LaTeX Kernel (Math Mode).

Centred ellipses ⋯ symbol. [§9.4]

`\centering`

Defined in: LaTeX Kernel.

Switches the paragraph alignment to centred. [§2.12]

`\cfrac[⟨pos⟩]{⟨numerator⟩}{⟨denominator⟩}`

Defined in: amsmath (Math Mode).

Displays a continued fraction. [§9.4]

`\chapter[⟨short title⟩]{⟨title⟩}`

Defined in: Book-style classes (such as scrbook or scrreprt) that have the concept of chapters.

Inserts a chapter heading. **This command has a moving argument.** [§5.3]

`\chaptername`

Defined in: Classes or packages that define chapters.

Number prefix used in chapter headings. [§8.2]

`\chi`

Defined in: LaTeX Kernel (Math Mode).

Greek lower case chi χ. [§9.4]

SUMMARY

\circ

Defined in: LaTeX Kernel (Math Mode).

Circle ∘ symbol. [§9.4]

\cite[⟨*text*⟩]{⟨*key list*⟩}

Defined in: LaTeX Kernel.

Inserts the citation markers of each reference identified in the key list. A second run is required to ensure the reference is correct. [§5.6]

\color[⟨*model*⟩]{⟨*specs*⟩}

Defined in: color and xcolor packages.

A declaration that switches the current foreground colour to the given specification. [§8.0]

\cong

Defined in: LaTeX Kernel (Math Mode).

Relational ≅ symbol. [§9.4]

\contentsname

Defined in: Classes or packages that define a table of contents.

Text used for table of contents heading. [§8.2]

\coprod

Defined in: LaTeX Kernel (Math Mode).

Co-product ∐ symbol (may take limits). [§9.4]

\copyright

Defined in: LaTeX Kernel.

Copyright © symbol. [§4.3]

\cos

Defined in: LaTeX Kernel (Math Mode).

Typesets cos function name. [§9.4]

\cosh

Defined in: LaTeX Kernel (Math Mode).

Typesets cosh function name. [§9.4]

\cot

Defined in: LaTeX Kernel (Math Mode).

Typesets cot function name. [§9.4]

\coth

Defined in: LaTeX Kernel (Math Mode).

Typesets coth function name. [§9.4]

\csc

Defined in: LaTeX Kernel (Math Mode).

Typesets csc function name. [§9.4]

\cup

Defined in: LaTeX Kernel (Math Mode).

Operator ∪ symbol. [§9.4]

\currenttime

Defined in: datetime package.

Inserts into the output file the time when the LaTeX application created it from the source code. [§4.2]

D

\d{⟨*c*⟩}

Defined in: LaTeX Kernel.

Dot under ⟨*c*⟩. Example: \d{o} produces ọ. [§4.3]

\dag

Defined in: LaTeX Kernel.

Dagger † symbol. [§4.3]

\dagger

Defined in: LaTeX Kernel (Math Mode).

Binary operator † symbol. [§9.4]

\dashv

Defined in: LaTeX Kernel (Math Mode).

Relational ⊣ symbol. [§9.4]

SUMMARY

\date{⟨*text*⟩}

Defined in: Most classes that have the concept of a title page.

Specifies the document date. This command doesn't display any text so may be used in the preamble, but if it's not in the preamble it must be placed before \maketitle. If omitted, most classes assume the current date (as provided by \today). [§5.1]

\ddag

Defined in: LaTeX Kernel.

Double-dagger ‡ symbol. [§4.3]

\ddagger

Defined in: LaTeX Kernel (Math Mode).

Binary operator ‡ symbol. [§9.4]

\ddmmyyyydate

Defined in: datetime package.

Changes the format of \today so that it displays the date in the form 07/10/2012 (day/month/year in digits). [§4.2]

\ddots

Defined in: LaTeX Kernel (Math Mode).

Diagonal ellipses $\ddots$ symbol. [§9.4]

\DeclareCaptionLabelFormat {⟨*name*⟩}{⟨*code*⟩}

Defined in: caption.

Used to defined your own caption label formats. [§7.4]

\DeclareGraphicsExtensions{⟨*ext-list*⟩}

Defined in: graphicx package.

Specify the file extensions to look for if no extension is used in \includegraphics [§6.0]

\DeclareMathOperator{⟨*cmd*⟩} {⟨*operator-name*⟩}

Defined in: amsmath package (Preamble Only).

Defines a new maths operator. The starred version allows limits. [§9.4]

\deg

Defined in: LaTeX Kernel (Math Mode).

Typesets deg function name. [§9.4]

\Delta

Defined in: LaTeX Kernel (Math Mode).

Greek upper case delta Δ. [§9.4]

\delta

Defined in: LaTeX Kernel (Math Mode).

Greek lower case delta δ. [§9.4]

\begin{description}

Defined in: Most class files.

Labelled list. [§4.4]

\det

Defined in: LaTeX Kernel (Math Mode).

Typesets det function name (may have limits via _ or ^). [§9.4]

\diamond

Defined in: LaTeX Kernel (Math Mode).

Binary operator $\diamond$ symbol. [§9.4]

\dim

Defined in: LaTeX Kernel (Math Mode).

Typesets dim function name. [§9.4]

\ding{⟨*n*⟩}

Defined in: pifont package.

Inserts PostScript ZapfDingbats character with code ⟨*n*⟩, which must be an integer. [§8.2]

`\begin{dinglist}{`⟨*number*⟩`}`

Defined in: pifont package.

A list where the item marker is given by character ⟨*number*⟩ in the Zapf Dingbats font. [§8.2]

`\displaybreak[`⟨*n*⟩`]`

Defined in: amsmath package.

Allows a page break in multi-lined maths environments, such as align. [§9.3]

`\div`

Defined in: LaTeX Kernel (Math Mode).

Division operator ÷ symbol. [§9.4]

`\begin{document}`

Defined in: LaTeX Kernel.

The body of the document. [§4.0]

`\documentclass[`⟨*option-list*⟩`]{`⟨*class-name*⟩`}`

Defined in: LaTeX Kernel.

Loads the document class file, which sets up the type of document you wish to write. [§4.0]

`\doteq`

Defined in: LaTeX Kernel (Math Mode).

Relational $\doteq$ symbol. [§9.4]

`\dotsb`

Defined in: amsmath (Math Mode).

Ellipses ⋯ for dots with binary operators/relations. [§9.4]

`\dotsc`

Defined in: amsmath (Math Mode).

Ellipses ... for dots with commas. [§9.4]

`\dotsi`

Defined in: amsmath (Math Mode).

Ellipses ⋯ for dots with integrals. [§9.4]

`\dotsm`

Defined in: amsmath (Math Mode).

Ellipses ⋯ for dots with multiplications. [§9.4]

`\dotso`

Defined in: amsmath (Math Mode).

Ellipses ... for general dots. [§9.4]

`\doublebox{`⟨*text*⟩`}`

Defined in: fancybox package.

Puts a double-lined frame around its contents, prohibiting a line break in the contents. [§4.7]

`\Downarrow`

Defined in: LaTeX Kernel (Math Mode).

Double-lined down arrow ⇓. (May be used as a delimiter.) [§9.4]

`\downarrow`

Defined in: LaTeX Kernel (Math Mode).

Down arrow ↓. (May be used as a delimiter.) [§9.4]

E

`\em`

Defined in: LaTeX Kernel.

Toggles the upright and italic/slanted form of the current font family. [§4.5]

`\begin{em}`

Defined in: LaTeX Kernel.

Typesets the environment contents in an emphasized font. (Switches to italic/slanted if the surrounding font is upright, or switches to upright if the surrounding font is italic/slanted.) [§4.5]

`\emph{`⟨*text*⟩`}`

Defined in: LaTeX Kernel.

Toggles the upright and italic/slanted rendering of ⟨*text*⟩. [§4.5]

\end{⟨*env-name*⟩}

Defined in: LATEX Kernel.

Ends an environment. (Must have a matching \begin.) [§2.15]

\enspace

Defined in: LATEX Kernel.

Horizontal spacing command (half as wide as \quad). [§2.13]

\begin{enumerate}

Defined in: LATEX Kernel.

Ordered list. [§4.4]

\epsilon

Defined in: LATEX Kernel (Math Mode).

Greek lower case epsilon ϵ. [§9.4]

\eqref{⟨*label*⟩}

Defined in: amsmath package.

Short cut for (\ref{⟨*label*⟩}) for referencing equations. [§9.2]

\begin{equation}

Defined in: LATEX Kernel.

Displays its contents as a single-lined numbered equation. [§9.2]

\equiv

Defined in: LATEX Kernel (Math Mode).

Relational $\equiv$ symbol. [§9.4]

\eta

Defined in: LATEX Kernel (Math Mode).

Greek lower case eta η. [§9.4]

\exp

Defined in: LATEX Kernel (Math Mode).

Typesets exp function name. [§9.4]

F

\familydefault

Defined in: LATEX Kernel.

Specifies the default font family. Defaults to \rmdefault but may be redefined by certain classes. [§8.2]

\fbox{⟨*text*⟩}

Defined in: LATEX Kernel.

Puts a frame around its contents, prohibiting a line break in the contents. [§4.7]

\begin{figure}[⟨*placement*⟩]

Defined in: Most classes that define sectioning commands.

Floats the contents to the nearest location according to the preferred placement options, if possible. Within the environment, \caption may be used one or more times, as required. The caption will usually include the prefix given by \figurename. [§7.1]

\figurename

Defined in: Classes or packages that define figures.

Number prefix used in figure captions. [§8.2]

\fnsymbol{⟨*counter*⟩}

Defined in: LATEX Kernel.

Displays counter value as footnote symbol. (∗ † ‡ § ¶ ‖ ∗∗ †† ‡‡) [§11.0]

\footnote[⟨*number*⟩]{⟨*text*⟩}

Defined in: LATEX Kernel.

Inserts a footnote. [§4.1]

\footnotesize

Defined in: Most document classes.

Switches to footnote sized text. [§4.5]

\footnotesize

\forall

Defined in: LaTeX Kernel (Math Mode).

"For all" ∀ symbol. [§9.4]

\foreignlanguage{⟨*language name*⟩}{⟨*text*⟩}

Defined in: babel package.

Typesets the given text using any predefined names or date formats supplied by the given language. [§5.8]

\frac{⟨*numerator*⟩}{⟨*denominator*⟩}

Defined in: LaTeX Kernel (Math Mode).

Displays a fraction. [§9.4]

\framebox[⟨*width*⟩][⟨*align*⟩]{⟨*text*⟩}

Defined in: LaTeX Kernel.

Puts a frame around its contents, prohibiting a line break in the contents. [§4.7]

\frenchspacing

Defined in: LaTeX Kernel.

Switch to French spacing. [§2.13]

\frontmatter

Defined in: Most book-style classes, such as scrbook.

Switches to lower case Roman numeral page numbering. Also suppresses chapter and section numbering, but still adds unstarred sectional units to the table of contents. (See also \mainmatter and \backmatter.) [§5.7]

\frown

Defined in: LaTeX Kernel (Math Mode).

Relational ⌢ symbol. [§9.4]

G

\Gamma

Defined in: LaTeX Kernel (Math Mode).

Greek upper case gamma Γ. [§9.4]

\gamma

Defined in: LaTeX Kernel (Math Mode).

Greek lower case gamma γ. [§9.4]

\gcd

Defined in: LaTeX Kernel (Math Mode).

Typesets gcd function name (may have limits via _ or ^). [§9.4]

\ge

Defined in: LaTeX Kernel (Math Mode).

Relational ≥ symbol. [§9.4]

\geq

Defined in: LaTeX Kernel (Math Mode).

Relational ≥ symbol. [§9.4]

\gets

Defined in: LaTeX Kernel (Math Mode).

Left arrow ←. [§9.4]

\gg

Defined in: LaTeX Kernel (Math Mode).

Relational ≫ symbol. [§9.4]

H

\H{⟨*c*⟩}

Defined in: LaTeX Kernel.

Double acute diacritic over ⟨*c*⟩. Example: \H{o} produces ő. [§4.3]

\heavyrulewidth

Defined in: booktabs package.

Length register specifying the thickness of \toprule and \bottomrule. [§4.6]

\hom

Defined in: LaTeX Kernel (Math Mode).

Typesets hom function name. [§9.4]

`\hookleftarrow`

Defined in: LaTeX Kernel (Math Mode).

Hooked left arrow ↩. [§9.4]

`\hookrightarrow`

Defined in: LaTeX Kernel (Math Mode).

Hooked right arrow ↪. [§9.4]

`\hspace{⟨length⟩}`

Defined in: LaTeX Kernel.

Inserts a horizontal gap of the given width. [§4.6]

`\Huge`

Defined in: Most document classes.

Switches to extra-huge sized text. [§4.5]

`\huge`

Defined in: Most document classes.

Switches to huge sized text. [§4.5]

`\hyphenation{⟨word⟩}`

Defined in: LaTeX Kernel.

Specifies hyphenation points. [§2.14]

I

`\i`

Defined in: LaTeX Kernel.

Dotless i character: ı. [§4.3]

`\iflanguage{⟨language name⟩}{⟨true text⟩}{⟨false text⟩}`

Defined in: babel package.

Tests the current language. [§5.8]

`\ignorespaces`

Defined in: LaTeX Kernel.

Used in begin environment code to suppress any spaces occurring at the start of the environment (see also `\ignorespacesafterend`). [§10.0]

`\ignorespacesafterend`

Defined in: LaTeX Kernel.

Used in end environment code to suppress any spaces following the end of the environment. [§10.0]

`\in`

Defined in: LaTeX Kernel (Math Mode).

Relational ∈ symbol. [§9.4]

`\includegraphics[⟨key vals⟩]{⟨filename⟩}`

Defined in: graphicx package.

Inserts a graphics file into the document. [§6.0]

`\index{⟨text⟩}`

Defined in: LaTeX Kernel.

Adds indexing information to an external index file. The command `\makeindex` must be used in the preamble to enable this command. The external index file must be post-processed with an indexing application, such as `makeindex`. [§8.0]

`\indexname`

Defined in: Classes or packages that define an index section.

Text used for index heading. [§8.2]

`\inf`

Defined in: LaTeX Kernel (Math Mode).

Typesets inf function name (may have limits via _ or ^). [§9.4]

`\infty`

Defined in: LaTeX Kernel (Math Mode).

Infinity ∞ symbol. [§9.4]

`\injlim`

Defined in: amsmath (Math Mode).

Typesets inj lim function name (may have limits via _ or ^). [§9.4]

\int

Defined in: LATEX Kernel (Math Mode).

Integral ∫ symbol (may take limits). [§9.4]

\intertext{⟨*text*⟩}

Defined in: amsmath package (Math Mode).

Used for a short interjection in the middle of a multi-line displayed maths, such as in an align environment. May only appear right after \\. [§9.3]

\iota

Defined in: LATEX Kernel (Math Mode).

Greek lower case iota ι. [§9.4]

\item[⟨*marker*⟩]

Defined in: LATEX Kernel.

Specifies the start of an item in a list. (Only allowed inside one of the list making environments.) [§4.4]

\begin{itemize}

Defined in: LATEX Kernel.

Unordered list. [§4.4]

\begin{itshape}

Defined in: LATEX Kernel.

Typesets the environment contents in an italic font. [§4.5]

\itshape

Defined in: LATEX Kernel.

Switches to the italic form of the current font family, if it exists. [§4.5]

J

\j

Defined in: LATEX Kernel.

Dotless j character: ȷ. [§4.3]

K

\kappa

Defined in: LATEX Kernel (Math Mode).

Greek lower case kappa κ. [§9.4]

\ker

Defined in: LATEX Kernel (Math Mode).

Typesets ker function name. [§9.4]

L

\L

Defined in: LATEX Kernel.

Upper case L-bar Ł character. [§4.3]

\l

Defined in: LATEX Kernel.

Lower case l-bar ł character. [§4.3]

\label{⟨*string*⟩}

Defined in: LATEX Kernel.

Assigns a unique textual label linked to the most recently incremented cross-referencing counter in the current scope (see also \ref). [§5.5]

\labelformat{⟨*ctr*⟩}{⟨*defn*⟩}

Defined in: fncylab package.

Defines how the label for the counter ⟨*ctr*⟩ should be formatted. The definition ⟨*defn*⟩ should use #1 to indicate the label value. [§7.4]

\labelitemi

Defined in: Classes that define the itemize environment.

The default label for the first level itemize. [§8.2]

\labelitemii

Defined in: Classes that define the itemize environment.

The default label for the second level itemize. [§8.2]

\labelitemiii

Defined in: Classes that define the itemize environment.

The default label for the third level itemize. [§8.2]

\labelitemiv

Defined in: Classes that define the itemize environment.

The default label for the fourth level itemize. [§8.2]

\Lambda

Defined in: LaTeX Kernel (Math Mode).

Greek upper case lambda Λ. [§9.4]

\lambda

Defined in: LaTeX Kernel (Math Mode).

Greek lower case lambda λ. [§9.4]

\langle

Defined in: LaTeX Kernel (Math Mode).

Left-angled $\langle$ delimiter. [§9.4]

\LARGE

Defined in: Most document classes.

Switches to extra-extra-large sized text. [§4.5]

\Large

Defined in: Most document classes.

Switches to extra-large sized text. [§4.5]

\large

Defined in: Most document classes.

Switches to large sized text. [§4.5]

\LaTeX

Defined in: LaTeX Kernel.

Typesets the LaTeX logo. [§2.6]

\LaTeXe

Defined in: LaTeX Kernel.

Typesets the LaTeX 2_ε logo. [§5.6]

\lceil

Defined in: LaTeX Kernel (Math Mode).

Left ceil $\lceil$ delimiter. [§9.4]

\ldots

Defined in: LaTeX Kernel.

Ellipses ... symbol. [§4.3]

\le

Defined in: LaTeX Kernel (Math Mode).

Relational $\leq$ symbol. [§9.4].

\left⟨*delimiter*⟩

Defined in: LaTeX Kernel (Math Mode).

Indicates a left stretchable delimiter. Must have a matching \right. [§9.4]

\Leftarrow

Defined in: LaTeX Kernel (Math Mode).

Double-lined left arrow $\Leftarrow$. [§9.4]

\leftarrow

Defined in: LaTeX Kernel (Math Mode).

Left arrow $\leftarrow$. [§9.4]

\leftharpoondown

Defined in: LaTeX Kernel (Math Mode).

Left down harpoon $\leftharpoondown$. [§9.4]

\leftharpoonup

Defined in: LaTeX Kernel (Math Mode).

Left up harpoon $\leftharpoonup$. [§9.4]

\Leftrightarrow

Defined in: LaTeX Kernel (Math Mode).

\Leftrightarrow

Double-ended double-lined horizontal arrow ⇔. [§9.4]

\leftrightarrow

Defined in: LaTeX Kernel (Math Mode).

Double-ended horizontal arrow ↔. [§9.4]

\leq

Defined in: LaTeX Kernel (Math Mode).

Relational ≤ symbol. [§9.4]

\lfloor

Defined in: LaTeX Kernel (Math Mode).

Left floor ⌊ delimiter. [§9.4]

\lg

Defined in: LaTeX Kernel (Math Mode).

Typesets lg function name. [§9.4]

\lightrulewidth

Defined in: booktabs package.

Length register specifying the thickness of \midrule. [§4.6]

\lim

Defined in: LaTeX Kernel (Math Mode).

Typesets lim function name (may have limits via _ or ^). [§9.4]

\liminf

Defined in: LaTeX Kernel (Math Mode).

Typesets lim inf function name (may have limits via _ or ^). [§9.4]

\limsup

Defined in: LaTeX Kernel (Math Mode).

Typesets lim sup function name (may have limits via _ or ^). [§9.4]

\linebreak[⟨n⟩]

Defined in: LaTeX Kernel.

Requests a line break, ensuring the paragraph remains justified. This may cause excess white space in the paragraph. [§B.29]

\linewidth

Defined in: LaTeX Kernel.

A length containing the desired current line width. This is usually the width of the typeblock, but inside a minipage or \parbox it will be the width the box. Note that the actual contents of the line may fall short of the line width (underfull hbox) or extend beyond it (overfull hbox). [§4.7]

\listfigurename

Defined in: Classes or packages that define a list of figures.

Text used for list of figures heading. [§8.2]

\listoffigures

Defined in: Most classes that have the concept of document structure.

Inserts the list of figures. A second (possibly third) run is required to ensure the page numbering is correct. [§7.1]

\listoftables

Defined in: Most classes that have the concept of document structure.

Inserts the list of tables. A second (possibly third) run is required to ensure the page numbering is correct. [§7.2]

\listtablename

Defined in: Classes or packages that define a list of tables.

Text used for list of tables heading. [§8.2]

\leftrightarrow

\ll

Defined in: LaTeX Kernel (Math Mode).

Relational ≪ symbol. [§9.4]

\ln

Defined in: LaTeX Kernel (Math Mode).

Typesets ln function name. [§9.4]

\log

Defined in: LaTeX Kernel (Math Mode).

Typesets log function name. [§9.4]

\Longleftarrow

Defined in: LaTeX Kernel (Math Mode).

Long double-lined left arrow ⟸. [§9.4]

\longleftarrow

Defined in: LaTeX Kernel (Math Mode).

Long left arrow ⟵. [§9.4]

\Longleftrightarrow

Defined in: LaTeX Kernel (Math Mode).

Long double-lined double-ended horizontal arrow ⟺. [§9.4]

\longleftrightarrow

Defined in: LaTeX Kernel (Math Mode).

Long double-ended horizontal arrow ⟷. [§9.4]

\longmapsto

Defined in: LaTeX Kernel (Math Mode).

Long mapping arrow ⟼. [§9.4]

\Longrightarrow

Defined in: LaTeX Kernel (Math Mode).

Long double-lined right arrow ⟹. [§9.4]

\longrightarrow

Defined in: LaTeX Kernel (Math Mode).

Long right arrow ⟶. [§9.4]

\lVert

Defined in: amsmath (Math Mode).

Left double vertical bar ‖ delimiter. [§9.4]

\lvert

Defined in: amsmath (Math Mode).

Left vertical bar | delimiter. [§9.4]

M

\mainmatter

Defined in: Most book-style classes, such as scrbook.

Switches to Arabic page numbering and enables chapter and section numbering. (See also \frontmatter and \backmatter.) [§5.7]

\makeindex

Defined in: LaTeX Kernel (Preamble Only).

Enables \index. [§8.0]

\maketitle

Defined in: Most classes that have the concept of a title page.

Generates the title page (or title block). This command is usually placed at the beginning of the document environment. [§5.1]

\mapsto

Defined in: LaTeX Kernel (Math Mode).

Mapping arrow ↦. [§9.4]

\markboth{⟨*left head*⟩}{⟨*right head*⟩}

Defined in: LaTeX Kernel.

Specifies information for the left and right page headers. Not all page styles use this information, in which case the arguments are ignored. [§5.7]

\markright{⟨*right head*⟩}

Defined in: LaTeX Kernel.

Specifies information for the right (odd) page header. Not all page styles use this information, in which case the argument is ignored. [§5.7]

\begin{math}

Defined in: LaTeX Kernel.

Sets its contents in in-line math mode. [§9.1]

\mathbb{⟨*maths*⟩}

Defined in: amsfonts package (Math Mode).

Typesets its argument in the blackboard bold font. Example: \(\mathbb{R}\) produces ℝ. [§9.4]

\mathbf{⟨*maths*⟩}

Defined in: LaTeX Kernel (Math Mode).

Renders ⟨*maths*⟩ in the predefined maths bold font. (Doesn't work with numbers and nonalphabetical symbols.) See also \boldsymbol. [§9.4]

\mathcal{⟨*maths*⟩}

Defined in: LaTeX Kernel (Math Mode).

Typesets its argument in the maths calligraphic font. Example: \(\mathcal{S}\) produces 𝒮. [§9.4]

\mathfrak{⟨*maths*⟩}

Defined in: amsfonts package (Math Mode).

Typesets its argument in Euler Fraktur letters. Example: \(\mathfrak{U}\) produces 𝔘. [§9.4]

\mathit{⟨*maths*⟩}

Defined in: LaTeX Kernel (Math Mode).

Renders ⟨*maths*⟩ in the predefined maths italic font. [§9.4]

\mathrm{⟨*maths*⟩}

Defined in: LaTeX Kernel (Math Mode).

Renders ⟨*maths*⟩ in the predefined maths serif font. [§9.4]

\mathsf{⟨*maths*⟩}

Defined in: LaTeX Kernel (Math Mode).

Renders ⟨*maths*⟩ in the predefined maths sans-serif font. [§9.4]

\mathtt{⟨*maths*⟩}

Defined in: LaTeX Kernel (Math Mode).

Renders ⟨*maths*⟩ in the predefined maths typewriter font. [§9.4]

\begin{matrix}

Defined in: amsmath package (Math Mode).

Like the array environment, but doesn't have an argument. [§9.4]

\max

Defined in: LaTeX Kernel (Math Mode).

Typesets max function name (may have limits via _ or ^). [§9.4]

\mbox{⟨*text*⟩}

Defined in: LaTeX Kernel.

Ensures that the given text doesn't contain a line break. [§4.7]

\mdseries

Defined in: LaTeX Kernel.

Switches to the medium weight in the current font family. [§4.5]

\medspace

Defined in: amsmath package.

Medium space. [§9.4]

\mid

Defined in: LaTeX Kernel (Math Mode).

Relational | symbol. [§9.4]

\midrule[⟨*wd*⟩]

Defined in: booktabs package.

Horizontal rule to go below headings row of a tabular environment. [§4.6]

\min

Defined in: LATEX Kernel (Math Mode).

Typesets min function name (may have limits via _ or ^). [§9.4]

\begin{minipage}[⟨*pos*⟩][⟨*height*⟩] {⟨*width*⟩}

Defined in: LATEX Kernel.

Makes a box with line-wrapped contents. (See also \parbox.) [§4.7]

\minisec{⟨*heading*⟩}

Defined in: scrartcl, scrreprt and scrbook classes.

An unnumbered heading not associated with any structuring level. [§5.3]

\mod{⟨*maths*⟩}

Defined in: amsmath (Math Mode).

Modulo operator without parentheses. [§9.4]

\models

Defined in: LATEX Kernel (Math Mode).

Relational |= symbol. [§9.4]

\mp

Defined in: LATEX Kernel (Math Mode).

Minus or plus operator ∓ symbol. [§9.4]

\mu

Defined in: LATEX Kernel (Math Mode).

Greek lower case mu μ. [§9.4]

\multicolumn{⟨*cols spanned*⟩}{⟨*col specifier*⟩}{⟨*text*⟩}

Defined in: LATEX Kernel.

Spans multiple columns in a tabular-style environment. [§4.6]

N

\nearrow

Defined in: LATEX Kernel (Math Mode).

North-East arrow ↗. [§9.4]

\negmedspace

Defined in: amsmath package.

Negative medium space. [§9.4]

\negthickspace

Defined in: amsmath package.

Negative thick space. [§9.4]

\negthinspace

Defined in: LATEX Kernel.

Negative thin space. [§9.4]

\neq

Defined in: LATEX Kernel (Math Mode).

Relational ≠ symbol. [§9.4]

\newcommand{⟨*cmd*⟩}[⟨*n-args*⟩] [⟨*default*⟩]{⟨*text*⟩}

Defined in: LATEX Kernel.

Defines a new command. [§8.0]

\newcounter{⟨*counter*⟩}[⟨*outer counter*⟩]

Defined in: LATEX Kernel.

Defines a new counter. [§11.0]

\newenvironment{⟨*env-name*⟩}[⟨*n-args*⟩][⟨*default*⟩]{⟨*begin-code*⟩}{⟨*end-code*⟩}

Defined in: LATEX Kernel.

Defines a new environment. [§10.0]

\newline

Defined in: LaTeX Kernel.

Forces a line break. [§B.29]

\ni

Defined in: LaTeX Kernel (Math Mode).

Relational $\ni$ symbol. [§9.4]

\noindent

Defined in: LaTeX Kernel.

Suppress the indentation that would usually occur at the start of the next paragraph. [§10.0]

\nonfrenchspacing

Defined in: LaTeX Kernel.

Switch to English spacing. [§2.13]

\normalfont

Defined in: LaTeX Kernel.

Switches to the default font style. [§4.5]

\normalsize

Defined in: LaTeX Kernel.

Switches to normal sized text. [§4.5]

\not⟨*symbol command*⟩

Defined in: LaTeX Kernel (Math Mode).

Negates the following symbol. Example: \not\subset produces $\not\subset$. [§9.4]

\notag

Defined in: amsmath package.

Suppresses equation numbering for the current row in environments such as align. [§9.3]

\notin

Defined in: LaTeX Kernel (Math Mode).

Relational $\notin$ symbol. [§9.4]

\nu

Defined in: LaTeX Kernel (Math Mode).

Greek lower case nu ν. [§9.4]

\nwarrow

Defined in: LaTeX Kernel (Math Mode).

North-West arrow $\nwarrow$. [§9.4]

O

\O

Defined in: LaTeX Kernel.

Upper case slashed-O Ø character. [§4.3]

\o

Defined in: LaTeX Kernel.

Lower case slashed-o ø character. [§4.3]

\odot

Defined in: LaTeX Kernel (Math Mode).

Operator $\odot$ symbol. [§9.4]

\OE

Defined in: LaTeX Kernel.

Œ ligature. [§4.3]

\oe

Defined in: LaTeX Kernel.

œ ligature. [§4.3]

\oint

Defined in: LaTeX Kernel (Math Mode).

Closed path integral $\oint$ symbol (may take limits). [§9.4]

\Omega

Defined in: LaTeX Kernel (Math Mode).

Greek upper case omega Ω. [§9.4]

\omega

Defined in: LaTeX Kernel (Math Mode).

SUMMARY

Greek lower case omega ω. [§9.4]

`\ominus`

Defined in: LaTeX Kernel (Math Mode).

Operator $\ominus$ symbol. [§9.4]

`\oplus`

Defined in: LaTeX Kernel (Math Mode).

Operator $\oplus$ symbol. [§9.4]

`\oslash`

Defined in: LaTeX Kernel (Math Mode).

Operator $\oslash$ symbol. [§9.4]

`\begin{otherlanguage}{⟨language name⟩}`

Defined in: babel package.

Within the environment contents, predefined textual elements, such as the date given by `\today` or prefixes like "Chapter", are set to those supplied by the given language. [§5.8]

`\otimes`

Defined in: LaTeX Kernel (Math Mode).

Operator $\otimes$ symbol. [§9.4]

`\Ovalbox{⟨text⟩}`

Defined in: fancybox package.

Puts a thick-lined oval frame around its contents, prohibiting a line break in the contents. [§4.7]

`\ovalbox{⟨text⟩}`

Defined in: fancybox package.

Puts a thin-lined oval frame around its contents, prohibiting a line break in the contents. [§4.7]

`\overleftarrow{⟨maths⟩}`

Defined in: LaTeX Kernel (Math Mode).

Puts an extendible left arrow over ⟨*maths*⟩ [§9.4]

`\overleftrightarrow{⟨maths⟩}`

Defined in: amsmath package (Math Mode).

Puts an extendible left-right arrow over ⟨*maths*⟩ [§9.4]

`\overrightarrow{⟨maths⟩}`

Defined in: LaTeX Kernel (Math Mode).

Puts an extendible right arrow over ⟨*maths*⟩ [§9.4]

P

`\P`

Defined in: LaTeX Kernel.

Paragraph ¶ symbol. [§4.3]

`\pagenumbering{⟨style⟩}`

Defined in: LaTeX Kernel.

Sets the style of the page numbers. [§5.7]

`\pageref{⟨string⟩}`

Defined in: LaTeX Kernel.

Similar to `\ref` but inserts the page number where the given label was defined. A second (possibly third) run of LaTeX is required to ensure the cross-references are up-to-date. [§5.5]

`\pagestyle{⟨style⟩}`

Defined in: LaTeX Kernel.

Sets the style of the headers and footers. [§5.7]

`\par`

Defined in: LaTeX Kernel.

Insert a paragraph break. [§4.0]

`\paragraph[⟨short title⟩]{⟨title⟩}`

Defined in: Most classes that have the concept of document structure.

Inserts a subsubsubsection header. Most classes default to an unnumbered running header for this sectional unit. **This command has a moving argument.** [§5.3]

`\parallel`

Defined in: LaTeX Kernel (Math Mode).

Relational ∥ symbol. [§9.4]

`\parbox[⟨pos⟩][⟨height⟩]{⟨width⟩}{⟨text⟩}`

Defined in: LaTeX Kernel.

Makes a box with line-wrapped contents. (More restrictive than minipage.) [§4.7]

`\parindent`

Defined in: LaTeX Kernel.

A length register that stores the indentation at the start of paragraphs. [§2.17]

`\parskip`

Defined in: LaTeX Kernel.

A length register that stores the spacing between paragraphs. (If you're using one of the KOMA-Script classes, use the `parskip` option to set it to full or half line height.) [§2.17]

`\part[⟨short title⟩]{⟨title⟩}`

Defined in: Most classes that have the concept of document structure.

Inserts a part sectional unit. **This command has a moving argument.** [§5.3]

`\partial`

Defined in: LaTeX Kernel (Math Mode).

Partial ∂ symbol. [§9.4]

`\partname`

Defined in: Classes or packages that define parts with a number prefix.

Number prefix used in part headings. [§8.2]

`\perp`

Defined in: LaTeX Kernel (Math Mode).

Relational ⊥ symbol. [§9.4]

`\Phi`

Defined in: LaTeX Kernel (Math Mode).

Greek upper case phi Φ. [§9.4]

`\phi`

Defined in: LaTeX Kernel (Math Mode).

Greek lower case phi φ. [§9.4]

`\Pi`

Defined in: LaTeX Kernel (Math Mode).

Greek upper case pi Π. [§9.4]

`\pi`

Defined in: LaTeX Kernel (Math Mode).

Greek lower case pi π. [§9.4]

`\pm`

Defined in: LaTeX Kernel (Math Mode).

Operator ± symbol. [§9.4]

`\begin{pmatrix}`

Defined in: amsmath package (Math Mode).

Like the array environment, but doesn't have an argument and adds round bracket delimiters. [§9.4]

`\pmb{⟨symbol⟩}`

Defined in: amsmath package (Math Mode).

"Poor man's bold." Overlays multiple copies of the symbol to produce a bold effect for symbols that don't work with \boldsymbol. [§9.4]

\pmod{⟨*maths*⟩}

Defined in: LaTeX Kernel (Math Mode).

Modulo operator with parentheses. [§9.4]

\pod{⟨*maths*⟩}

Defined in: amsmath (Math Mode).

Modulo operator with parentheses but no "mod". [§9.4]

\pounds

Defined in: LaTeX Kernel.

Pound £ symbol. [§4.3]

\Pr

Defined in: LaTeX Kernel (Math Mode).

Typesets Pr function name (may have limits via _ or ^). [§9.4]

\prec

Defined in: LaTeX Kernel (Math Mode).

Relational ≺ symbol. [§9.4]

\preceq

Defined in: LaTeX Kernel (Math Mode).

Relational ⪯ symbol. [§9.4]

\printindex

Defined in: makeidx package.

Prints the index. Must be used with \makeindex and \index. (The external index file must first be processed by an indexing application.) [§8.0]

\prod

Defined in: LaTeX Kernel (Math Mode).

Product ∏ symbol (may take limits). [§9.4]

\projlim

Defined in: amsmath (Math Mode).

Typesets proj lim function name (may have limits via _ or ^). [§9.4]

\propto

Defined in: LaTeX Kernel (Math Mode).

Relational ∝ symbol. [§9.4]

\protect⟨*command*⟩

Defined in: LaTeX Kernel.

Used in a moving argument to prevent a fragile command from expanding. [§2.9]

\Psi

Defined in: LaTeX Kernel (Math Mode).

Greek upper case psi Ψ. [§9.4]

\psi

Defined in: LaTeX Kernel (Math Mode).

Greek lower case psi ψ. [§9.4]

\publishers{⟨*text*⟩}

Defined in: scrartcl, scrreprt, scrbook classes.

Specifies the publisher (typeset after all the other titling information). [§5.1]

Q

\qquad

Defined in: LaTeX Kernel.

Horizontal spacing command (twice as wide as \quad). [§9.4]

\quad

Defined in: LaTeX Kernel.

Horizontal spacing command equal to the current font's em value. [§9.4]

R

\r{⟨*c*⟩}

Defined in: LaTeX Kernel.

Ring over ⟨*c*⟩. Example: \r{u} produces ů. [§4.3]

\raggedleft

Defined in: LaTeX Kernel.

Ragged-left paragraph justification. [§2.12]

\raggedright

Defined in: LaTeX Kernel.

Ragged-right paragraph justification. [§2.12]

\rangle

Defined in: LaTeX Kernel (Math Mode).

Right-angled ⟩ delimiter. [§9.4]

\rceil

Defined in: LaTeX Kernel (Math Mode).

Right ceil ⌉ delimiter. [§9.4]

\ref{⟨*string*⟩}

Defined in: LaTeX Kernel.

References the value of the counter linked to the given label. A second (possibly third) run of LaTeX is required to ensure the cross-references are up-to-date. [§5.5]

\reflectbox{⟨*text*⟩}

Defined in: graphicx package.

Reflects the specified contents in the *y*-axis.) [§6.1]

\refname

Defined in: Article style classes that define a bibliography section.

Text used for bibliography section heading. (See also \bibname.) [§8.2]

\refstepcounter{⟨*counter*⟩}

Defined in: LaTeX Kernel.

Increments the value of the given counter by one and allows the counter to be cross-referenced using \ref and \label. [§11.0]

\renewcommand{⟨*cmd*⟩}[⟨*n-args*⟩] [⟨*default*⟩]{⟨*text*⟩}

Defined in: LaTeX Kernel.

Redefines an existing command. [§8.2]

\renewenvironment{⟨*env-name*⟩}[⟨*n-args*⟩][⟨*default*⟩]{⟨*begin-code*⟩}{end-code}

Defined in: LaTeX Kernel.

Redefines an existing environment. [§10.1]

\resizebox{⟨*h length*⟩}{⟨*v length*⟩}{⟨*text*⟩}

Defined in: graphicx package.

Scales the specified contents to the given dimensions. [§6.1]

\rfloor

Defined in: LaTeX Kernel (Math Mode).

Right floor ⌋ delimiter. [§9.4]

\rho

Defined in: LaTeX Kernel (Math Mode).

Greek lower case rho ρ. [§9.4]

\right⟨*delimiter*⟩

Defined in: LaTeX Kernel (Math Mode).

Indicates a right stretchable delimiter. Must have a matching \left. [§9.4]

\Rightarrow

Defined in: LaTeX Kernel (Math Mode).

Double-lined right arrow $\Rightarrow$. [§9.4]

\rightarrow

Defined in: LaTeX Kernel (Math Mode).

Right arrow →. [§9.4]

\rightharpoondown

Defined in: LaTeX Kernel (Math Mode).

Right down harpoon ⇁. [§9.4]

\rightharpoonup

Defined in: LaTeX Kernel (Math Mode).

Right up harpoon ⇀. [§9.4]

\rightleftharpoons

Defined in: LaTeX Kernel (Math Mode).

Right-left harpoons ⇌. [§9.4]

\rmdefault

Defined in: LaTeX Kernel.

The name of the default serif family as used by \rmfamily. Defaults to cmr (Computer Modern Roman). [§8.2]

\rmfamily

Defined in: LaTeX Kernel.

Switches to the predefined serif font. (Defaults to Computer Modern Roman.) [§4.5]

\Roman{⟨counter⟩}

Defined in: LaTeX Kernel.

Displays counter value as an upper case Roman number. (I, II, III, ...) [§11.0]

\roman{⟨counter⟩}

Defined in: LaTeX Kernel.

Displays counter value as a lower case Roman number. (i, ii, iii, ...) [§11.0]

\rotatebox[⟨option list⟩]{⟨angle⟩}{⟨text⟩}

Defined in: graphicx package.

Rotates the given contents by the given angle. [§6.1]

\rVert

Defined in: amsmath (Math Mode).

Right double vertical bar ‖ delimiter. [§9.4]

\rvert

Defined in: amsmath (Math Mode).

Right vertical bar | delimiter. [§9.4]

S

\S

Defined in: LaTeX Kernel.

Sectional § symbol. [§4.3]

\sb{⟨maths⟩}

Defined in: LaTeX Kernel (Math Mode).

Displays its argument as a subscript. [§9.4]

\scalebox{⟨h scale⟩}[⟨v scale⟩]{⟨text⟩}

Defined in: graphicx package.

Scales the specified contents. [§6.1]

\scriptsize

Defined in: Most document classes.

Switches to sub- or superscript sized text. [§4.5]

\scshape

Defined in: LaTeX Kernel.

Switches to the small-caps form of the current font family, if it exists. [§4.5]

\searrow

Defined in: LaTeX Kernel (Math Mode).

South-East arrow ↘. [§9.4]

\sec

Defined in: LaTeX Kernel (Math Mode).

Typesets sec function name. [§9.4]

`\section[⟨short title⟩]{⟨title⟩}`

Defined in: Most classes that have the concept of document structure.

Inserts a section header. **This command has a moving argument.** [§5.3]

`\selectlanguage{⟨language name⟩}`

Defined in: babel package.

Switches to the named language. Predefined textual elements, such as the date given by \today or prefixes like "Chapter", are redefined to those supplied by the given language. [§5.8]

`\setcounter{⟨counter⟩}{⟨number⟩}`

Defined in: LaTeX Kernel.

Sets the value of a counter. [§11.0]

`\setlength{⟨register⟩}{⟨dimension⟩}`

Defined in: LaTeX Kernel.

Sets the value of a length register. [§2.17]

`\setminus`

Defined in: LaTeX Kernel (Math Mode).

Operator \ symbol. [§9.4]

`\sfdefault`

Defined in: LaTeX Kernel.

The name of the default sans-serif family as used by \sffamily. Defaults to cmss (Computer Modern Sans-serif). [§8.2]

`\sffamily`

Defined in: LaTeX Kernel.

Switches to the predefined sans-serif font. (Defaults to Computer Modern Sans.) [§4.5]

`\shadowbox{⟨text⟩}`

Defined in: fancybox package.

Puts a shadow frame around its contents, prohibiting a line break in the contents. [§4.7]

`\begin{sidewaysfigure}`

Defined in: rotating package.

Like the figure environment but rotates the entire figure (including caption) sideways. [§7.3]

`\begin{sidewaystable}`

Defined in: rotating package.

Like the table environment but rotates the entire table (including caption) sideways. [§7.3]

`\Sigma`

Defined in: LaTeX Kernel (Math Mode).

Greek upper case sigma Σ. [§9.4]

`\sigma`

Defined in: LaTeX Kernel (Math Mode).

Greek lower case sigma σ. [§9.4]

`\sim`

Defined in: LaTeX Kernel (Math Mode).

Relational $\sim$ symbol. [§9.4]

`\simeq`

Defined in: LaTeX Kernel (Math Mode).

Relational $\simeq$ symbol. [§9.4]

`\sin`

Defined in: LaTeX Kernel (Math Mode).

Typesets sin function name. [§9.4]

`\sinh`

Defined in: LaTeX Kernel (Math Mode).

Typesets sinh function name. [§9.4]

`\slash`

Defined in: LaTeX Kernel.

Forward slash / symbol. [§4.3]

`\slshape`

Defined in: LaTeX Kernel.

Switches to the slanted form of the current font family, if it exists. [§4.5]

`\small`

Defined in: Most document classes.

Switches to small sized text. [§4.5]

`\begin{smallmatrix}`

Defined in: amsmath package (Math Mode).

Like the array environment but doesn't have an argument and is designed for in-line maths. [§9.4]

`\smile`

Defined in: LaTeX Kernel (Math Mode).

Relational $\smile$ symbol. [§9.4]

`\sp{`⟨*maths*⟩`}`

Defined in: LaTeX Kernel (Math Mode).

Displays its argument as a superscript. [§9.4]

`\sqcap`

Defined in: LaTeX Kernel (Math Mode).

Operator $\sqcap$ symbol. [§9.4]

`\sqcup`

Defined in: LaTeX Kernel (Math Mode).

Operator $\sqcup$ symbol. [§9.4]

`\sqrt[`⟨*order*⟩`]{`⟨*operand*⟩`}`

Defined in: LaTeX Kernel (Math Mode).

Displays a root. [§9.4]

`\sqsubseteq`

Defined in: LaTeX Kernel (Math Mode).

Relational $\sqsubseteq$ symbol. [§9.4]

`\sqsupseteq`

Defined in: LaTeX Kernel (Math Mode).

Relational $\sqsupseteq$ symbol. [§9.4]

`\SS`

Defined in: LaTeX Kernel.

SS (upper case ß). [§4.3]

`\ss`

Defined in: LaTeX Kernel.

Eszett ß character. [§4.3]

`\star`

Defined in: LaTeX Kernel (Math Mode).

Operator $\star$ symbol. [§9.4]

`\stepcounter{`⟨*counter*⟩`}`

Defined in: LaTeX Kernel.

Increments the value of the given counter by one. [§11.0]

`\begin{subfigure}[`⟨*pos*⟩`]{`⟨*width*⟩`}`

Defined in: subcaption package.

Used to form a subfigure within a figure environment. The `\caption` command may be used in this environment to produce a subcaption. [§7.4]

`\subject{`⟨*text*⟩`}`

Defined in: scrartcl, scrreprt, scrbook classes.

Specifies the subject (typeset just above the title). [§5.1]

`\subparagraph[`⟨*short title*⟩`]{`⟨*title*⟩`}`

Defined in: Most classes that have the concept of document structure.

Inserts a subsubsubsection header. Most classes default to an unnumbered running header for this sectional unit. **This command has a moving argument.** [§5.3]

\subref{⟨*label*⟩}

Defined in: subcaption package.

Analogous to \ref but only references the subfigure or subtable caption. [§7.4]

\subsection[⟨*short title*⟩]{⟨*title*⟩}

Defined in: Most classes that have the concept of document structure.

Inserts a subsection header. **This command has a moving argument.** [§5.3]

\subset

Defined in: LaTeX Kernel (Math Mode).

Subset $\subset$ symbol. [§9.4]

\subseteq

Defined in: LaTeX Kernel (Math Mode).

Relational $\subseteq$ symbol. [§9.4]

\substack{⟨*maths*⟩}

Defined in: amsmath package.

Can be used to produce a multiline subscript or superscript. Lines are separated using \\. [§9.4]

\subsubsection[⟨*short title*⟩]{⟨*title*⟩}

Defined in: Most classes that have the concept of document structure.

Inserts a subsubsection header. **This command has a moving argument.** [§5.3]

\begin{subtable}[⟨*pos*⟩]{⟨*width*⟩}

Defined in: subcaption package.

Used to form a subtable within a table environment. The \caption command may be used in this environment to produce a subcaption. [§7.4]

\subtitle{⟨*text*⟩}

Defined in: scrartcl, scrreprt, scrbook classes.

Specifies the subtitle (typeset just below the title). [§5.1]

\succ

Defined in: LaTeX Kernel (Math Mode).

Relational $\succ$ symbol. [§9.4]

\succeq

Defined in: LaTeX Kernel (Math Mode).

Relational $\succeq$ symbol. [§9.4]

\sum

Defined in: LaTeX Kernel (Math Mode).

Summation $\sum$ symbol (may take limits). [§9.4]

\sup

Defined in: LaTeX Kernel (Math Mode).

Typesets sup function name (may have limits via _ or ^). [§9.4]

\supset

Defined in: LaTeX Kernel (Math Mode).

Relational $\supset$ symbol. [§9.4]

\supseteq

Defined in: LaTeX Kernel (Math Mode).

Relational $\supseteq$ symbol. [§9.4]

\swarrow

Defined in: LaTeX Kernel (Math Mode).

South-West arrow $\swarrow$. [§9.4]

T

\t{⟨*characters*⟩}

Defined in: LaTeX Kernel.

Tie over ⟨*characters*⟩. Example: \t{xy} produces $\widetilde{xy}$. [§4.3]

\tabcolsep

Defined in: LaTeX Kernel.

Length register specifying half the gap between columns in a tabular environment. [§4.6]

\begin{table}[⟨*placement*⟩]

Defined in: Most classes that define sectioning commands.

Floats the contents to the nearest location according to the preferred placement options, if possible. Within the environment, \caption may be used one or more times, as required. The caption will usually include the prefix given by \tablename. [§7.2]

\tablename

Defined in: Classes or packages that define tables.

Number prefix used in table captions. [§8.2]

\tableofcontents

Defined in: Most classes that have the concept of document structure.

Inserts the table of contents. A second (possibly third) run is required to ensure the page numbering is correct. [§5.4]

\begin{tabular}[⟨*v-pos*⟩]{⟨*column specifiers*⟩}

Defined in: LaTeX Kernel (Text Mode).

Environment for lining things up in rows and columns. Use array for math mode. [§4.6]

\tabularnewline

Defined in: LaTeX Kernel.

Behaves like \\ in a tabular-like environment but helps to disambiguate a line break in a paragraph cell from a row separator. [§4.6]

\tag{⟨*tag*⟩}

Defined in: amsmath package.

Overrides equation numbering for the current row in environments such as align. [§9.3]

\tan

Defined in: LaTeX Kernel (Math Mode).

Typesets tan function name. [§9.4]

\tanh

Defined in: LaTeX Kernel (Math Mode).

Typesets tanh function name. [§9.4]

\tau

Defined in: LaTeX Kernel (Math Mode).

Greek lower case tau τ. [§9.4]

\TeX

Defined in: LaTeX Kernel.

Typesets the TeX logo. [§2.6]

\text{⟨*text*⟩}

Defined in: amsmath package (Math Mode).

Displays its argument in the normal text font (as opposed to the current maths font). [§9.2]

\textasciicircum

Defined in: LaTeX Kernel.

Circumflex ^ symbol. [§4.3]

\textasciitilde

Defined in: LaTeX Kernel.

Tilde ~ symbol. (If you are typing an URL, use the url package, which provides \url{⟨*address*⟩} that allows you to directly type ~ in the address.) [§4.3]

\textbackslash

Defined in: LaTeX Kernel (Text Mode).

Backlash \ symbol. (Use \backslash for math mode.) [§4.3]

\textbar

Defined in: LaTeX Kernel.

Vertical bar | symbol. [§4.3]

\textbf{⟨*text*⟩}

Defined in: LaTeX Kernel.

Renders ⟨*text*⟩ with a bold weight in the current font family, if it exists. [§4.5]

\textbullet

Defined in: LaTeX Kernel (Text Mode).

Bullet • symbol. [§4.3]

\textcolor[⟨*model*⟩]{⟨*specs*⟩}{⟨*text*⟩}

Defined in: color and xcolor packages.

Sets ⟨*text*⟩ with the foreground colour according to the given ⟨*specs*⟩. [§8.0]

\textemdash

Defined in: LaTeX Kernel.

Em-dash — symbol. (Normally used to indicate omissions or interruptions or to highlight a parenthetical element.) See also ---. [§4.3]

\textendash

Defined in: LaTeX Kernel.

En-dash – symbol. (Normally used for number ranges.) See also --. [§4.3]

\textexclamdown

Defined in: LaTeX Kernel.

Upside-down exclamation mark ¡ symbol. [§4.3]

\textgreater

Defined in: LaTeX Kernel (Text Mode).

Greater than > symbol. (Just use > in math mode.) [§4.3]

\textheight

Defined in: LaTeX Kernel.

A length containing the height of the typeblock. Note that the actual contents of the page may fall short of the text height (underfull vbox) or extend beyond it (overfull vbox). This measurement does not include the header and footer areas. [§6.0]

\textit{⟨*text*⟩}

Defined in: LaTeX Kernel.

Renders ⟨*text*⟩ with the italic form of the current font family, if it exists. [§4.5]

\textless

Defined in: LaTeX Kernel (Text Mode).

Less than < symbol. (Just use < in math mode.) [§4.3]

\textmd{⟨*text*⟩}

Defined in: LaTeX Kernel.

Renders ⟨*text*⟩ with a medium weight in the current font family. [§4.5]

\textnormal{⟨*text*⟩}

Defined in: LaTeX Kernel.

Renders ⟨*text*⟩ in the default font style. [§4.5]

\textperiodcentered

Defined in: LaTeX Kernel (Text Mode).

Centred period · symbol. [§4.3]

\textquestiondown

Defined in: LaTeX Kernel.

Upside-down question mark ¿ symbol. [§4.3]

\textquotedblleft

Defined in: LaTeX Kernel.

Opening double quote " symbol. [§4.3]

SUMMARY

\textbar

`\textquotedblright`

Defined in: LaTeX Kernel.

Closing double quote " symbol. [§4.3]

`\textquoteleft`

Defined in: LaTeX Kernel.

Opening single quote ' symbol. [§4.3]

`\textquoteright`

Defined in: LaTeX Kernel.

Closing single quote (or apostrophe) ' symbol. [§4.3]

`\textregistered`

Defined in: LaTeX Kernel.

Registered ® symbol. [§4.3]

`\textrm{⟨text⟩}`

Defined in: LaTeX Kernel.

Renders ⟨text⟩ in the predefined serif font. (Defaults to Computer Modern Roman.) [§4.5]

`\textsc{⟨text⟩}`

Defined in: LaTeX Kernel.

Renders ⟨text⟩ with the small-caps form of the current font family, if it exists. [§4.5]

`\textsf{⟨text⟩}`

Defined in: LaTeX Kernel.

Renders ⟨text⟩ in the predefined sans-serif font. (Defaults to Computer Modern Sans.) [§4.5]

`\textsl{⟨text⟩}`

Defined in: LaTeX Kernel.

Renders ⟨text⟩ with the slanted form of the current font family, if it exists. [§4.5]

`\texttrademark`

Defined in: LaTeX Kernel.

Trademark ™ symbol. [§4.3]

`\texttt{⟨text⟩}`

Defined in: LaTeX Kernel.

Renders ⟨text⟩ in the predefined monospaced font. (Defaults to Computer Modern Typewriter.) [§4.5]

`\textunderscore`

Defined in: LaTeX Kernel.

Underscore _ symbol (see also `\textunderscore`). [§4.3]

`\textup{⟨text⟩}`

Defined in: LaTeX Kernel.

Renders ⟨text⟩ with the upright form of the current font family. [§4.5]

`\textwidth`

Defined in: LaTeX Kernel.

A length containing the width of the typeblock. Note that the actual contents of the line may fall short of the line width (underfull hbox) or extend beyond it (overfull hbox). This width does not include the area for marginal notes. [§2.17]

`\thanks{⟨text⟩}`

Defined in: Most classes that have the concept of a title page.

Inserts a special type of footnote in one of the titling fields, such as `\author` or `\title`. Usually used for some form of acknowledgement or affiliation. [§5.1]

`\the⟨register⟩`

Defined in: LaTeX Kernel.

Displays the value of the given register (such as a length register). Not to be confused with `\the⟨ctr⟩` commands, such as `\thefigure`. [§2.17]

`\the`

`\begin{thebibliography}{`*⟨widest entry label⟩*`}`

Defined in: Most classes that define sectioning commands.

Bibliographic list. (See also \bibitem and \cite). [§5.6]

`\thechapter`

Defined in: LaTeX Kernel.

Displays the current value of the chapter counter [§11.0]

`\thefigure`

Defined in: LaTeX Kernel.

Displays the current value of the figure counter [§11.0]

`\thefootnote`

Defined in: LaTeX Kernel.

Displays the current value of the footnote counter [§11.0]

`\thepage`

Defined in: LaTeX Kernel.

Displays the current value of the page counter [§11.0]

`\thesection`

Defined in: LaTeX Kernel.

Displays the current value of the section counter [§11.0]

`\Theta`

Defined in: LaTeX Kernel (Math Mode).

Greek upper case theta Θ. [§9.4]

`\theta`

Defined in: LaTeX Kernel (Math Mode).

Greek lower case theta θ. [§9.4]

`\thickspace`

Defined in: amsmath package.

Thick space. [§9.4]

`\thinspace`

Defined in: LaTeX Kernel.

Thin space. [§9.4]

`\thispagestyle{`*⟨style⟩*`}`

Defined in: LaTeX Kernel.

Like \pagestyle but only affects the current page. [§5.7]

`\times`

Defined in: LaTeX Kernel (Math Mode).

Operator $\times$ symbol. [§9.4]

`\tiny`

Defined in: Most document classes.

Switches to tiny sized text. [§4.5]

`\title{`*⟨text⟩*`}`

Defined in: Most classes that have the concept of a title page.

Specifies the document title. This command doesn't display any text so may be used in the preamble, but if it's not in the preamble it must be placed before \maketitle. [§5.1]

`\titlehead{`*⟨text⟩*`}`

Defined in: scrartcl, scrreprt, scrbook classes.

Specifies the title header (typeset at the top of the title page). [§5.1]

`\to`

Defined in: LaTeX Kernel (Math Mode).

Right arrow $\to$. [§9.4]

`\today`

Defined in: Most of the commonly-used classes.

Inserts into the output file the date when the LaTeX application created it from the source code. [§4.1]

`\toprule[⟨wd⟩]`

Defined in: booktabs package.

Horizontal rule for the top of a tabular environment. [§4.6]

`\triangleleft`

Defined in: LaTeX Kernel (Math Mode).

Binary operator ◁ symbol. [§9.4]

`\triangleright`

Defined in: LaTeX Kernel (Math Mode).

Binary operator ▷ symbol. [§9.4]

`\ttdefault`

Defined in: LaTeX Kernel.

The name of the default typewriter family as used by `\ttfamily`. Defaults to cmtt (Computer Modern Typewriter). [§8.2]

`\ttfamily`

Defined in: LaTeX Kernel.

Switches to the predefined monospaced font. (Defaults to Computer Modern Typewriter.) [§4.5]

U

`\u{⟨c⟩}`

Defined in: LaTeX Kernel.

Breve diacritic over ⟨c⟩. Example: `\u{o}` produces ŏ. [§4.3]

`\underleftarrow{⟨maths⟩}`

Defined in: amsmath package (Math Mode).

Puts an extendible left arrow under ⟨maths⟩ [§9.4]

`\underleftrightarrow{⟨maths⟩}`

Defined in: amsmath package (Math Mode).

Puts an extendible left-right arrow under ⟨maths⟩ [§9.4]

`\underrightarrow{⟨maths⟩}`

Defined in: amsmath package (Math Mode).

Puts an extendible right arrow under ⟨maths⟩ [§9.4]

`\Uparrow`

Defined in: LaTeX Kernel (Math Mode).

Double-lined up arrow ⇑. (May be used as a delimiter.) [§9.4]

`\uparrow`

Defined in: LaTeX Kernel (Math Mode).

Up arrow ↑. (May be used as a delimiter.) [§9.4]

`\Updownarrow`

Defined in: LaTeX Kernel (Math Mode).

Double-ended double-lined vertical arrow ⇕. (May be used as a delimiter.) [§9.4]

`\updownarrow`

Defined in: LaTeX Kernel (Math Mode).

Double-ended vertical arrow ↕. (May be used as a delimiter.) [§9.4]

`\uplus`

Defined in: LaTeX Kernel (Math Mode).

Operator ⊎ symbol. [§9.4]

`\upshape`

Defined in: LaTeX Kernel.

Switches to the upright form of the current font family. [§4.5]

`\Upsilon`

Defined in: LaTeX Kernel (Math Mode).

Greek upper case upsilon Υ. [§9.4]

`\upsilon`

Defined in: LaTeX Kernel (Math Mode).

Greek lower case upsilon υ. [§9.4]

`\url{⟨address⟩}`

Defined in: url package.

Typesets an URL in a typewriter font and allows you to use characters such as ~. [§4.5]

`\usepackage[⟨option-list⟩]{⟨package-list⟩}`

Defined in: LaTeX Kernel.

Loads the named packages. [§4.2]

V

`\v{⟨c⟩}`

Defined in: LaTeX Kernel.

Caron diacritic over ⟨c⟩. Example: `\v{o}` produces ǒ. [§4.3]

`\value{⟨counter⟩}`

Defined in: LaTeX Kernel.

References the value of the given counter where a number rather than a counter name is required. [§11.0]

`\varepsilon`

Defined in: LaTeX Kernel (Math Mode).

Variant Greek lower case alpha ε. [§9.4]

`\varinjlim`

Defined in: amsmath (Math Mode).

Typesets $\varinjlim$ function name (may have limits via _ or ^). [§9.4]

`\varliminf`

Defined in: amsmath (Math Mode).

Typesets $\varliminf$ function name (may have limits via _ or ^). [§9.4]

`\varlimsup`

Defined in: amsmath (Math Mode).

Typesets $\varlimsup$ function name (may have limits via _ or ^). [§9.4]

`\varphi`

Defined in: LaTeX Kernel (Math Mode).

Variant Greek lower case phi φ. [§9.4]

`\varpi`

Defined in: LaTeX Kernel (Math Mode).

Variant Greek lower case pi ϖ. [§9.4]

`\varprojlim`

Defined in: amsmath (Math Mode).

Typesets $\varprojlim$ function name (may have limits via _ or ^). [§9.4]

`\varrho`

Defined in: LaTeX Kernel (Math Mode).

Variant Greek lower case rho ϱ. [§9.4]

`\varsigma`

Defined in: LaTeX Kernel (Math Mode).

Variant Greek lower case sigma ς. [§9.4]

`\vartheta`

Defined in: LaTeX Kernel (Math Mode).

A variant Greek lower case theta ϑ. [§9.4]

`\vdash`

Defined in: LaTeX Kernel (Math Mode).

Relational $\vdash$ symbol. [§9.4]

`\vdots`

Defined in: LaTeX Kernel (Math Mode).

Vertical ellipses $\vdots$ symbol. [§9.4]

\vec{⟨c⟩}

Defined in: LaTeX Kernel (Math Mode).

Typesets its argument as a vector (defaults to a right arrow accent). [§9.4]

\vee

Defined in: LaTeX Kernel (Math Mode).

Operator ∨ symbol. [§9.4]

\begin{Vmatrix}

Defined in: amsmath package (Math Mode).

Like the array environment, but doesn't have an argument and adds double vertical bar delimiters. [§9.4]

\begin{vmatrix}

Defined in: amsmath package (Math Mode).

Like the array environment, but doesn't have an argument and adds single vertical bar delimiters. [§9.4]

\vref{⟨string⟩}

Defined in: varioref package.

Like \ref but also adds information about the location, such as "on page ⟨n⟩" or "on the following page". [§5.5]

\vspace{⟨length⟩}

Defined in: LaTeX Kernel.

Inserts a vertical gap of the given height. [§11.0]

W

\wedge

Defined in: LaTeX Kernel (Math Mode).

Operator ∧ symbol. [§9.4]

\wr

Defined in: LaTeX Kernel (Math Mode).

Operator ≀ symbol. [§9.4]

X

\Xi

Defined in: LaTeX Kernel (Math Mode).

Greek upper case xi Ξ. [§9.4]

\xi

Defined in: LaTeX Kernel (Math Mode).

Greek lower case xi ξ. [§9.4]

\xleftarrow[⟨subscript⟩] {⟨superscript⟩}

Defined in: amsmath package (Math Mode).

An extendible left arrow with a superscript and optionally a subscript. [§9.4]

\xrightarrow[⟨subscript⟩] {⟨superscript⟩}

Defined in: amsmath package (Math Mode).

An extendible right arrow with a superscript and optionally a subscript. [§9.4]

Z

\zeta

Defined in: LaTeX Kernel (Math Mode).

Greek lower case zeta ζ. [§9.4]

SUMMARY

Page numbers in *italic* indicate the primary reference. Page numbers in **bold** indicate the entry definition in the summary.

INDEX

INDEX

INDEX

INDEX

INDEX

\scalebox

INDEX

GNU Free Documentation License

Version 1.2, November 2002
Copyright © 2000,2001,2002 Free Software Foundation, Inc.

51 Franklin St, Fifth Floor, Boston, MA 02110-1301 USA

Everyone is permitted to copy and distribute verbatim copies of this license document, but changing it is not allowed.

Preamble

The purpose of this License is to make a manual, textbook, or other functional and useful document "free" in the sense of freedom: to assure everyone the effective freedom to copy and redistribute it, with or without modifying it, either commercially or noncommercially. Secondarily, this License preserves for the author and publisher a way to get credit for their work, while not being considered responsible for modifications made by others.

This License is a kind of "copyleft", which means that derivative works of the document must themselves be free in the same sense. It complements the GNU General Public License, which is a copyleft license designed for free software.

We have designed this License in order to use it for manuals for free software, because free software needs free documentation: a free program should come with manuals providing the same freedoms that the software does. But this License is not limited to software manuals; it can be used for any textual work, regardless of subject matter or whether it is published as a printed book. We recommend this License principally for works whose purpose is instruction or reference.

1. APPLICABILITY AND DEFINITIONS

This License applies to any manual or other work, in any medium, that contains a notice placed by the copyright holder saying it can be distributed under the terms of this License. Such a notice grants a world-wide, royalty-free license, unlimited in duration, to use that work under the conditions stated herein. The "**Document**", below, refers to any such manual or work. Any member of the public is a licensee, and is addressed as "**you**". You accept the license if you copy, modify or distribute the work in a way requiring permission under copyright law.

A "**Modified Version**" of the Document means any work containing the Document or a portion of it, either copied verbatim, or with modifications and/or translated into another language.

A "**Secondary Section**" is a named appendix or a front-matter section of the Document that deals exclusively with the relationship of the publishers or authors of the Document to the Document's overall subject (or to related matters) and contains nothing that could fall directly within that overall subject. (Thus, if the Document is in part a textbook of mathematics, a Secondary Section may not explain any mathematics.) The relationship could be a matter of historical connection with the subject or with related matters, or of legal, commercial, philosophical, ethical or political position regarding them.

The "**Invariant Sections**" are certain Secondary Sections whose titles are designated, as being those of Invariant Sections, in the notice that says that the Document is released under this License. If a section does not fit the above definition of Secondary then it is not allowed to be designated as Invariant. The Document may contain zero Invariant Sections. If the Document does not identify any Invariant Sections then there are none.

The "**Cover Texts**" are certain short passages of text that are listed, as Front-Cover Texts or Back-Cover Texts, in the notice that says that the Document is released under this License. A Front-Cover Text may be at most 5 words, and a Back-Cover Text may be at most 25 words.

A "**Transparent**" copy of the Document means a machine-readable copy, represented in a format whose specification is available to the general public, that is suitable for revising the document straightforwardly with generic text editors or (for images composed of pixels) generic paint programs or (for drawings) some widely available drawing editor, and that is suitable for input to text formatters or for automatic translation to a variety of formats suitable for input to text formatters. A copy made in an otherwise Transparent file format whose markup, or absence of markup, has been arranged to thwart or discourage subsequent modification by readers is not Transparent. An image format is not Transparent if used for any substantial amount of text. A copy that is not "Transparent" is called "**Opaque**".

Examples of suitable formats for Transparent copies include plain ASCII without markup, Texinfo input format, LaTeX input format, SGML or XML using a publicly available DTD, and standard-conforming simple HTML, PostScript or PDF designed for human modification. Examples of transparent image formats include PNG, XCF and JPG. Opaque formats include proprietary formats that can be read and edited only by proprietary word processors, SGML or XML for which the DTD and/or processing tools are not generally available, and the machine-generated HTML, PostScript or PDF produced by some word processors for output purposes only.

The "**Title Page**" means, for a printed book, the title page itself, plus such following pages as are needed to hold, legibly, the material this License requires to appear in the title page. For works in formats which do not have any title page as such, "Title Page" means the text near the most prominent appearance of the work's title, preceding the beginning of the body of the text.

A section "**Entitled XYZ**" means a named subunit of the Document whose title either is precisely XYZ or contains XYZ in parentheses following text that translates XYZ in another language. (Here XYZ stands for a specific section name mentioned below, such as "**Acknowledgements**", "**Dedications**", "**Endorsements**", or "**History**".) To "**Preserve the Title**" of such a section when you modify the Document means that it remains a section "Entitled XYZ" according to this definition.

The Document may include Warranty Disclaimers next to the notice which states that this License applies to the Document. These Warranty Disclaimers are considered to be included by reference in this License, but only as regards disclaiming warranties: any other implication that these Warranty Disclaimers may have is void and has no effect on the meaning of this License.

2. VERBATIM COPYING

You may copy and distribute the Document in any medium, either commercially or noncommercially, provided that this License, the copyright notices, and the license notice saying this License applies to the Document are reproduced in all copies, and that you add no other conditions whatsoever to those of this License. You may not use technical measures to obstruct or control the reading or further copying of the copies you make or distribute. However, you may accept compensation in exchange for copies. If you distribute a large enough number of copies you must also follow the conditions in section 3.

You may also lend copies, under the same conditions stated above, and you may publicly display copies.

3. COPYING IN QUANTITY

If you publish printed copies (or copies in media that commonly have printed covers) of the Document, numbering more than 100, and the Document's license notice requires Cover Texts, you must enclose the copies in covers that carry, clearly and legibly, all these Cover Texts: Front-Cover Texts on the front cover, and Back-Cover Texts on the back cover. Both covers must also clearly and legibly identify you as the publisher of these copies. The front cover must present the full title with all words of the title equally prominent and visible. You may add other material on the covers in addition. Copying with changes limited to the covers, as long as they preserve the title of the Document and satisfy these conditions, can be treated as verbatim copying in other respects.

If the required texts for either cover are too voluminous to fit legibly, you should put the first ones listed (as many as fit reasonably) on the actual cover, and continue the rest onto adjacent pages.

If you publish or distribute Opaque copies of the Document numbering more than 100, you must either include a machine-readable Transparent copy along with each Opaque copy, or state in or with each Opaque copy a computer-network location from which the general network-using public has access to download using public-standard network protocols a complete Transparent copy of the Document, free of added material. If you use the latter option, you must take reasonably prudent steps, when you begin distribution of Opaque copies in quantity, to ensure that this Transparent copy will remain thus accessible at the stated location until at least one year after the last time you distribute an Opaque copy (directly or through your agents or retailers) of that edition to the public.

It is requested, but not required, that you contact the authors of the Document well before redistributing any large number of copies, to give them a chance to provide you with an updated version of the Document.

4. MODIFICATIONS

You may copy and distribute a Modified Version of the Document under the conditions of sections 2 and 3 above, provided that you release the Modified Version under precisely this License, with the Modified Version filling the role of the Document, thus licensing distribution and modification of the Modified Version to whoever possesses a copy of it. In addition, you must do these things in the Modified Version:

A. Use in the Title Page (and on the covers, if any) a title distinct from that of the Document, and from those of previous versions (which should, if there were any, be listed in the History section of the Document). You may use the same title as a previous version if the original publisher of that version gives permission.

B. List on the Title Page, as authors, one or more persons or entities responsible for authorship of the modifications in the Modified Version, together with at least five of the principal authors of the Document (all of its principal authors, if it has fewer than five), unless they release you from this requirement.

C. State on the Title page the name of the publisher of the Modified Version, as the publisher.

D. Preserve all the copyright notices of the Document.

E. Add an appropriate copyright notice for your modifications adjacent to the other copyright notices.

F. Include, immediately after the copyright notices, a license notice giving the public permission to use the Modified Version under the terms of this License, in the form shown in the Addendum below.

G. Preserve in that license notice the full lists of Invariant Sections and required Cover Texts given in the Document's license notice.

H. Include an unaltered copy of this License.

I. Preserve the section Entitled "History", Preserve its Title, and add to it an item stating at least the title, year, new authors, and publisher of the Modified Version as given on the Title Page. If there is no section Entitled "History" in the Document, create one stating the title, year, authors, and publisher of the Document as given on its Title Page, then add an item describing the Modified Version as stated in the previous sentence.

J. Preserve the network location, if any, given in the Document for public access to a Transparent copy of the Document, and likewise the network locations given in the Document for previous versions it was based on. These may be placed in the "History" section. You may omit a network location for a work that was published at least four years before the Document itself, or if the original publisher of the version it refers to gives permission.

K. For any section Entitled "Acknowledgements" or "Dedications", Preserve the Title of the section, and preserve in the section all the substance and tone of each of the contributor acknowledgements and/or dedications given therein.

L. Preserve all the Invariant Sections of the Document, unaltered in their text and in their titles. Section numbers or the equivalent are not considered part of the section titles.

M. Delete any section Entitled "Endorsements". Such a section may not be included in the Modified Version.

N. Do not retitle any existing section to be Entitled "Endorsements" or to conflict in title with any Invariant Section.

O. Preserve any Warranty Disclaimers.

If the Modified Version includes new front-matter sections or appendices that qualify as Secondary Sections and contain no material copied from the Document, you may at your option designate some or all of these sections as invariant. To do this, add their titles to the list of Invariant Sections in the Modified Version's license notice. These titles must be distinct from any other section titles.

You may add a section Entitled "Endorsements", provided it contains nothing but endorsements of your Modified Version by various parties–for example, statements of peer review or that the text has been approved by an organization as the authoritative definition of a standard.

You may add a passage of up to five words as a Front-Cover Text, and a passage of up to 25 words as a Back-Cover Text, to the end of the list of Cover Texts in the Modified Version. Only one passage of Front-Cover Text and one of Back-Cover Text may be added by (or through arrangements made by) any one entity. If the Document already includes a cover text for the same cover, previously added by you or by arrangement made by the same entity you are acting on behalf of, you may not add another; but you may replace the old one, on explicit permission from the previous publisher that added the old one.

The author(s) and publisher(s) of the Document do not by this License give permission to use their names for publicity for or to assert or imply endorsement of any Modified Version.

5. COMBINING DOCUMENTS

You may combine the Document with other documents released under this License, under the terms defined in section 4 above for modified versions, provided that you include in the combination all of the Invariant Sections of all of the original documents, unmodified, and list them all as Invariant Sections of your combined work in its license notice, and that you preserve all their Warranty Disclaimers.

The combined work need only contain one copy of this License, and multiple identical Invariant Sections may be replaced with a single copy. If there are multiple Invariant Sections with the same name but different contents, make the title of each such section unique by adding at the end of it, in parentheses, the name of the original author or publisher of that section if known, or else a unique number. Make the same adjustment to the section titles in the list of Invariant Sections in the license notice of the combined work.

In the combination, you must combine any sections Entitled "History" in the various original documents, forming one section Entitled "History"; likewise combine any sections Entitled "Acknowledgements", and any sections Entitled "Dedications". You must delete all sections Entitled "Endorsements".

6. COLLECTIONS OF DOCUMENTS

You may make a collection consisting of the Document and other documents released under this License, and replace the individual copies of this License in the various documents with a single copy that is included in the collection, provided that you follow the rules of this License for verbatim copying of each of the documents in all other respects.

You may extract a single document from such a collection, and distribute it individually under this License, provided you insert a copy of this License into the extracted document, and follow this License in all other respects regarding verbatim copying of that document.

7. AGGREGATION WITH INDEPENDENT WORKS

A compilation of the Document or its derivatives with other separate and independent documents or works, in or on a volume of a storage or distribution medium, is called an "aggregate" if the copyright resulting from the compilation is not used to limit the legal rights of the compilation's users beyond what the individual works permit. When the Document is included in an aggregate, this License does not apply to the other works in the aggregate which are not themselves derivative works of the Document.

If the Cover Text requirement of section 3 is applicable to these copies of the Document, then if the Document is less than one half of the entire aggregate, the Document's Cover Texts may be placed on covers that bracket the Document within the aggregate, or the electronic equivalent of covers if the Document is in electronic form. Otherwise they must appear on printed covers that bracket the whole aggregate.

8. TRANSLATION

Translation is considered a kind of modification, so you may distribute translations of the Document under the terms of section 4. Replacing Invariant Sections with translations requires special permission from their copyright holders, but you may include translations of some or all Invariant Sections in addition to the original versions of these Invariant Sections. You may include a translation of this License, and all the license notices in the Document, and any Warranty Disclaimers, provided that you also include the original English version of this License and the original versions of those notices and disclaimers. In case of a disagreement between the translation and the original version of this License or a notice or disclaimer, the original version will prevail.

If a section in the Document is Entitled "Acknowledgements", "Dedications", or "History", the requirement (section 4) to Preserve its Title (section 1) will typically require changing the actual title.

9. TERMINATION

You may not copy, modify, sublicense, or distribute the Document except as expressly provided for under this License. Any other attempt to copy, modify, sublicense or distribute the Document is void, and will automatically terminate your rights under this License. However, parties who have received copies, or rights, from you under this License will not have their licenses terminated so long as such parties remain in full compliance.

10. FUTURE REVISIONS OF THIS LICENSE

The Free Software Foundation may publish new, revised versions of the GNU Free Documentation License from time to time. Such new versions will be similar in spirit to the present version, but may differ in detail to address new problems or concerns. See http://www.gnu.org/copyleft/.

Each version of the License is given a distinguishing version number. If the Document specifies that a particular numbered version of this License "or any later version" applies to it, you have the option of following the terms and conditions either of that specified version or of any later version that has been published (not as a draft) by the Free Software Foundation. If the Document does not specify a version number of this License, you may choose any version ever published (not as a draft) by the Free Software Foundation.

ADDENDUM: How to use this License for your documents

To use this License in a document you have written, include a copy of the License in the document and put the following copyright and license notices just after the title page:

> Copyright © YEAR YOUR NAME. Permission is granted to copy, distribute and/or modify this document under the terms of the GNU Free Documentation License, Version 1.2 or any later version published by the Free Software Foundation; with no Invariant Sections, no Front-Cover Texts, and no Back-Cover Texts. A copy of the license is included in the section entitled "GNU Free Documentation License".

If you have Invariant Sections, Front-Cover Texts and Back-Cover Texts, replace the "with ... Texts." line with this:

> with the Invariant Sections being LIST THEIR TITLES, with the Front-Cover Texts being LIST, and with the Back-Cover Texts being LIST.

If you have Invariant Sections without Cover Texts, or some other combination of the three, merge those two alternatives to suit the situation.

If your document contains nontrivial examples of program code, we recommend releasing these examples in parallel under your choice of free software license, such as the GNU General Public License, to permit their use in free software.

HISTORY

25th Sept 2012 (Version 1.4)

- Paperback edition 1 produced.

- Added TeXWorks section.

- Moved "Text editor and Terminal approach", "TeXnicCenter" and "WinEdt" sections to new supplementary material.

- Added hardcopy-related code.

- Change to KOMA-Script classes (both for examples and for pdf versions of this document).

- Changed from using subfloat to subcaption package.

- Added section on inter-sentence spacing.

- Moved "Errors" and "Where to get Help?" to appendices.

- Moved section "Downloading and Installing Packages" to new appendix chapter.

- Moved introduction to packages to "Creating a Simple Document".

- Moved datetime section to "Creating a Simple Document" chapter. (Removed reference to ukdate package.)

- Moved babel section to "Structuring Your Document" chapter.

- Moved graphicx section to its own chapter.

- Added section on align.

- Added \cfrac, \substack and amsmath ellipses to maths chapter.

- Added extensible arrows and \bigl etc to maths chapter.

- Added booktabs.

- Moved lengths chapter to section in definitions.

- Added summary chapter with commands hyperlinked to their definitions in the summary.

- Changed definitions chapter to use a glossary structure.

- Moved bibliography into bib file.

- Added varioref.

- Removed dependency on html package (for pdf versions) to avoid conflict between html and varioref (html package functions not defined by hyperref now emulated; comment package loaded to provide htmlonly environment).

- Removed image of equation written in Word (Microsoft have improved their equation rendering) and added link to Murray Sargent III blog [12].

- Added section on what a terminal/command prompt is.

- Added section on auxiliary files.

- Added section on Perl.

- Added information about latexmk

- Mentioned grffile package.

- Mentioned on-the-fly EPS conversion.

- Mentioned etoolbox's \appto and babel's \addto.

- Changed to UTF-8 and mostly changed to using code points instead of named entities in HTML files.

- Moved the document's home page from http://theoval.cmp.uea.ac.uk/~nlct/latex/novices/ to http://www.dickimaw-books.com/latex/novices/.

15th Jan 2008 (Version 1.3)

The main reason behind this change was to increase accessibility and conform to W3C guidelines. If you are experiencing problems relating to accessibility, please let me know (clearly stating the problem).

- Corrected error in the university's post code on the title page

- Added alternative text tags to more of the images, and made some of the images hyperlinks to a more detailed description of the image.

- Added information on how to break ligatures.

- Moved information on TeX to the introduction, and removed section on TeX that was in the "Some Definitions" chapter.

- Document nodes now have permanent names instead of the generic node⟨n⟩.htm which LaTeX2HTML generates by default.

- Went back to using straight double quotes in the HTML document as the fancy typographic double quotes are nonstandard.

8th May 2007 (Version 1.2)

- Links to UK FAQ [19] added.

- Overview made into a separate section, and tidied up a bit.

- Added some extra definitions: moving arguments and fragile commands, robust commands, short and long commands.

- Changed "Text editor and Terminal approach" to deal with Unix-type systems rather than MS-DOS.

- Moved section on tabular environment.

- Added section on boxes and mini-pages.

- Segmented section on font changing commands.

- Segmented section describing graphicx.

- Added section on the babel package.

- Updated and segmented section on downloading and installing new packages.

- Added section on side-by-side figures.

- Updated section on sub-figures to use the new subfloat package instead of the obsolete subfigure package.

- Added "Need More Help?" chapter.

Back Cover Text

(See http://www.gnu.org/licenses/fdl-howto-opt.html#SEC2.)

If you choose to buy a copy of this book, Dickimaw Books asks for your support through buying the Dickimaw Books edition to help cover costs.

Printed in March 2021
by Rotomail Italia S.p.A., Vignate (MI) - Italy